Praise for *Saved by a*

"**Saved by a Poem** is, quite simply, transfor[m]... keep by my bedside. I have never before appreciate[d] ... been talked out of it in school. Kim Rosen redeemed poetry for me. And a who[le] new world has opened up. I love this book (and the audio that goes with it)."

— **Christiane Northrup, M.D.**, author of *The Secret Pleasures of Menopause* and *Women's Bodies, Women's Wisdom*

"*Rarely in one's life does a book come along that touches a tender place in the heart that knows truth.* **Saved by a Poem** *did that for me. It reawakened my love of poetry, filled my soul with the beauty of its words, and fueled my creative spirit with the vital nourishment that only poetry can offer. What a gift. Thank you, Kim Rosen.*"

— **Cheryl Richardson**, author of *The Art of Extreme Self-Care*

"*Kim Rosen's work is a unique and important means to help us embody the word in a time when reality is becoming more and more virtual.*"

— **Roger Housden**, author of *Ten Poems to Change Your Life*

"*Kim Rosen's work is infinitely more important than it might appear. I have no doubt that our highly distressed society could be saved by poetry. Kim tells us here how a poem wakens and nourishes the soul and gives us the insight and sensitivity we need to live as creative individuals and as a peaceful society. She tells us how and what to read, not just appreciating some surface pleasantness but taking in the life-changing perspectives of real poetry. You will be educated and healed by this book.*"

— **Thomas Moore**, author of *Care of the Soul* and *Writing in the Sand*

"*Intimate and wise, personal and encyclopedic, this book is about the fully embodied life that steps forward when great language is spoken aloud. Kim Rosen opens—and holds open—poetry's first door: the intimate and unobstructed voice. She shows how the practice of saying a poem can be limitless, revealing our fullest capacities of heart and mind, and returning those capacities to us in times when we have forgotten our way. This is a book both profoundly useful and usefully profound. It comes straight from the original fires in which poems are forged.*"

— **Jane Hirshfield**, author of *Nine Gates: Entering the Mind of Poetry*

"*Kim Rosen's terrific and moving book invites everyone into the inspiring power of poetry to transform not only perceptions of the world but also how we act within it. This is a brave, powerful, passionate book that will bring healing joy to anyone who reads it.*"

— **Andrew Harvey**, author of *The Way of Passion: A Celebration of Rumi* and *The Hope: A Guide to Sacred Activism*

saved by a poem

saved by a poem

THE TRANSFORMATIVE
POWER OF WORDS

Kim Rosen

HAY HOUSE, INC.
Carlsbad, California • New York City
London • Sydney • Johannesburg
Vancouver • Hong Kong • New Delhi

Published and distributed in the United States by: Hay House, Inc.: www.hay house.com • *Published and distributed in Australia by:* Hay House Australia Pty. Ltd.: www.hayhouse.com.au • *Published and distributed in the United Kingdom by:* Hay House UK, Ltd.: www.hayhouse.co.uk • *Published and distributed in the Republic of South Africa by:* Hay House SA (Pty), Ltd.: www.hayhouse.co.za • *Distributed in Canada by:* Raincoast Books: www.raincoast.com • *Published in India by:* Hay House Publishers India: www.hayhouse.co.in

Design: Tricia Breidenthal

Cover poem: "I have faith in all that is not yet spoken" by Rainer Maria Rilke, translated by Kim Rosen and Karin Aarons.

Library of Congress Cataloging-in-Publication Data

Rosen, Kim
Saved by a poem : the transformative power of words / Kim Rosen.
    p. cm.
Includes bibliographical references.
ISBN 978-1-4019-2146-0 (pbk. : alk. paper) 1. Poetry--Appreciation.
2. Poetry--Psychological aspects. 3. Literature and morals. I. Title.

PN1075.R58 2009
808.1--dc22

                                    2009013825

ISBN: 978-1-4019-2146-0

1st edition, October 2009

Printed in the United States of America

Dedicated to all the poets
whose words have shaped my life
and
to Karin
who listened this book into being

CONTENTS

RECITING POEMS IN THE MOONLIGHT,
RIDING A PAINTED BOAT . . .
EVERY PLACE THE WIND CARRIES ME IS HOME.

— YU XUANJI (A.D. 843–868), TRANSLATED BY JANE HIRSHFIELD

FOREWORD

When I was 16 years old, I found poetry. I was in Florida for the summer and worked as a lifeguard at a lonely pool. It was the same August I discovered my freedom and independence and sexuality. I had my brother's volume of T. S. Eliot's *Collected Poetry*. I remember his special sticker with his name imprinted on it sealed in the front of the book. It made me guilty all summer because I had taken it from him without asking. I stole it away because I desperately wanted to believe I was not stupid, that I could understand T. S. Eliot like my very smart 18-year-old brother.

Each day I would sit on the beach and read "The Love Song of J. Alfred Prufrock" out loud. I said it to the sand and the sky and the clouds and the sea. I spoke it to the wind and the hot sun. It became a chorus, a mantra that floated through my August, through my kissing, my dreaming, my swimming. *Let us go then, you and I, / When the evening is spread out against the sky . . . Let us go then, you and I . . . Let us go then.* I remember lying on the hot sand, this poem entering me, entering my bloodstream like a kind of verbal tattoo, forever marking my consciousness.

But it wasn't just the poem; it was poetry itself that entered me. It was the way words created loss and possibility simultaneously, made sense and made no sense, begged for understanding and invited dislocation.

It was as if another world, a parallel world, opened for me that summer. That world became my sanctuary, my home. It allowed me to become a nomad, to surrender nation and family as identity. Ever since, poetry has been a place to go back to when there is no way forward. Poetry makes sense of things that are incomprehensible—or it makes perfect no-sense of them. It is in that nuanced beauty where meaning is supplanted with motion, logic with rhythm, arrival with contemplation.

In the last ten years I have spent time in refugee camps, war-torn counties, homeless shelters, prisons, and post-disaster sites.

Most recently I have been in the Democratic Republic of the Congo, where some of the greatest atrocities of this century are being perpetrated on the bodies of thousands of women. What form can give adequate expression to the scope of such pain? What language can invite our connection, our care, our action without compelling us to cover our ears and flee from the horror?

Poetry is the language of our time. It is a verbal excavation, digging us into and under that which is inarticulate, that which cannot be said but can be felt, that which cannot be stated but can be conjured. Poetry is a form of revolution. It rearranges our thinking, our perception, our dialogue. It takes us out of the literal so that we can see what is real.

These are volatile and epic times. Buildings, concepts, and economies are collapsing in our midst. Our greed, our overconsumption, has come back to haunt us in every respect. This book puts forward poetry as literary ecology, concerned with the protection and preservation of our souls. It is a call, a guide, an invitation to know poetry, to find poetry, to remember poetry. It suggests that turning to poetry can become a necessary practice, like turning off a water faucet or not using a plastic bag.

Really what this book is calling for is attention—to detail, to nuance, to each other. It teaches us that by bringing poetry deeply into our lives, our hearts, and our bodies we strengthen our muscle for care, our capacity for intricate metaphoric thinking, our appreciation for ambiguity. This book encourages our longing not for answers but for ever-expanding questions. *Let us go then, you and I, / When the evening is spread out against the sky . . .*

Eve Ensler

PROLOGUE

Nearly every day, poetry saves me. Some favorite line or surprising image will rescue my vagrant attention from the careening bandwagon of my thoughts and redirect it to the path of my soul. My mind quiets, my breath deepens, and I remember what matters most to me.

For many years, poetry was not a big part of my life. Though I wrote poems as a child and went to college hoping to become a great poet, the intellectuality of the academic approach I encountered as an undergrad disheartened me. Suddenly poetry became a foreign language, and I couldn't crack the code. So I turned away.

Then, through a miracle I describe in Chapter 2, poetry poured back into my life, cracking the encrustation of depression that was then gripping me. The healing did not come through writing poems or even through reading them. It came when I discovered that taking a poem I loved deeply into my life and speaking it aloud caused a profound integration of every aspect of me—physical, emotional, mental, and spiritual. I felt a wholeness I had never before experienced. I felt like I was flying. I was speaking the truth, and the truth was setting me free.

For the first time in my life, I had found the voice of my soul.

On Entering the Language of Poetry

Many people have confessed to me, "I want to like poetry, but I just don't understand most of it!" I know what they mean. For decades, I felt the same way. Until I realized that the language of poetry, like the "language" of music or art, is not (usually) about the kind of understanding I had been taught. Most Western education focuses on analytical thinking, much of which happens in the left hemisphere of the brain. But, while poetry happens in both sides of the brain, it primarily calls on the holistic, intuitive, and imagistic functioning that is the work of the right hemisphere. And, since it arrives in words, poetry can be deceiving. The left brain, which is the primary processor of language, can mistakenly perceive the poem as part of its own domain and apply its highly tuned rational capacities—often to no avail. When asked how to help young readers appreciate poetry, the poet Mary Oliver said, "Emphasize their response in terms of feeling. We give far too much focus to understanding in our educational systems. Don't ask them what the poem is about. Ask them, 'How does it make you feel?'"[1] Billy Collins wrote a poem about this dilemma called "Introduction to Poetry." In it, he talks about how, even though he invites people to look at the light through a poem like a color slide, or "press an ear against its hive," all they want to do is beat it with a hose to "find out what it really means."

In order to enter poetry's language, your grip on habitual, left-brained ways of processing information needs to soften. Somehow we know how to do this with music and art. You probably wouldn't try to figure out the exact meaning of Beethoven's Ninth Symphony or Ella Fitzgerald's scat singing. Nor are you likely to do a pragmatic analysis of an abstract painting by Georgia O'Keeffe or Jackson Pollock. You feel these art forms. You allow associations to play through your awareness. You let your linear mind relax and go for the ride.

As you read poems, listen to them, and speak them aloud, try meeting them as you would a piece of music. Allow your rational brain to relax. Dare to not understand, to lose your grip on making sense of the words. Let the images, like musical notes, pour over you. The French philosopher Gaston Bachelard writes that poetry "comes before thought . . . [R]ather than being a phenomenology of the mind, [poetry] is a phenomenology of the soul."[2]

A Note about the Soul and Other Indefinables

Like several other words pointing to intangible realities—
God, spirit, love, and *heart* being only a few—the word *soul* is
frequently used to stand for some assumed territory, often with-
out delineating exactly what that territory is. The *Encyclopædia
Britannica* defines *soul* as "the immaterial aspect or essence of a
human being, that which confers individuality and humanity."[3]
But in the Bhagavad Gita, the soul is anything but individual and
human; it is the one unchanging, indestructible, indivisible pres-
ence within everything. In the Old Testament, the soul is some-
times referred to as breath and therefore necessary to the life of
the body. But Christian writers have portrayed the body and soul
as separate and, at times, in conflict with each other. Plato, quot-
ing his teacher Socrates, defined the soul as the immortal essence
of a being. Jungian psychologist James Hillman calls the soul "the
poetic basis of mind" and goes on to define it as "the imagina-
tive possibility in our natures, the experiencing through reflective
speculation, dream, image, fantasy."[4]

In his book *Care of the Soul,* Thomas Moore writes, "It is impos-
sible to define precisely what the soul is. Definition is an intel-
lectual enterprise anyway; the soul prefers to imagine. We know
intuitively that soul has to do with genuineness and depth, as
when we say certain music has soul or a remarkable person is soul-
ful."[5] Indeed, the very indefinability of the word gives us the need
for poetry. Poems can speak these ineffables with a kind of mys-
terious accuracy. "Poetry is a commitment of the soul," Gaston
Bachelard writes. "Forces are manifested in poems that do not pass
through the circuits of knowledge."[6]

In this book, I take the liberty of asking the word *soul* to include
all of these varied and even opposing definitions. I ask it to stand
for all that lives in us beyond the socialized, survival-oriented
self. I ask it to include the many realms of the "inner"[7] world:
the psychological self with its memories, wounds, imaginings, and
feelings; the oceanic movements of the emotions; the archetypal
themes, forces, and elements of the collective unconscious that

we share with all humanity; and the Self that is pure, formless, awake, eternal presence. What all of these have in common is a lack of concern with appearances, achievement, or even survival in worldly terms. According to Emily Dickinson, "The Soul selects her own Society— / Then—shuts the Door—."[8] Chariots stop at her gate. Emperors kneel on her doormat. She opens and closes "the Valves of her attention" when she pleases. She is beholden only to herself.

This book is an invitation to discover what happens when you merge the power of the word with the language of the soul. The potency of the words we speak is not a new discovery. From the Proverbs in the Old Testament to a recent flood of books on the creative power of thoughts, many teachers have revealed how words, whether silent or spoken, can cause hurt and healing, war and peace—within and around us. To take a poem into your life is to fill yourself with words that ignite your true essence, aligning your thoughts, words, and deeds with your heart's wisdom and longing. The simple and powerful act of creating a deep relationship with a poem you love can change your life and, through your spoken words, the lives of those around you.

Each chapter in this book invites you into a different dimension of relationship with a poem. Although I speak of them sequentially, you can start anywhere and explore each chapter with or without reading the others. For instance, you can directly experience the powerful healing medicine of poetry in the chapter called "The Anatomy of a Poem," regardless of whether you ever go on to speak it aloud to others. You can read the chapters on learning a poem by heart to discover new and transformative ways to commit just about anything to memory: a prose passage, a speech, or lines in a play. And the lessons in "Undressing Your Voice" may help you speak authentically in public, whether you are delivering poetry, telling your life story, or teaching a class.

At the end of each chapter you will find a poem. Sometimes I've chosen the poem because it speaks one of the themes in the preceding pages, sometimes because I referred to it in the text, and sometimes for the sheer beauty of how it opens the mind and graces the movement of the journey at that particular moment. Like coming upon a mountain stream after a long hike or listening to music after much conversation, I hope you'll let the poems wash over you, tuning your inner listening to "the one who talks to the deep ear in / your chest."[9]

No exploration of the healing power of poetry would be complete without an opportunity to directly experience the magic that can happen when you listen to a poem delivered by someone who has deeply embodied its wisdom. On the accompanying audio (download instructions at the end of this book), the voices of several esteemed spiritual teachers and poets, each reading and discussing a favorite poem, are woven among my own insights on hearing and speaking poetry.

My greatest hope is that this work will inspire you to find the poems that are the language of your soul, take them into your life, feel them in your body, and speak them to those whose lives you touch. As you embody the poems you love, you may meet yourself, your imagination, and your true voice in ways you never dreamed of. As you speak the words aloud, you can change the world around you with poetry's medicine—dissolving lines of separation, fostering intimacy and truthfulness, and awakening the heart.

Love after Love

The time will come
when, with elation,
you will greet yourself arriving
at your own door,
in your own mirror,
and each will smile at the other's welcome
and say, sit here. Eat.
You will love again the stranger who was your self.
Give wine. Give bread.
Give back your heart
to itself, to the stranger who has loved you

all your life, whom you ignored
for another, who knows you by heart.
Take down the love letters from the bookshelf,

the photographs, the desperate notes,
peel your own image from the mirror.
Sit. Feast on your life.

— Derek Walcott

INVITATION

Sometimes you hear a voice through
the door calling you, as fish out of

water hear the waves or a hunting
falcon hears the drum's come back.

This turning toward what you deeply love
saves you.

— Rumi, translated by Coleman Barks

Poetry is the language of the soul. From below the surface of your life, the truth of who you are calls to you through the poems you love. Even if you have been touched by only one poem, or just a single line heard at a crucial moment and remembered, those words are an invitation from within. To take them deeply into your life and speak them aloud brings every level of who you are—your thoughts, your words, your feelings, and even your physical energies—into alignment with what matters most to you. You are receiving and giving voice not only to the poem but also to your own soul.

Many of us have searched for guides to help unravel the riddles of our existence and point us toward aspects of ourselves we cannot uncover on our own. We have turned to gurus, friends, lovers, and mentors for help. A poem you love can be such a teacher.

Before written language took words out of our mouths and onto the page, and long before "virtual" communication lifted them off the page and into intangible space, our ancestors knew that a poem, spoken aloud, could change us with its vital, voiced wisdom. Even today, in many cultures throughout the world, poetry still resides in its original home—in the sounds, sensations, and feelings of the human body.

I invite you to take a poem you love into your heart and your body. Develop a vibrant relationship with it. Become intimate with it, and allow it to guide you into intimacy with yourself. Receive the poem's gifts as it illuminates undiscovered realms within you. And give the poem the gift of a home in your particular human-ness. If you do this, that poem can become a teacher that is always with you, touching and changing every moment of your life.

As you go deeper into your relationship with a poem, it may guide you to discover treasures that you did not know you had. Perhaps there are hidden talents or creative visions that will appear. Perhaps the poem will call forth a long-buried memory, magnetized by the words to the surface of your consciousness for healing or inspiration. Perhaps it will open you to a new way of seeing the world, or a feeling of grief you have avoided, or an experience of joy you didn't know was in you.

A poem is a physical event. The rhythm may quicken or slow your pulse. The flow of the language may expand your breathing. The music woven into the words may change the very texture of your voice. A poem even entrains your brainwaves, altering your biochemistry and allowing shifts in consciousness that can bring healing, understanding, and unexpected insight.

Spending time with a poem is a way of choosing what you're going to do with your attention. In this world of iPods, e-mails, cell phones, and spam, opportunities for fragmentation of con-sciousness are thick and fast. It can be lifesaving to return to the sanctuary of a poem that you hold within you. Like singing a song you love or blasting it on the stereo, like reading a favorite Psalm or the Heart Sutra several times a day, it is a choice to fill your thoughts with what you hold precious and believe in, instead of the plethora of commercial jingles, self-criticisms, or anxiet-ies about the past and the future that usually overrun the mind. When I focus on a poem I love, my thoughts stop spinning and become quiet. My body relaxes. My breathing finds the rhythm of the poem. Whether I'm in the car, on the subway, walking on the beach, or sitting on a meditation cushion, that poem becomes as real a refuge as any church, synagogue, or mosque.

To develop a relationship with a poem is something like falling in love—with all the wonder and challenge that can bring. It begins with infatuation: the curiosity to get to know the poem, to learn everything you can about its meaning, rhythm, sound, and silence. At the same time, you are allowing the poem to carry you into yourself, evoking feelings, reflections, and new experiences of the world.

Then, as with any relationship, inevitable difficulties arise and the hard work comes: suddenly you find you don't like the last stanza after all, or you repeatedly stumble over the third line, or a certain turn of phrase inexplicably brings up a sense of discomfort you'd rather avoid. But you hang in there anyway, allowing the poem to take you beyond your comfort zone.

A new and enriching experience invariably waits behind every resistance. Ultimately there is the pleasure and grace that comes when the poem has become yours. You know it intimately and can share it with others or simply read it to yourself for your own pleasure. The spoken poem is a wondrous new creation born of the unique convergence between words that have been written by someone else, even someone who may have lived centuries ago in a faraway country, and your own voice.

Once you know a poem deeply, you have a gift you can give others as well as yourself. There are those who might need to hear this poem at crucial moments in their lives as only you can speak it. I have that experience almost every day. When my neighbor, who had never before liked poetry, lost her daughter in a car accident, she asked me if I knew of a poem that might help her. I read to her from Rilke's "First Elegy." When I got to the final stanza, which speaks of how grief for the death of a child can become "the source of our spirit's growth" and "pierce through the barren numbness," she started to sob. She tried to stifle her tears at first, but as I read on, wave after wave surged through her. Later, when the flood of grief had subsided, she told me she had been unable to cry for her daughter until her own numbness was pierced by the poem.

During the fiercest period of her chemotherapy, my friend Melanie often asked me to speak poems to help her through the ordeal. "That Eliot poem about the darkness," she murmured one day as she sat on her hospital bed and stared at her pillow, which was covered with strands of her beautiful bright red hair, "I need to hear it right now." I put my arm around her and spoke the lines from *Four Quartets:* "I said to my soul be still, and let the dark come upon you / Which shall be the darkness of God." I will never forget how her breath deepened as I spoke, her features softened, and she lay back onto the pillow, letting the fear and pain flow through her more gently.

When you get to know a poem well, you may find that you naturally begin to remember the words. Lines may come to you, seemingly out of the blue, or you may find yourself quoting a phrase at a crucial moment when nothing else will do. At that point you may choose to go even deeper: to learn your poem by heart.

Often people balk at the idea of committing a poem to memory. Phantoms of childhood humiliations and middle-aged failures crowd the mind: that second-grade performance of *Snow White and the Seven Dwarfs* where you played Sneezy and forgot your only line, your fumbled solo in the high school glee club's *Messiah,* last week's embarrassing failure to remember the name of your best friend's cat.

But none of these has anything to do with remembering a poem. Learning by heart is not the same as memorizing. Strangely enough, it does not require a good memory. I have a terrible memory. I can't remember where I hid my computer password, much less the password itself! I, too, forget the name of my brother-in-law's mother and who wrote the Declaration of Independence. Yet when I fall in love with a poem, because of my hunger to taste it again and again, enter its world, and discover what new territory it will show me within myself, the process of learning it happens naturally.

I have stood with many trembling students at the brink of poems they never thought they could learn, watched them finally dive into the process, submerge, and rise up spouting the words in a way no one else ever could. So I know this is possible for anyone. When you love a poem enough to allow it to guide you into your own intimate experience of its words, breath, and pulse, learning it by heart happens effortlessly.

Regardless of whether you ever learn a poem by heart, there are hundreds of other ways to nourish your connection with the poems that move you. Create a poetry journal by filling blank books with handwritten copies of your favorites in the order in which they touch your life. Or start a salon with a group of kindred souls to meet regularly and share aloud the poems that are speaking most deeply to you. You can also create your own poetry cards, each with lines from your favorite poems. Call on them for inspiration and guidance as you might a divination deck, or give them to loved ones at pivotal moments when only poetry can express what cannot be told in ordinary speech.

One of America's great poets, Stanley Kunitz, said a poet's work is not only to avoid clichés of language but also to avoid clichés of thought and feeling. Clichés are familiar patterns of reaction that arise automatically, without consciousness. These habitual responses can be the cause of much suffering because they lead to the same painful situations again and again. As William Wordsworth said, "Not choice but habit rules the unreflecting herd." Because it goes underneath conventional thought, poetry can cut through these patterns, waking you up to the vibrancy of the moment.

In this way, filling your mind with poetry can offer a profound, paradoxical medicine. It strengthens the mind and disarms it at once. Among spiritual seekers, there is sometimes a tendency to disparage the mind, as if it were essentially adversarial to the experience of truth. Yet while the reality of the true self cannot fit into the borders of the mind, that same mind has one extraordinary capacity that makes it essential to the path of awakening. The mind can use itself to shatter itself.

In the "Aha!" that happens when the mind bursts open—at a breathtaking metaphor or an insight or a chiming among the words—all levels of being human come into alignment. You feel a sudden integration of body, mind, heart, and soul. The fragmentation that many experience in the multitasking onrush of modern life cannot withstand a good poem. Whether it is a mystical song by Kabir asking, "What is God?" or a poem by June Jordan about being homeless in New York City, you are called into presence by the resonance of truth. And when you are present, you are open to your feelings. And when you feel, the rigid boundaries that divide you from others can melt. In that moment, the man sleeping on the subway vent, the child shot in Falluja, the little girl in the FEMA trailer, and your own mother, whether or not she seemed to love you, are no longer separate from you; they are you.

On a bombed-out street that was once a beautiful section of downtown Baghdad, a large tent was erected on August 28, 2006, in the midst of explosions and clashes. It was the first of many gatherings of poets in what came to be called the Freedom Space events. There, while Sunni and Shiite militias roamed the streets propagating terror, men and women from both factions gathered to speak poetry together. The Shiites sat opposite the Sunnis, as if it were a competition. But by the end of the event, they were embracing and dancing together because the poems from both sides voiced the same words, the same longings, the same wounds.

There were 25 people in the tent at that first gathering. Since then the movement has proliferated throughout Baghdad and the surrounding areas. Large monthly events in central locations draw hundreds of listeners. Smaller weekly events bring together poets and musicians from all factions. Though some of these gatherings are held in areas where people have been killed for speaking poetry, more and more are risking their lives to be a part of the surge of hope shining from the Freedom Space. Even soldiers from both Sunni and Shiite militias have joined the celebration, volunteering to guard the space and speaking poetry from the stage. Some have left their posts in the army because they see in these poetry gatherings a more powerful form of peacemaking than any militia. The Freedom Space of March 2008 was held at the Theatre Hall of the technical university in downtown Baghdad. Though

armed guards surrounded the space and the sound of bombs punc-
tuated the poetry, inside, an audience of a thousand—Sunni and
Shiite—danced, wept, and cheered.[1]

No wonder speaking poetry can be an act of peacemaking.
When you meet a poem as a partner, friend, and teacher, you can
be carried by its voice into your own true voice. When you allow
yourself to be opened and changed by the poem, you can open
and change those around you when you speak it. You and anyone
listening are drawn into a fertile wholeness from which healing,
inspiration, and service can spring. In those moments you feel as
if something far greater than you is speaking the poem, as if you
are part of a mystery that goes beyond both you and the poem.
Perhaps this is what D. H. Lawrence experienced when he wrote:

> Not I, not I, but the wind that blows through me!
> A fine wind is blowing the new direction of Time.
> If only I let it bear me, carry me, if only it carry me!
> If only I am sensitive, subtle, oh, delicate, a winged gift!
> If only, most lovely of all, I yield myself and am borrowed
> By the fine, fine wind that takes its course through
>   the chaos of the world . . .[2]

Eternity

A poem written three thousand years ago

about a man who walks among horses
grazing on a hill under the small stars

comes to life on a page in a book

and the woman reading the poem
in her kitchen filled with a gold metallic light

finds the experience of living in that moment

so vividly described as to make her feel known
to another, until the woman and the poet share

not only their souls but the exact silence

between each word. And every time the poem is read,
no matter her situation or her age,

this is more or less what happens.

— Jason Shinder

Chapter 1

EMBODYING
A POEM

A word is dead
When it is said
Some say.
I say it just
Begins to live
That day.

— Emily Dickinson

Poetry was created to be experienced in the body and spoken aloud. Made of breath, sound, rhythm, meaning, and silence, a poem is a physical event. It needs a human body to give it life. To celebrate a poem's natural expression means giving it a life inside your own body—in your voice, your breathing, and your pulse, not to mention your feelings and thoughts. As you take it in, the poem can become an inner teacher, changing you from the inside out. And you can change the poem as well, giving it a voice in a way no one else ever could.

There was a time before language when all communication may have been a kind of poetry. Many archaeologists and anthropologists speculate that our ancestors spoke to each other through song-like sounds that conveyed rhythmic, holographic, emotional messages. This "musilanguage"[1] used by the early hominids was predominantly a function of the right hemisphere of the brain. It communicated through the feeling and intuitive faculties, not the cognitive thinking process. In *The Singing Neanderthals,* archaeologist Steven Mithen named this system of relating *Hmmmmm,* an acronym for holistic, multi-modal, manipulative, mimetic, and musical. He theorizes that it was *Homo ergaster,* our ancestor of 1.8 million years ago, who initially invented Hmmmmm. Mithen's research suggests that over the eons the language may have evolved to become a highly complex and emotionally rich form of interactive bonding used by the Neanderthals about 250,000 years ago.[2] Personally, I cannot help but think of the elaborate soundings of dolphins and whales, which also seem to communicate in a very sophisticated, holographic manner through vocalizations more like song and verse than linear thought.

Even after this "musilanguage" turned into words in about 50,000 B.C.,[3] it was dozens of millennia before writing evolved (circa 3500 B.C.). During this time, the only way to carry words from a spontaneous present into the future was to commit them to memory. Poetry, with its rhythms, repeated sounds, and rhymes, helped our predecessors to retain their stories, secrets, and revelations. Before there was the alphabet, hieroglyphics, or cuneiform, spoken poems were the way wisdom passed from one generation to another. As the poet Jane Hirshfield says, "The earliest vessel for holding consciousness that has lasted, poetry is the progenitor of all the technologies of memory to come."[4]

Even today, poetry remains a musical language of the body and feelings, regardless of the subject matter. As Hmmmmm became spoken poetry, which became cuneiform script on clay tablets, then ink marks on paper, and, later, signals on an LCD display, it has retained its allegiance to these acoustic devices. "Poetry is words music-ed," poet Amiri Baraka once said.

That sound-play not only aids memory, it is a primary ingredient of poetry's magic. Its rhythms and echoing tones entrain your body and mind, transporting you out of your ordinary thoughts to a realm where the unspeakable is, miraculously, spoken. Because of this, to take a poem into your life can be an extraordinary gift to your soul. And to give voice to that poem from your heart can infuse the world around you with truth and beauty.

Freeing the Words from the Page

As a child, I was a very slow reader. I would labor over a few pages of biology for the same three hours that it took my best friend to finish all her assigned reading plus a few chapters of Nancy Drew. Somewhere around eighth grade I discovered that if I read the text out loud to myself, key words and phrases would inscribe themselves in my memory. It's not that I was particularly good at memorizing. Rather, I was particularly slow at reading, and my incapacity drove me to this invention. So instead of reading my assignments silently to myself in the library, I took my textbooks to the woods where I could hear my own voice free the words from their written cages and turn them to living sound in the air. As I heard them aloud, the phrases and ideas would become lodged in my memory. In this way, I began memorizing key points, hoping desperately that I had guessed accurately where the teacher would focus. Fortunately, I was often right.

I see now that what began as a compensation for my limitation gave me, like my ancient predecessors, a connection with language untethered from the page. Language for me was not the written word. It was the sensation of sound in my body, the vibration of voice on my breath. For the most part, I was learning prosaic treatises like the chapter summaries in *The World and Its People* or the table of contents in *Essential Biology*. But even these would come alive in me when I lifted them from the page to my voice.

I grew up in a time in America when the art of speaking poems aloud was latent, if not extinct. My friend Judith, on the other hand, tells of being a girl in Hungary in the 1930s where, to pass the time as they waited for the bus, she and her friends would recite the work of the contemporary Hungarian poets to each other. "I would go home each night and pick a new poem to learn for the kids at the bus stop," she remembers. "Everybody did. It was like a game. And besides, there was this feeling of impending war everywhere. Any material possession could be taken in a moment. The only things you knew you could hold on to were what you had inside you."

In many other countries as well, poetry holds a central place in the culture. The most popular prime-time TV show in the Middle East is The Million's Poet, boasting an audience of over 70 million viewers and ratings higher than sports or the news. Within a format similar to American Idol, poets from throughout the Gulf region, many from very poor Bedouin tribes, perform poems on all themes imaginable. As one journalist reporting on the show put it, "It is as common today as it was centuries ago to recite on the topics close to one's heart as well as what is affecting people around them."[5] The show has even inspired a TV channel completely dedicated to poetry.

Speaking poetry, in these countries, is not relegated to the poets. People who never dreamed of writing poetry carry their favorite poems in their hearts and often speak them aloud. In many parts of Latin America, Ireland, and the Middle East, for instance, it is not unusual for spoken poetry to be heard as part of everyday conversations. Poems are spoken at parties, at the family dinner table, on the street. My students from Wales and Ireland describe how the poems of Dylan Thomas or William Butler Yeats are exchanged into the night at almost any local pub. My Iranian friend's father knows many poems by Rumi and Hafiz. He knows them in Farsi, but if you give him time, he'll recite a dozen or more, then figure out the translations for you. An Israeli friend tells me poets are regarded there as national heroes: readers line up in the bookstores of Tel Aviv for a newly released collection of poetry with the eagerness Americans reserve for best-selling novels. In Havana, lines from the Spanish poet Antonio Machado are emblazoned in spray paint on the sides of houses. Almost every time I find myself on a plane next to someone from outside the U.S., I am gifted with a recitation of at least one of the poems he or she holds most precious. I still have the page in my diary where the Pakistani accountant wrote, first in Urdu then underneath in stumbling English, the poem that had won the heart of his wife 45 years earlier. I hope to dig that journal out of storage one day.

In recent years, hip-hop, rap, and poetry slams, as well as a variety of other spoken-word art forms, are returning embodied poetry to the American language. One of the initiatives most exciting to me is the "Poetry Out Loud" contest for high-school students in the United States, sponsored by the Poetry Foundation. In 2009, over 300,000 students from all 50 states and the District of Columbia learned great classical and modern poems in the hopes of winning a trip to the finals in Washington, D.C., and a chance for first prize: a $20,000 college scholarship. "Poetry was never something I thought I'd get involved with," admitted the winner, 16-year-old Shawntay Henry of the United States Virgin Islands. "But I realized I had a hidden talent." I imagine many of the other participants felt the same way. Through encouraging students not only to read but also to embody poems, the Poetry Foundation is fulfilling its objective of bringing "new energy to an ancient art by returning it to the classrooms of America."[6] Poetry may indeed be resurrecting as the oral art it was, in only a slightly different form, in the days of Homer.

And just in time. When I see the word *soul* used to sell a bank, *love* to sell an airline, and *security* selling a war, I can feel the vital force of these words struggling like an animal on the verge of extinction. The breakdown of language is a serious issue, one for which poetry can be a medicine. Poems return us to the power of words to tell the truth. They develop our capacity to speak the complexities of our lives in all the wonder and horror, grace, mystery, and ambiguity. In his eulogy for Robert Frost, John F. Kennedy said, "When power leads man toward arrogance, poetry reminds him of his limitations. When power narrows the areas of man's concern, poetry reminds him of the richness and diversity of his existence. When power corrupts, poetry cleanses."[7]

I hope this book inspires you to allow the poems you love to infiltrate your daily conversations, shaking up the rules of distance woven into the infrastructure of ordinary communication. Perhaps you will remember a couple of lines from a love poem and whisper them to your sweetheart in a tender moment: "in your most frail gesture are things which enclose me / or which i cannot touch because they are too near."[8] Perhaps you will read a verse of political outrage onto the voice mail of your senator: "Tell me why it is we don't lift our voices these days / And cry over what is happening?"[9] Or as your heart swells to breaking at the beauty of a sunset, you might recall a few lines from Rilke: "For beauty is nothing / but the beginning of terror, which we still are just able to endure."[10] Or, at your nephew's seventh birthday party, you might delight the kids with "Today you are you! That is truer that true! / There is no one alive who is you-er than you!"[11]

Embodying a poem can be an extremely powerful medicine for you and anyone who has the good fortune to be listening. Often poetry is a very private experience. Poems are usually written alone and often they are read in solitude and silence as well. A poem can talk to your most interior self, revealing truths that might seem too intimate to speak aloud—perhaps too personal, perhaps too sacred. Yet this is exactly why it is essential to give it voice. Speaking those words aloud can connect you viscerally with your deepest self. Speaking them to someone else can be lifesaving in this "Information Age" when communication can be so impersonal. It is an opportunity to slow down, look into another's eyes, and share what matters most.

Whether you are new to poetry, a lifetime lover of poetry, or a poet yourself, lift the poems off the page and into your embodied experience. Let them live in your pulse and your breath and your voice. Let them pour out of you, into the space between you and others. Your whole being will come into alignment. And that wholeness is contagious. You will touch other people and bring them into resonance with their own souls as well.

Poetry

And it was at that age . . . Poetry arrived
in search of me. I don't know, I don't know where
it came from, from winter or a river.
I don't know how or when,
no, they were not voices, they were not
words, nor silence,
but from a street I was summoned,
from the branches of night,
abruptly from others,
among violent fires
or returning alone,
there I was without a face
and it touched me.

I did not know what to say, my mouth
had no way
with names,
my eyes were blind,
and something started in my soul,
fever or forgotten wings,
and I made my own way,
deciphering
that fire,
and I wrote the first faint line,
faint, without substance, pure
nonsense,
pure wisdom
of someone who knows nothing,
and suddenly I saw
the heavens
unfastened
and open,
planets,
palpitating plantations,

shadow perforated,
riddled
with arrows, fire and flowers,
the winding night, the universe.

And I, infinitesimal being,
drunk with the great starry
void,
likeness, image of
mystery,
felt myself a pure part of the abyss,
I wheeled with the stars,
my heart broke loose on the wind.

— Pablo Neruda, translated by Alastair Reid

Chapter 2

HOW POETRY SAVED MY LIFE

It is difficult
to get the news from poems
*   yet men die miserably every day*
*   for lack*
of what is found there.

— William Carlos Williams

The first time I actually lived a poem by heart, it happened inadvertently. I was 15. Mr. Barclay, the public speaking teacher at Weston High, had assigned the sophomore class the task of memorizing a poem.

Of course I had memorized before. At ten, I had learned my lines as Mr. Bumble in the (all-girl) production of *Oliver!* (*Catch him! Snatch him! Hold him! Scold him!*). At about 12, I discovered the trick of memorizing chapter summaries from my textbooks to hide the fact that I couldn't read all the pages my teachers assigned. And of course I had memorized the requisite lists of state capitals

(Augusta, Albany, Cheyenne, Memphis . . .), how to spell *Missis-sippi,* and even the first 15 lines of *The Canterbury Tales* in Middle English (*Whan that Aprill, with his shoures soote . . .*), assigned in seventh grade and learned by rote. Not to mention the plethora of rhymes, lyrics, and commercial jingles (*What do you get when you fall in love? Have it your way! The inky dinky spider . . .*) that accidentally find a way into everyone's memory without invitation or choice.

I had memorized all of these. I had not learned them by heart.

Several weeks before Mr. Barclay decreed that we memorize and recite a poem, my new friend Samantha had given me a gift of *100 Selected Poems* by E. E. Cummings. In the year since I had met her, Samantha had introduced me to books unlike any I had ever known, books that seemed to reach right through me into an inner sanctum where my most private wonderings and knowings lived—until then, in loneliness. She seemed to see through my awkward, overly articulate mask to a depth that no one had recognized in me before. She taught me how to throw the I Ching and to make tea of dried herbs (long before anyone had put them in bags to market them.) After school, over chamomile tea, we would read aloud the writings of Cummings, Dag Hammarskjöld, and Carl Jung. For the first time in my life, through the revelations and agonies in these books, I was discovering that there were others like me.

So I chose my favorite Cummings poem for the assignment, "somewhere i have never travelled,gladly beyond." This poem had become a kind of sanctuary for me ever since I had found it.

Intending to learn the words by rote, I curled up in the window seat of my bedroom and opened the book to the dog-eared page where the words glowed with the yellow of my highlighter.

The first few lines were relatively easy. I learned them like I learned the "Minuet in G" for my piano lesson, drilling myself over and over in the places where I made mistakes until my fingers knew the notes or someone screamed from elsewhere in the house, "Stop that! You're going to drive me crazy!"

It was the same with learning words. When I came to something

I couldn't remember, I repeated it in a sing-song way until it virtually lost meaning and was inscribed as a pattern of sound in my memory. It seemed a bit sad that a poem that had brought me so much joy was now being stripped of meaning in the name of memorization, but I accepted that as the price of the task. I settled in for a long and boring evening.

Then I came to these lines:

you open always petal by petal myself as Spring opens
(touching skillfully,mysteriously) her first rose.[1]

Suddenly I could go no further. There was something so naked about the statement that it scared me. I couldn't imagine ever saying it in front of other people. What had I been thinking when I chose this poem? Even to imagine speaking it out loud caused a collision inside me between the self-conscious girl who hid behind her horn-rimmed glasses and another self who was magnetized by the desire and tenderness in the words.

Even at 15 I knew I was imprisoned by my inhibitions. While my friends screamed for the Beatles and learned to slow dance with the boys, I hid in the bathroom. While they went shopping for tight jeans and experimented with mascara, I made infirmaries in the garage for hurt pigeons and squirrels.

In those days, it seemed there was no bridge between my inner life and the world around me. I sensed there was another language, one that could tell the surgings inside me, but I did not know how to speak it. What I did know was that the hungers of my heart were crushed behind a mask of distance, intelligence, and control. I desperately wanted out.

I tasted the words tentatively. The sensuality in them frightened me. The closeness. The simple, undisguised longing. In that moment I recognized that I had to make a choice between my habitual control and the truth of my inner being. The price of the authenticity I longed for was my willingness to take this plunge.

It quickly became clear to me that learning these words was not about the assignment at all. I needed to invite these words into me and to speak them aloud, regardless of what happened in class. It was a matter of life and death. The poem was a deep medi-cine I had inadvertently prescribed for myself. I could not com-mit the poem to memory without living it directly. And I could not live it directly without courageously confronting the strictures that had imprisoned my spontaneity.

I began speaking the phrases aloud. At first it was frightening. Each time I let myself feel the full impact of an image, it caused tinglings, hungers, visions, and memories to stream through me. Though I had never before fallen in love, within the world of this poem I was the lover being touched "skillfully,mysteriously," opened "petal by petal," then shut by "the snow carefully every-where descending."

As I rode the waves of sensation, emotion, and imagery, a remarkable process unfolded. The words began to naturally root in my memory. I could remember them without effort, without rote repetition, without "memorization."

At the time I did not understand how the rhythms, tones, and movement of a passage permeate the body so that the experience described becomes the experience directly lived. I only knew that I loved to say those words over and over and over. The delicate inter-play of sound and meaning unlocked a realm within me where I was loved and unashamed. When I was frustrated by the friction between my mother and me at the height of my adolescent rebel-lion, I would crawl into my bed in the far corner of our house and speak the words to myself. It was not so much an escape as a return to a part of myself that was tender and unstained. When I galloped my mare across the neighbor's field, I would chant the words to the cadence of her pounding hooves. When I hit a wall doing my science homework, I would whisper them. When I was bored out of my mind in geometry class, I would secretly recite them under my breath. When I was shunned by the girl who lived across the street because I wasn't part of her clique, I would go to the stable and weep the words into Miss Jessy's pungent mane.

In this way, the poem became a part of me. It found me—a sen-sual, yearning, and undefended me that I had never met before. I discovered myself not only through the meaning, which challenged and shook open the cage of my personality, but also through the breathing, the song, the pulse of the poem, which entered me and became a Never Never Land where, it turned out, I knew how to fly. I did not memorize those words, I lived them by heart.

An Accidental Grace

It would be decades before poetry again "arrived in search of me," as Pablo Neruda says. Twenty-three years later, in 1994, the practice of living poems by heart seized me and became a path that would save my life.

It was the threshold of winter. A thin sheen of ice coated the naked tree branches and the light slanted gray into my little house in Upstate New York. Somewhere in the preceding months I had lost my muse—and with her, my will to live. Though I was working as a spiritual teacher and therapist, I had lost faith in what I was teaching. Though I was in a graduate program for writing poetry, I couldn't find a thing to write. I was leading workshops and teaching classes about the creative spark but I couldn't find even a warm ember within myself.

This was terrifying. Since I had left my family home at 16, some mysterious inspiration had fueled my life and given me enough juice to come up with some rather innovative ways of making money and helping people. I'd done everything from starting a theater company in New York City to taking groups swimming with dolphins in workshops on self-transformation. Now that spark was nowhere to be found. All my searching in the worlds of psychology and spirituality had brought me learning and insight and fantastic adventures. But now the same articulations that had once freed me seemed to flatten and skew everything they touched. I felt I had come to the end of language. I had lost faith in words. I couldn't communicate my reality.

And on top of that, my family was in crisis. My mother and father had had major heart attacks within months of each other. A depression engulfed me. I functioned well enough to show up for work and meetings with friends. But when I returned home alone, the emptiness inside me was unbearable.

When I can't do anything else, I clean. At least in that domain I have some control. The more difficult a period in my life, the cleaner my house. One day, as I was cleaning yet again, I came upon a battered, unmarked cassette tape under a radiator in the waiting room outside my therapy office. Mildly curious, I dropped it into the stereo and proceeded to do the dishes.

A man's voice speaking poetry filled my house. "To find the great silence / asking so little," he intoned. "One word. / One word only."

My life is not one of those speckled with sensational, inexplicable acts of grace. I am way too skeptical to believe that some *deus ex machina* will drop into my living room and point out the next step of my life. But as the poetry went on, I had to admit a miracle was in progress. Something in the voice of the speaker and the power of the poems spoken aloud pierced the thick skin of my depression. I felt like I was hearing poetry for the first time. I was drinking in an entirely new language, one that could actually cut through the calloused layers of my mind and touch my inner self. I put down my sponge. I lay on the couch and wept.

It took a lot of phone calls to sleuth out the fact that the tape had accidentally slipped out of the handbag of one of my clients as she waited for her session the week before. She told me the speaker was a poet named David Whyte. She described how he had dozens of poems in his memory, his own work and others', which he spoke as part of the lectures he gave.

Inspired by David's example, I decided that if I couldn't write poems, at least I could commit the ones I loved to memory. It seemed to me that writing required a visitation by the muse, a grace over which I had no control. Learning poems by heart, on the other hand, appeared to be an act of choice. Since no amount of invitation, seduction, or demand had resulted in an appointment with the muse, I opted to focus on something that I could actually do.

During this time I was driving at least once a month to visit my mother and father in Massachusetts as they recovered their health. The four-hour trip was mostly composed of one long, straight highway between Upstate New York and their home. In those hours on the Mass Pike, I learned the power of taking a poem into my life as my teacher and friend.

With my hands on the wheel and the poem of the day on the passenger seat beside me, my eyes would furtively grab each line in the split second that I could afford to shift my focus from the unfurling asphalt. I would speak, sing, shout, whisper, and weep the words, taking them deeper and deeper into me, letting them call out voices and feelings and memories that I did not know existed inside me.

I devoured the poems of Mary Oliver, Johann Wolfgang von Goethe, and Rainer Maria Rilke, letting their rich imagery and truth-telling fill my emptiness. I learned ancient, mystical poems by Kabir and Lalla, rhyming poems by William Butler Yeats and Edna St. Vincent Millay, modern poems by Sharon Olds, Leonard Cohen, and Marie Howe. I discovered myself in the words of Jelaluddin Rumi and T. S. Eliot. "You will love again the stranger who was your self," Derek Walcott promises in his poem "Love after Love." As I took these poems into my breath, voice, and heart, that promise was coming true.

A Path of Living Poetry

As the miles and months passed, I took many poems to heart— some I committed to memory and others became companions and guides for me from the page. I realized that learning the poems by heart was only a part of the experience that was quietly, inexorably freeing me from the grip of the depression. More impactful than having the poems in my memory was the experience of living them: inviting them into my voice, body, feelings, and thoughts, where they were causing profound shifts in my energy and consciousness. I was returning to a forgotten language that had once been mine. The poems seemed to know me better than I knew myself. They sparked insights and reflected my deepest feelings more intimately than words alone could touch. For though a poem is made of words, what touches us is between and beyond them. The words might be simple or complex. Of themselves, they have no magic. But together the words become part of a structure that encloses intimate space. Once again I was realizing what I had discovered as a teenager: It is possible to speak the mystery, the silence, the unnamable joys and sorrows of my inner reality. To touch the wordless through a gathering of words.

I have experienced this phenomenon even in poems that have no intention of being spiritual. There are moments when an unexpected metaphor, or the startling way the poet uses a word, or the rhythm of a particular phrase takes you by surprise and suddenly you have fallen into yourself, freed of the trappings of your mind. It can happen in a mystical poem by Catherine of Siena from the 14th century:

There the soul dwells—
like the fish in the sea
and the sea in the fish.²

or one by Lucille Clifton, written in 1996 on her father's 90th birthday:

what he has forgotten
is more than i have seen.
what i have forgotten
is more than i can bear.³

The mind meets something it can't conceive of and yet conception occurs. A completely new, yet somehow remembered, experience is born. There is a gasp, a closing of eyes, a sense of being recognized by this stranger, the poem.

As I took more and more poems into my life, what began as a self-prescribed therapy for depression became the unwitting discovery of a transformational path. It turned out that receiving a poem so completely caused profound shifts in my consciousness. Some of this came through the self-inquiry required to find the authentic experience of each word of the poem within me. Some of it came through the transformative power of the body of the poem as it entered my body: the rhythm of it beating in my pulse; the lines and phrases changing my breathing; the song of the consonants, vowels, and rhymes making music on my tongue. Some of it came through giving my voice to the voice of the poem, which required dissolving restrictions that had censored my sound since I was a toddler. Rumi's words—"Forget your life! Say God is great. Get up!"[4]—summoned a jubilant demand I'd never before permitted myself to express. A poem by W. B. Yeats brought a raunchy seductiveness into my voice that I didn't know I had within me:

> A woman can be proud and stiff
> When on love intent;
> But Love has pitched his mansion in
> The place of excrement;
> For nothing can be sole or whole
> That has not been rent.[5]

A spontaneity and freedom was returning to my life. Poem by poem, the depression that had cloaked me was lifting.

Somewhere in those miles of macadam, I discovered a very particular path for taking poetry into my life as a transformative agent. I say I discovered it because the experience was less an act of invention than it was like coming upon an intricate underground city and meticulously brushing the dust off its elaborate mosaic walls. And this discovery was changing the very shape of my life.

somewhere i have never
travelled,gladly beyond

somewhere i have never travelled,gladly beyond
any experience,your eyes have their silence:
in your most frail gesture are things which enclose me,
or which i cannot touch because they are too near

your slightest look easily will unclose me
though I have closed myself as fingers,
you open always petal by petal myself as Spring opens
(touching skillfully,mysteriously) her first rose

or if your wish be to close me,i and
my life will shut very beautifully,suddenly,
as when the heart of this flower imagines
the snow carefully everywhere descending;

nothing which we are to perceive in this world equals
the power of your intense fragility:whose texture
compels me with the colors of its countries,
rendering death and forever with each breathing

(i do not know what it is about you that closes
and opens;only something in me understands
the voice of your eyes is deeper than all roses)
nobody,not even the rain,has such small hands

— E. E. Cummings

Chapter 3

THE MEDICINE OF POETRY

Poetry is a life-cherishing force. For poems are not words, after all, but fires for the cold, ropes let down to the lost, something as necessary as bread in the pockets of the hungry. Yes indeed.

— Mary Oliver

As I learned more poems, I was astounded at the power of their medicine. It seemed that just about every aspect of my life was being infused by the gathering wellspring of poetry inside me. Like a convert to some new religion, I was giddy with enthusiasm. I wanted to share it with everyone I met. My excitement was enough to propel me through the wall of shyness that had surrounded me since I was a child and launch me into surprisingly deep conversations with all sorts of people. I spoke poems to anyone who would listen—friends, clients, students, even the stranger sitting next to me on the plane if she or he happened to ask about my life. It was as if I had come upon an elixir that would instantly open the heart, and I wanted to tell everyone.

Naïvely, I imagined this discovery to be my own. But as I shared the poems with others and talked about my experience, a remarkable phenomenon occurred. All sorts of people started telling me about poems that had saved *their* lives. More than a few pulled index cards ragged with age from their wallets to show me the lines that had seen them through the hard times. Several reached back decades in memory to speak a poem learned in high school, which, even today, they whisper to themselves when in need. My own father, who had never revealed any interest in poetry, launched into John Milton's famous sonnet "On His Blindness" upon learning of my passion. He had memorized the poem in high school in 1933, and it had lived within him for 75 years. Almost everyone I spoke to knew a person who had found a path through some dark jungle by the light of a poem. It turned out that poetry—carried on scraps of paper, or taped to the fridge, or committed to memory—was a resource that had a long history, a lineage of great teachers, and an entire heritage that, born as I was in the middle of the 20th century in America, I had completely missed out on.

Finding a Voice

One of the most resonant voices for the potency and necessity of spoken poetry is Dr. Maya Angelou. We met in September 2005 at a conference called "Women and Power." I was to deliver a closing poem after an evening of extraordinary keynote speakers. Dr. Angelou's speech was the last, just before my poem. Her voice rang out from the stage as I sat in the front row, not wanting to miss a word, waiting for the last possible moment to slip backstage and prepare myself to go on.

She spoke about the vital need for our voices to arise and be heard, the courage to set them free, and the necessity of support and community as each woman dares to speak. Every time she walks onto a stage, she told us, she imagines her grandmother out in the audience. Sometimes she adds her mother and other women in her life who have loved and supported her. Without them, she said, she could not stand on that stage alone. As she spoke, she punctuated her words and memories with poems that she recited by heart, her voice rich and swaying, a wide river of sound.

Then she spoke of her childhood. How she had found her own voice at the age of 12, after years of being mute. I'm sure many in the audience had read her autobiography, *I Know Why the Caged Bird Sings,* and remembered that she had been raped by her mother's lover when she was eight. After he was murdered, she went mute because she imagined her own words had caused his death. "Just my breath, carrying my words out, might poison people and they'd curl up and die like the black fat slugs that only pretended,"[1] she explains in the autobiography. So the young Maya stopped talking for almost six years.

When I was about 12, I read and reread *I Know Why the Caged Bird Sings.* The story of those years of mutism fascinated me. An extremely quiet child myself, I wished I had known the young Marguerite, as she was then called. I was sure we would have been best friends. Perhaps she would have been a companion in the loneliness of my alienation from most conversations. At family gatherings and school dances, my silence bordered on the antisocial, and I was reprimanded for not being more outgoing. I wondered what it would be like to give up talking completely, without apology. I was haunted by questions about Marguerite's silence. What did she do with all that space while the rest of the world filled even the slightest pause with small talk? Did she ever speak, even to herself? And what brought her voice out at last? What was important enough to make her break her vow?

In three and a half decades, I hadn't forgotten these questions. As Dr. Angelou's rich, buttery voice poured into the audience, they floated through my mind.

"What did I do in the silence?" She plucked the question right out of my thoughts, as if we had indeed been best friends when I was 12. "Poetry! I memorized poetry. I memorized 60 Shakespearean sonnets. And some of the things I memorized, I'd never heard them spoken, so I memorized them according to the cadence that I heard in my head. I loved Edgar Allan Poe, and I memorized everything I could find. And I loved Paul Laurence Dunbar—still do. It was like putting a CD on. If I wanted to, I'd just run through my memory and think, that's one I want to hear."[2] As she walked the dirt roads of Stamps, Arkansas, speaking to no one, the poems would play through her mind like invisible friends.

In her autobiography, Angelou draws a portrait of Mrs. Flowers, the teacher who eventually reached through her mutism and coaxed out her voice. This wise woman appealed to her love of literature. "Words mean more than what is set down on paper," she told the girl. "It takes the human voice to infuse them with meaning." She brought out freshly baked cookies and lemonade. Then she read to the child from *A Tale of Two Cities*. "Her voice slid in and curved down through and over the words," Angelou writes, astonished. "She was nearly singing. I wanted to look at the pages. Were they the same that I had read? Or were there notes, music, lined on the pages, as in a hymn book?"[3]

While she describes her meeting with Mrs. Flowers in *I Know Why the Caged Bird Sings*, Angelou never tells the story of her first spoken words. So it was not until that evening in 2005 that I learned it was poetry that compelled her to crack her vow of silence.

"Mrs. Flowers knew I loved poetry," Dr. Angelou told the audience. "She knew I had been memorizing. And she said to me, 'You don't love poetry.' It was the cruelest thing I think she could have said. She seemed to be taking my only friend! 'In order to love poetry you must speak it! You must feel it come across your tongue, through your teeth, over your lips.'"[4]

She told Marguerite to take home a book of poetry, to learn one by heart, and, next time they met, to recite it. The mute child was so upset by this challenge that she ran away from Mrs. Flowers and avoided her for six months.

Then, one day, after not speaking for almost six years, she went under her house to see if she could recite a poem out loud. She chose a sonnet from Shakespeare.

"And I had a voice! I had a voice."

The Gossamer Thread

Several years after I met Dr. Angelou, I was introduced to her son, the poet and novelist Guy Johnson. He told me a story of how his mother's love of poetry had helped him through a turning point in his own life. In December 2002, he called her from a hospital room in Miami.

"Mom, could you recite 'Invictus' for me?"

"Of course!" she answered.

It was Guy's ninth spinal surgery. Paralyzed in 1982 by a car accident, he had frequently drawn on his mother's reservoir of poems during the most difficult periods of dealing with the loss of his body's capacities.

"I had to assess if it was worth living. I was at a point where Hell was close. You see, before the accident, my body had been my vehicle. I was six feet five, muscular, not a bad physical presence. So part of my dynamism had to do with my physicality. But when I was paralyzed, it all turned to lard. I was just a head. I could still talk, but I could not turn, I could not move anything below my neck."

As I sit with Guy in his writing office, his powerful energy fills the room and beyond. I feel like I am plugged in to a vibrant current, a voltage that runs through everything he says and does. Frequently as we speak, tears come to his eyes. Not when he tells his own story, but when he speaks of those he loves—his family, friends, and the poems that have touched his life. Every few minutes in the course of our conversation, he grabs a book to read a poem to me—Paul Lawrence Dunbar's "Little Brown Baby," which his mother read to him as a boy and he read to his own son; Countee Cullen's "What is Africa to me?"; Langston Hughes' "Harlem Sweeties"; James Weldon Johnson's "O Black and Unknown Bards":

O black and unknown bards of long ago,
How came your lips to touch the sacred fire?
How, in your darkness, did you come to know
The power and beauty of the minstrel's lyre?

As he reads the next five stanzas of the poem, his lush, musical voice fills with so much intensity that it seems to crack open and spill out through his tears. I, too, am weeping. Guy is introducing me to a rich vein of poetry I have never before encountered. Until this moment, I had not realized that the scope of my knowledge was limited to mostly white, mostly "mystical" poets. Now he is reading to me the words of African Americans—some from the late 1800s and some from today—and I feel myself personally touched at the deepest level as if by an intimate friend or teacher. "The great thing about poetry," he tells me, "is that no matter what lonely street you are on, someone has been there before you. And survived."

"Invictus," the poem Guy asked his mother to say to him over the phone in the hospital, is such a poem of survival. William Ernest Henley, the poet, was a journalist, writer, and adventurer. "But what isn't known about him," Guy explains, "is that his leg was amputated and he had an eye put out by a branch in a riding accident. So he had real physical difficulties at a time when having physical difficulties generally meant your social death." Henley wrote "Invictus" as he learned to survive these losses.

As we sit together in the creative ferment of Guy's office, surrounded by photographs of children, grandchildren, and friends and shelves of well-worn books that seem to have overflowed their places and scattered onto every surface, it is clear to me that Guy's story is not so different from the poet he lauds. Here, too, is a man who has survived impossible physical and psychological obstacles to become a living inspiration through his presence and words.

"It must have been quite a lot of work to learn how to move everything again." I am watching him reach for a notebook on the other side of the room.

"It wasn't my doing. I mean I worked, but I was given a divine gift. There were a lot of people working hard who never got there."

He tells me it took him a long time to learn to use a typewriter because he couldn't control his movements. He wrote his own poem "The Psalm of Severed Strings" while he was paralyzed, struggling to teach each finger to hit the right keys. In the poem he speaks of the "marionettes" who "strive against flaccid muscles and confused reflexes . . . to regain that which nature has freely given and fate stolen away." He goes on in the final stanza:

Yet, if spirit remains,
a human can still be seen
amidst the disobedient flesh.
And, if the will has fiber,
even wood can be made to dance.
Thus, when you see them among the crowds,
you have seen the true puppeteers,
for with gossamer thread
each ligament, nerve and limb is moved
to rejoin life's wild carousel.

Guy's ninth surgery, in combination with a lot of hard work and miracles, made it possible for him to connect with that "gossamer thread" and move again. It was ten days after that operation that he called on his mother to recite William Ernest Henley's poem "Invictus."

"That was my grandfather's poem." He uses the possessive as if his grandfather owned the deed to the work. But I understand what he means. There is many a poem that I associate with whoever passed it on to me, so complete is their embodiment of its essence. Guy goes on, "Because of that, it was my mother's poem, and she taught it to me."

"As I began to speak the poem to him in the hospital," Angelou recalled later in an interview, "I remembered the eight-year-old to whom I had taught it. I remembered that little person, stomping around, marching like he was a soldier. And now, here he was, a man, needing something to hold on to, something to repeat to himself."[5]

She spoke the opening stanza as her son listened from his hospital room:

Out of the night that covers me,
Black as the Pit from pole to pole,
I thank whatever gods may be
For my unconquerable soul.[6]

She continued through to the famous final lines: "I am the master of my fate: / I am the captain of my soul." When she had finished speaking, her son thanked her and reminded her that she had forgotten a verse. Then he asked her, "Now would you do the poem with me? Use your cadence, I'll follow you." So they spoke it together over the phone. When they'd finished, he said, "Thanks, Mom. While we were saying that poem, the doctors were digging all the stitches out of my back."[7]

As I'm leaving, I ask Guy a question that has been haunting me since the United States dropped the first bombs on Iraq: "Why poetry at a time like this? In this world that seems to be so full of need for the basics—peace, human kindness, food, clothing, shelter—why do we need poetry?"

"When could be a better time for poetry than now?" His deep voice explodes with passion. "Poets can be truly courageous people who are willing to stand up for what they believe. Who else to say what needs to be said but a poet? In times of pain, you need to know that other human beings have felt as you feel. And that feeling is not confined to race or class or issue or country or nation. It is the heart of the human being."

Passing On the Gift

At the same "Women and Power" conference where I met Dr. Angelou, I also met the dynamo spoken-word poet C. C. Carter. C. C. was there to receive an award from an organization called V-Day, which works to stop violence against women and girls all over the world. She was being honored for a miracle she created on Chicago's South Side. Every Tuesday, up to 100 people crowd into Lee's Unleaded Blues Club to cheer each other on in an evening of spoken-word poetry and community. Most, if not all, are survivors of violence, abuse, or incest, and most, but not all, are women. (Once a month, at "Men on the Mike Night Out," male writers and performers serenade women, tackling issues of misogyny through hip-hop and rap music.) The heart of what gathers them together is the need to give voice, as only poetry can, to what has remained unspoken and unspeakable. Women who have never before felt safe enough to talk about their lives take the microphone as the rest of the people cheer, laugh, and cry to hear their own hopes and fears, wounds and wildness given voice. The gathering is organized by C. C.'s organization, POW-WOW, which is an acronym for "Performers or Writers for Women on Women's Issues."

Those who crowd into the club receive healing even beyond the poetry spoken there. "We know women survivors have a hard time with being touched," C. C. explained to me. "And we know that many of the women have not experienced a positive feeling all week long. They have been stressed out at their job or unappreciated in their family. So we start the evening by going around to every single woman and telling her, 'We are glad you are here! We are glad you made it! We are glad to see you back for another week.' And we hug everybody."

When C. C. receives the award, she takes the mike with the grace of a master conductor picking up her baton. One shoulder bare, the rest of her wrapped in a red silky dress just tight enough to show off her voluptuous hips, she raises one hand high above her head as if calling even the air to attention. She gives no acceptance speech. Instead, she does what she has made possible for so many others, what has earned her championships across the country. She dives right into one of her poems and takes us, the audience, with her.

What is it that you misunderstand about these hips
my hips?
These are my hips—
these forty-six-inch hips

attached to this twenty-four-inch waist
are my hips and they tell herstory
Perhaps you question the size of my hips—
the second largest continent in the world sired these hips
of course they would be as large—

The oldest civilization on earth gave birth to these hips
of course they would be as wide—[8]

Several stanzas later, as she careens toward the finish of the poem, the audience is on its feet, screaming and stamping. C. C. rides the swells of sound as if she'd spent lifetimes surfing the roar of 750 women all shouting at once. She is glowing. By the end of her poem each of us is wishing our hips were even wider and could swirl and flounce and pump and flutter like C. C.'s. As we leave the auditorium, I'm sure that I am not the only big-hipped woman to sashay a bit more sensually toward the dining hall, for the first time in my life feeling a little luckier and sexier than my less endowed friends.

C. C. was not always so at home in herself and her body. At the age of 11, she wanted to die. Her father was a minister and had to change parishes frequently, so her family was constantly moving. "Every time we got comfortable in a place and I finally started to make friends, he got a new church," C. C. told me.

On top of that, her body started to change. "I was from a family of very full-figured women. My grandmother was a Hottentot." C. C. explained to me that this was the name of a tribe from Southwestern Africa whose women became famous for their wide hips. They were horrifically mistreated in sideshow attractions when "imported" to Europe in the early 19th century.

"I developed these hips at 11. And walking in the world like that was not safe. Children can be cruel. Walking down the hallway, boys would grab me. Adults would chastise me. Even my own family would say, 'If you keep it up you'll be shaped just like your grandmother!'"

C. C.'s grandmother took care of her on Tuesdays and Thursdays. "She was this amazing poet who had given up everything for her family." One day years earlier, when C. C. was in the third grade, a chance homework assignment opened up the world of poetry between them and they forged a connection that would guide C. C.'s life. "I came home with the poem by Langston Hughes, 'Hold Fast to Dreams.' I was supposed to learn it by heart for my assignment. That's when we discovered that we had this hidden language that bonded us."

Later C. C. wrote about what happened that afternoon. "I didn't understand the intention of the poem, what it meant to 'hold fast to dreams.' Grandma said that was because I was mumbling, trying to learn it under my breath. 'You can't feel a poem just by reading it—you got to speak the poem, act out the poem, then you can know its true meaning.' And there in the mirror, watching her perform 'In the Morning' by Paul Lawrence Dunbar entirely by memory, that's when I realized that my grandmother was magic."[9]

C. C. and her grandmother spent hours in front of the mirror practicing poems together. But as she grew older, crushed under the accumulated stress of repeated moves and the merciless teasing and disrespect she endured as her body changed, C. C. gradually started to shrink into herself, hiding her shape in oversized clothes and hiding her feelings behind a veil of depression.

Her withdrawal culminated one day in eighth grade when she came home utterly devastated. She didn't want to return to school. She didn't want to live.

"I literally wanted to check out of here. My grandmother sensed this and gave me Dr. Angelou's poem 'Phenomenal Woman.' She told me to put it on my mirror. Every morning before I walked out of my room I was to read it. And every night after I said my prayers, I was to say it out loud."

That poem saved C. C.'s life. Its medicine brought her back to herself from the barrage of insults, invasion, and loneliness she faced at school. After that, every time C. C. met some kind of obstacle, her grandmother would "prescribe" a poem that would be the perfect medicine. Mostly they were Maya Angelou's poems.

"I learned how to use poetry to silence my enemies—spouting off to the bullies in the hallway, 'You may write me down in history / With your bitter, twisted lies. / You may trod me in the very dirt. / But still, like dust, I'll rise.' Or to the mean, snotty girls, 'Pretty women wonder where my secret lies. / I'm not cute or built to suit a fashion model's size.' Every time I hit an obstacle, there was Dr. Maya Angelou, and a poem, and my grandmother."[10]

After her grandmother's death, C. C. became a nationally recognized performance poet. Like Maya Angelou, every time she took the stage, she brought her grandmother with her. She'd hear the familiar voice: "Hold your head up, look right in that mirror . . ." Then her grandmother would merge into her, and she would fulfill the dream they had shared.

Years later, on a September night in 2005, both C. C. and I listened, enraptured for our own reasons, to Maya Angelou's message. For each of us it was a culmination point. C. C. sat in the audience and wept with gratitude.

A long chain of poetry, passed from heart to heart, had led up to that moment. There was the poetry Maya Angelou learned by heart that helped her survive as a child when she was mute with the trauma she had experienced. And there was the poetry she spoke to her son that helped him survive his paralysis and the operation that finally set him free. Angelou's poem, passed from grandmother to granddaughter, helped C. C. Carter survive to find her own poetic voice. C. C., in turn, gave the healing power of poetry to the women of Chicago's South Side, helping them face their days and speak their truth. Finally now, because of that work, C. C. sat in the audience listening to Maya Angelou recite the very poem that began the journey that became her life, her passion, and her service to the world.

"We've come full circle, Grandma," C. C. whispered to her grandmother's spirit as she listened to Dr. Angelou speak the words of "Phenomenal Woman."

Sustaining the Heart in the Midst of the Heartless

I have heard story after story about the countless ways poetry can be a medicine that heals and sustains. Maya Angelou, Guy

Johnson, and C. C. Carter called on poems to see them through times of extreme trauma. My optometrist's assistant told me that poetry brought her back from a nervous breakdown, when she was "hanging by a thread" after the untimely death of her brother. "I memorized almost all of Shakespeare's sonnets. They literally saved my life." At 15, John Muir, who grew up to be one of the founders of the environmental movement, sneaked out behind his tyrannical father's back to a neighbor's library where he secretly read the works of Wordsworth, Blake, and Keats, seeding his romantic view of nature. Others, like Sonja Franeta, discovered that poems can give protection and guidance through soul-battering hours of mindless labor.

Sonja was a dedicated Socialist who took a series of jobs on assembly lines when she was in her 20s. Though she had a master's degree in literature, she held a vision that the Labor movement could transform society. Her chosen job was an expression of her identification with the working people as well as a connection to her own immigrant Eastern European background.

In the cacophony of clanging metal, dull repetitive tasks, and abusive interactions, poetry saved her. Years later, she wrote a short story called "The Can Factory Sonnets" based on her experience there:

> The noise was unbearable in the can plant. It was like jackhammers but more metallic and hollow sounding. Constant clamor of machinery and can tops—the drive was to keep the place going one hundred percent all the time. Monotonous, mechanical, assembly-line work! . . . Fewer workers meant fewer variables. All alone at my station, I got their strategy but was pretty much a slave.

Reflecting on the experience three decades later, she said, "Everyone had their own way of surviving. Some people did it by drinking, drugs, music, fantasy, and many things I never found out about. I survived by doing political work and my poetry."

Before she left for work every morning, Sonja would choose a poem she wanted to learn by heart. Sometimes it was from the work of W. H. Auden or Emily Dickinson. Sometimes it was a sonnet by William Shakespeare. She'd write it in letters as small as she could manage on a tiny piece of paper. It had to be tiny because she couldn't risk being caught by her abusive foreman.

> I tucked it into my jeans and reached for it whenever I had a hand free—to bask in the next line. Sometimes I'd lay the paper in a strategic position at my station; while I worked I could see it—on the shelf above my rows of can lids or near the pile of paper bags stamped with a big old number. "When my love swears she is made of truth, / I do believe her, though I know she lies." Over and over I'd say the lines, till Will's rhythms overpowered the ugly clamoring machines.

Sonja's first assembly-line job, before she worked at the can factory, was at the Ford automobile plant in Milpitas, California. She was the only woman in her section, surrounded by men who were terrifying to her with their abrasive banter and hurtful, crass comments. As time went on, though, she realized that this was the only way they knew to counteract the harshness of their working conditions. Many had been at the same mechanical job for 30 years and were just holding out for retirement.

There, in the din of clanging car parts and shouting men, it was to the rhythms and sensibilities of Walt Whitman that she turned. At this job she didn't even have time to glance at a piece of paper because the huge metal chunks of automobiles kept moving relentlessly overhead. Nor did she want to risk being teased by the men around her.

But the ride to the factory was a long one. Sonja discovered she could use that time to immerse herself in "Song of Myself" or "I Sing the Body Electric," planting Whitman's words inside her so that, in the midst of the assembly line, she could recall and meditate upon them.

"It was the rhythm of Whitman's lines that saved me," she told me as we drank tea together in her Oakland home. "Those long lines of verse counteracted the terrible push. It was a power-ful paradox. I was being forced, by the movement of the assembly line, to work very fast. At the same time, meditating on those verses was making me human." She recited a few lines from "Song of Myself":

I believe in you my soul . . . the other I am must not abase
     itself to you,
And you must not be abased to the other.

Loafe with me on the grass . . . loose the stop from
     your throat,
Not words, not music or rhyme I want . . . not custom
     or lecture, not even the best,
Only the lull I like, the hum of your valved voice.[11]

As she spoke the words, I could almost hear the voices of men vying for dominance over the driven staccato of machinery dissolving in the gentle liquidity of Whitman's presence.

One of Sonja's heroes at the time, Che Guevara, once said, "The true revolutionary is guided by a great feeling of love." For Sonja, the harsh working environment of the factory made it hard to remember that it was love that had inspired her to take the job. But without that love, there was no point. Whitman's words brought her back to her reason for being there.

A working-class poet, Whitman sings the praises of all the different people who provided the labor force in the industrial age. In "I Hear America Singing," he honors the carpenter, the mason, the boatman, the shoemaker, the hatter, the woodcutter, the ploughboy, the mother, the young wife, the girl, "each singing what belongs to him or her and no one else." Whitman's poems were the gift that connected Sonja to her heart in that heartless environment. I can only imagine that Sonja's awakened heart, infused by Whitman's poetry, was a gift to the people she worked with, even though they would never know the medicine that was sustaining her.

Miracle in Baghdad

Sonja placed herself in that inhuman circumstance out of choice, because of her political convictions. She had loved poetry all her life and called on its medicine because she knew the power it held. Others find poetry's healing power in the midst of circumstances beyond their choice. In the center of the Iraq War, on streets where explosions punctuate the air, Yanar Mohammed and a group of Sunni and Shiite poets gather people together to share poetry's magic against all odds. They founded the Freedom Space that I wrote of earlier, where brave and passionate poetry lovers from all over the country come together to share their inspiration.

Yanar is a pretty, petite powerhouse. Each time we meet, the first thing that strikes me is the gentleness of her voice and dark eyes. Yet this soft-spoken woman has become such a fierce champion of women's rights in Iraq that there have been several threats to her life and the government has prohibited her from appearing on television. As I watched her speak to an outdoor gathering of activists here in the U.S., her light jacket blew open and the waves of her jet-black hair flew freely about her face. She told us that she could no longer go out dressed in this way in Baghdad. I tried to imagine her shrouded in the headscarf she must wear to protect herself from violent Islamic fundamentalists as she negotiates the streets of the war zone that was once her neighborhood.

Yanar was a successful architect until the Iraq War. She and her family lived in a beautiful home in the suburbs of Baghdad. But when she witnessed the violations happening to women as a result of the occupation, she could not remain silent. The movement she founded, the Organization of Women's Freedom in Iraq, runs several women's shelters and helps women who have been unjustly thrown into prison, forced into prostitution, threatened with "honor killings," or caught in the sex-trafficking trade.

It was only by chance that the group began hosting poetry events. The first was a favor Yanar did for the young man she had hired to guard the office of the organization. Adham was a gentle being and the gun he had to carry as a guard seemed a strange counterpoint to his quiet, kind eyes. But only a year ago, not knowing where to turn in his urgency to take some action to save his country from the destruction he was witnessing, Adham had come close to becoming a suicide bomber. His friends had talked him out of it, and now he was pouring his passion for peacemaking into speaking poetry instead.

When Adham asked Yanar to organize a poetry event for a group of his friends, she balked at first. What did poetry have to do with women's rights? The young man confessed he had been eavesdropping on the conversations going on inside the office he guarded. "You women are talking about what really matters: freedom and life," he explained. "And so are we. That is what our poetry is about."

Yanar agreed to host the event on one condition: that there be equal numbers of Shiite and Sunni poets invited. She had no idea that that first Freedom Space would birth a movement that would spread rapidly throughout Baghdad and the surrounding areas, touching the lives of thousands.

Poetry is a powerful force in Iraq and always has been. As Yanar explained to me how some poets are heroes in her country and have tremendous influence on popular opinion, it was hard for me to conceive of a culture so different from my own. There, "poetry is like food and drink"—even and especially in the midst of war. Ibrahim al-Shawi, an Iraqi blogger, writes, "For centuries, poetry was the first religion for many people. Their collective wisdom, their history and heritage, their values and ideals, their pride and achievements are all preserved in poetry lines."[12]

Though she claims she is not a poet, Yanar's words are so alive with rhythm and imagination that I felt as if she were speaking directly into my heart. "How do you respond when you have in your cell phone, let us say, 30 phone numbers of your loved ones?" As she set up the scene, I had a foreboding about where we might be going. "And maybe eight of them have died already. But you were talking to them only yesterday or last week!" She was speaking in particular about a young poet named Amen al-Salmawi who was one of the shining stars at the first Freedom Space. "You know, there are some poets who can hypnotize an audience. Amen was like that. Though he couldn't have been more than 23, when he delivered his poems he was really charismatic and outspoken. Everybody fell in love with him. But then on the breaks he was so shy he wouldn't even talk. He just smiled and nodded."

Amen came to the first Freedom Space with a group of other poets from the Sunni suburb of Salman Pak. They sat opposite a group from Sadr City, a Shiite area. "There were wonderful poets on each side," Yanar remembered. She told me how a Sunni poet would recite a poem that would trigger someone from the Shiite side of the tent to speak his or her poem because it voiced the same theme or longing. This, in turn, would inspire a poem from the opposite side, and so on. "It was ping-pong poetry, with this ball of magic being bounced from one side to the other," Yanar told me. "They all turned out to be on the same team!"

One evening a few months later, Amen was exchanging impro-vised poetry with a group of friends when suddenly the door was flung open and al Qaeda militants, who believe poetry is heresy, sprayed them with bullets. Amen was the first to die.

"He will always be with us in the Freedom Spaces," Yanar said emphatically. "You might find this very naïve, but we keep an empty chair among the poets, and we put his picture on it."

Just over a year later, in the same city where Amen was mur-dered for speaking poetry, the 12th Freedom Space took place. "We decided to hold the event in Salman Pak even though it was very dangerous," Yanar told me. "We wanted to say to the youth, 'You are not a Shiite or a Sunni, you are a human being. There are many other ways to live than offending, assaulting, and kill-ing each other.' What better way for these young people to forget about their differences than to join together and speak the poetry of their longing, their suffering, their love. To find some reason to continue to live together."

The risky poetry venture won the hearts of the young people of the city. Even some of the soldiers from the local militias vol-unteered to guard the event. "We have no money to pay them,"

Yanar explained. "We cannot give them anything other than the spiritual feeling of the poetry. But they say they feel they have received a symbolic salary."

As a Shiite, Wissam al-Assadi risked his life to travel to the Salman Pak Freedom Space. Many other Shiite poets declined the invitation, knowing that the city's Sunni residents saw Shiites as perpetrators of horror. Indeed, for the previous five years Shiite militias had been terrorizing the population. They tortured youths for wearing shorts or smoking and killed them for speaking poetry. Schools for girls were bombed. By the time of the Freedom Space event, the tables had turned and Sunni soldiers, supported by the United States, were controlling the area. They were known to turn on almost any Shiite in sight for revenge.

But when Wissam was invited to speak his poetry at the Salman Pak Freedom Space, he immediately accepted. His choice was to be on the "front line," speaking his poems no matter what it took.

"He is a genius poet." Yanar glowed when she told me about him. "He brings people to tears almost instantly." Several years earlier, Wissam had sustained a head injury when he was hit by a car, and his verses always include a line or two about the fracture in his skull. "Please forgive me," he writes. "I am not drunk, I am not high. But this crack in my skull twists everything I see, and I can't understand what is happening around me."

"It is as if he speaks for his whole generation," Yanar reflected. "They are all caught in a fragmented reality. They do not understand this daily war. They are torn apart by al Qaeda pressures and the militias from all sides that they must hide from or join. They feel Wissam's wound as their own." Indeed, by the end of his performance the audience was on its feet, chanting his name. Even the armed Sunni soldiers had come in from the street and were cheering with the crowd.

"A few hours of poetic magic brought this group of people together," Yanar told me. "We felt like one family with no differences. People are desperate for this kind of positive connection. What we see in every face, regardless of denomination, is absolute love and an aspiration for freedom."

Feeling Out Loud

Another beloved speaker at the poetry gatherings was a young woman who went by the name of Hind because it was too dangerous for her to use her real name. When she took the microphone at a Freedom Space event in downtown Baghdad, a hush fell over 1000 people. Many had heard her speak poetry at previous gatherings and had been waiting with anticipation for her turn on the stage. Hind does not write poetry; rather, she has a gift for learning poems by heart. As she moved from a classical Qasida (a highly structured ode with intricate rhymes and rhythms) to the work of modern Iraqi poets, the textures of her voice changed to meet each poem. The whisper of an intimate love poem broke open into an emphatic shout that filled the auditorium as she spoke the truth of the 8th-century female mystic Rabia al-Adawiyya: "I am a Doorkeeper of the Heart, not a lump of wet clay!" In moments she even swept into song, like an osprey lifting onto the wind, singing the verses that poured out of her memory in a voice at once delicate and fierce.

It was almost impossible to conceive that this young woman had only recently been rescued from a nightmare of forced prostitution, torture, and imprisonment. After being kidnapped in her late teens, Hind was bought and sold repeatedly in the sex-trafficking industry that has become rampant since the occupation. When the last brothel that bought her was ambushed, she was thrown into the women's prison. This is where Yanar and her co-workers found her.

"We asked her if she wanted to change her life," Yanar remembered. "She did not believe it could happen. When we told her that we had a shelter for women and that she could work with us, she wept. 'But I have an 11-year-old son,' she said. 'What will happen to my son?'" Of course, her son was invited to come with her. "And that is why," Yanar told me, laughing, "in many of the newspaper photographs of our activists, there is often a young boy in the picture!"

As Hind embarked on her recovery from the years of trauma, she discovered tremendous healing in learning poetry by heart. Like most people from her village, she could neither read nor write. But this did not diminish her genius for remembering and speaking poetry. The inhabitants of southern Iraq, where Hind was born, have been deprived of development and education for many decades. In spite of this, Yanar told me, they are known to have a talent for poetry. "Expressing their emotions comes spontaneously. They are so eloquent! In their spare time, when they are sitting among their families or their tribes, they speak in poetry together." I could hear Yanar's profound respect for these people for whom "the only tool for expressing the chronic deprivation, pain, and anger is poetry."

In the West, when we think of a talent for poetry, we usually associate it with writing poems. But in Iraq and many other countries, poetic ability is not confined to composition. Many, like Hind, have a gift of memory that is startling to those of us in the Western world. Our minds are overcrowded with modern multitasking, and such indigenous abilities have been lost or submerged. Al-Shawi writes, "People in the countryside and the desert have truly astonishing capacity to remember poetry . . . I have met people who can remember 50 lines of a poem after hearing them once. The rhythm and the music in the words of course help. I once met a Bedouin who in the course of an (extended) evening must have recited several thousand lines of poetry, covering almost three centuries of his tribe's and region's history."[13]

Within a short time, Hind learned dozens of poems by classical and modern Iraqi poets and began delivering them at the Freedom Space events. "She has become one of the most well-loved voices," Yanar said with pride. "Just imagine turning your life from being a symbol of evil, which is how she was seen when she was a prostitute, to being a source of joy and a figure of strength for other women. After spending years of her life being treated as a sexual commodity for very bad men to enjoy, now she speaks so openly and passionately to crowds of more than a hundred people. She always knows the right poem to say at the right time and is not a bit bashful."

Yanar's voice was full of awe for the talent of all the young poets who have constellated around the Freedom Spaces. "They call me their Princess of Poetry," she admitted shyly. "I am very proud of that. I cannot write one word of poetry or recite it, but these young poets have taught me to feel it more and more." Then her voice clouded as she thought about the burdens that the younger generation of Iraqis must live with. "They do not know how to respond to the constant fighting, to holding a machine gun, to mullahs trying to gain power over them, to American tanks that come into their towns. But they do know how to feel and speak it out loud. And if we start feeling out loud with each other, this is a first step to being stronger within ourselves in the sea of barbarism that we live in."

Later in our conversation she added softly, "It happens many times during the Freedom Spaces that we hear the bombs going off, left and right. We give it a moment or two of silence. Then we go on with the poetry."

Unexpected Gifts

Like Hind and Yanar, most people in Iraq, as well as people in many other countries, are steeped in poetry from their earliest years, and this remains true even in the midst of the rising death toll and the daily trauma of the war. In America, on the other hand, it is possible to grow up with little or no connection to poetry. This was the case with Carl Upchurch, until he inadvertently discovered Shakespeare while doing time in prison. Upchurch, a fourth-grade dropout, was a member of a street gang until he was arrested for bank robbery. Even behind bars, he was so violent with his fellow prisoners that he was thrown into solitary confinement.

After a couple of months of staring at the gray walls of his cell, he noticed a book wedged under the leg of a table. He pulled it out and was disgusted to discover it was a collection of Shakespeare's sonnets. Believing that Shakespeare couldn't possibly have anything to say to him, he returned the book to its task of holding up the table. But after a few more days of boredom, he reluctantly pulled it out again.

"I won't pretend that Shakespeare and I immediately connected," Upchurch admits. "I must have read those damn sonnets 20 times before they started to make sense. Even then, comprehension came slowly—first a word, then a phrase, and finally a whole poem. Those sonnets began to take hold of me, transported me out of the gray world into a world I had never, ever imagined."[14]

In his memoir, *Convicted in the Womb,* Upchurch writes about the transformation he underwent as he read Shakespeare's sonnets. "I discovered the magic of learning, the thrill of going from not knowing to knowing. By struggling to understand Shakespeare, I came to see that ideas have a beauty all their own, beyond even the beauty of the words that frame them."

Upchurch read the sonnets over and over. Before long he had unintentionally learned quite a few by heart. Noticing the transformation that was in progress, the prison chaplain offered to bring more books from the library. Upchurch asked for everything Shakespeare had ever written. After he made his way through the 38 plays and additional poetry, the chaplain suggested he read T. S. Eliot and Mark Twain. Then he read all the major African American poets, historians, and visionaries from the 1920s to the present. Maya Angelou was his favorite, touching him like no one else, especially her later poem "And Still I Rise."

As he continued to devour everything in the prison library from Machiavelli to Nikki Giovanni, he discovered an insatiable passion for learning and ideas. "I felt like I'd been starving my whole life," he writes in his memoir, "and all of a sudden I'd come to a banquet where I could have as much as I wanted." Each poet and writer gave him a different gift, but all seemed to point in the same direction:

Nikki Giovanni affirmed my anger, but showed me that anger could be channeled in a spiritual direction rather than a violent one. Dostoyevsky had the words for my loneliness and isolation. And Mark Twain, in *The Mysterious Stranger,* made me think for the very first time what it means to kill, to maim, to destroy things, to be insensitive and uncaring, to be a savage—all the things I had been, had been proud to be, in my life up to that point. Twain laid the foundation for my subsequent understanding of how sickening it is to cling to violence as if it were decent or human or spiritual.[15]

When he was released from his cell, Carl Upchurch was a changed man. After such intimacy with the likes of Shakespeare and Angelou, he could never again treat anyone with the violence that had put him in solitary. Nor could he stand back and allow those around him to be abusive with each other. He searched for a way to communicate to his fellow inmates the lessons he had been taught through his immersion in poetry and literature. Eventually that search took him out of prison to become a leader of the civil rights movement with several graduate degrees.

While Upchurch's transformation through poetry began reluctantly and unintentionally, others consciously call on poetry's "transportation" to carry them into connection with the spiritual core of their beings—even in places that seem to have little resemblance to the temples and mosques that usually sanctify such endeavors. Recently my friend Ed told me of a miraculous cab ride in Washington, D.C. He described being picked up by a middle-aged Iranian man who seemed surprisingly gentle and relaxed in the midst of the charged buzz of the city. When my friend expressed his love for the poetry of Rumi and Hafiz, the driver said that he had learned dozens of Rumi's poems by heart in Farsi. He was thrilled at Ed's request that he recite some of them. Blaring horns and the din of midday traffic permeated the recitation as they weaved their way through the city. "Such sweetness perfumed the cab," Ed remembered, "as he struggled to translate the poems into English for us." When they arrived at the hotel, the driver pulled down his visor to reveal a whole stack of poems he was learning as he waited between fares. He was glowing. It seemed as if the opportunity to recite his beloved verses had filled him with as much light as his listeners. He thanked his passengers profusely for the opportunity to pass on the gift.

In his book *The Gift,* Lewis Hyde describes a wisdom that is at the heart of many indigenous cultures but seldom acknowledged in the Western world. "Whatever we have been given is supposed to be given away again, not kept. Or, if it is kept, something of similar value should move on in its stead . . . The only essential is this: *the gift must always move.*" Anyone who has been touched by a poem somehow knows this, whether consciously or not. Haven't you noticed that when poetry enters and changes you, you want to share it with others?

When I think about how I was introduced to most of my favorite poems, I realize that almost every one was a gift from someone—a friend who knew I needed that precise medicine, or a colleague who wanted to share the beauty of a line or two, or a student who brought the poem to class, or a teacher who spoke it from a podium. Like C. C. and Guy, I have been blessed again and again with exactly the poem I needed at exactly the moment when it could deeply heal me. And it has been my greatest joy to pass on the gift to others. Each poem in the archive of my heart is like a hub of connection from which spokes radiate to touch many kindred souls in a human network of gifts given and received.

Song of Myself
[Excerpt from part 20]

Shall I pray? Shall I venerate and be ceremonious?
I have pried through the strata and analyzed to a hair,
And counseled with doctors and calculated close and found no
    sweeter fat than sticks to my own bones.

In all people I see myself, none more and not one a
    barleycorn less,
And the good or bad I say of myself I say of them.

And I know I am solid and sound,
To me the converging objects of the universe
    perpetually flow,
All are written to me, and I must get what the
    writing means.

And I know I am deathless,
I know this orbit of mine cannot be swept by a
    carpenter's compass,
I know I shall not pass like a child's carlacue cut with a burnt
    stick at night.

I know I am august,
I do not trouble my spirit to vindicate itself or be
    understood,
I see that the elementary laws never apologize,
I reckon I behave no prouder than the level I plant my house
    by after all.

I exist as I am, that is enough,
If no other in the world be aware I sit content,
And if each and all be aware I sit content.

*One world is aware, and by far the largest to me, and that is
   myself,*
*And whether I come to my own today or in ten thousand or
   ten million years,*
*I can cheerfully take it now, or with equal cheerfulness I can
   wait.*

— Walt Whitman

Chapter 4

CHOOSING
A POEM

Very truly, I tell you, when you were younger, you used to fasten your own belt and go wherever you wished. But when you grow old, you will stretch out your hands, and someone else will fasten a belt around you and take you where you do not wish to go.

— John 21:18

Choosing a poem to be your companion and guide is a mysterious process that does not usually submit to your mind's agenda. Often are the times I have encountered a poem I thought I "should" get to know—for a workshop I am about to give, for a friend's wedding, for a presentation with a colleague who wants me to read a sonnet I don't really like. Sometimes I've tried to use verses for prideful reasons—to win over a new lover with a few succulent lines of Neruda or to impress a poetry teacher with a recitation from Dante's *Divine Comedy*. It never works. Either I end up discarding the effort, or I succeed, but the poem does not truly root in me. Within a week, I will have little memory of it.

On the other hand, I find myself absorbing with gusto poems that are of no use at all to my hungry ego, poems I may never have an opportunity to offer to another person: reading long sections of T. S. Eliot's *Four Quartets* every night just before sleep until the music of the words is singing through my dreams, or learning Dr. Seuss's *Happy Birthday to You* by heart in its entirety, which takes ten minutes to deliver. There is an uncanny inner guidance that compels the poems that I take into my life.

You can trust the poems you are drawn to. They hold a medicine for your life, whether you know what it is or not. Sonja had no idea that Whitman's long, loping lines would counteract the frenetic intensity of the factory. Yet she followed an unnamable, seemingly irrational urge to immerse herself in *Leaves of Grass* and found that the rhythms and images were exactly what she needed to open her heart in the harsh world of the assembly line.

Getting to know a poem is entering into a relationship. And, like developing any relationship of substance, it asks for commitment and focus.

This does not mean hard work. It does not mean painstaking discipline. It does not mean, as poet Mary Oliver says, walking "on your knees for a hundred miles through the desert." It means, again in Oliver's words, letting "the soft animal of your body love what it loves." It requires about the same amount of discipline as becoming a connoisseur of chocolate, or exploring the intricate auditory landscape of a piece of music that makes your heart sing. These endeavors do require focus. But the focus is a natural companion to pleasure and curiosity. When a poem touches you, these arise spontaneously.

Poems attract you for all sorts of reasons. Some, like those described in the last chapter, are medicine for difficult times. Perhaps they offer a clear message that speaks directly to the crux of a soul need, as "Invictus" did for Guy Johnson and "Phenomenal Woman" did for C. C. Carter. Perhaps they bring the vibration of a brighter, truer life, as *Leaves of Grass* did for Sonja in the car factory. Maya Angelou, Carl Upchurch, and Hind were not seeking specific messages from the poems they immersed themselves in.

Rather, it was the essential beauty and wisdom of the verses that attracted them and powerfully counteracted their traumatic situations. In the darkest of times, I, too, have turned to poems for help, for comfort, for affirmation of my inspirations and dreams. They have held me, like wise elders, reminding me of who I am and what really matters.

The Yoga of Poetry

At times, it is not for support or comfort or even affirmation that I am drawn to a poem. Instead it is for the stretch. A poem can summon me to an edge that scares me, but one I know I need to face. Sometimes it is the tone of the poem that stretches me beyond my comfort zone: the brashness of D. H. Lawrence's wild imagination, for instance ("Would you like to throw a stone at me? Here, take all that's left of my peach"), or Anna Swir's unabashed wonder and sexuality ("I make love with my dear / as if I were dying"). Or the poem might ask me to open myself to the pain of those suffering unbearable circumstances, as do Anna Akhmatova's "Epilogue," about the Stalinist Terror in Leningrad ("There I learned how faces fall apart"), and "The Memory of Her Face," by Eve Ensler ("When she woke up / her face was on fire"), about a woman in the midst of the Iraq War.

Each of these poems calls me into communion with people around the world and across time. I am invited into the inner life of someone I took to be a stranger and am shocked to find myself utterly connected. Either I can gratefully bow to the welcome disorientation and move on to the next page in the book or the next moment of my day, or I can choose to take this poem deeper into my life.

When you decide to develop an ongoing relationship with such a poem—to read it deeply and frequently, to discover its layers of meaning and music, to allow it to guide and teach you, perhaps even to learn it by heart—you are consciously inviting that poem to stretch you beyond yourself. I think of this as the "yoga of poetry."

While the word *yoga* has become associated with certain physical practices usually designed to strengthen and open the body, the original Sanskrit word has a much vaster meaning. B. K. S. Iyengar defines it in this way:

> The word *Yoga* is derived from the Sanskrit root *yuj* meaning to bind, join, attach and yoke, to direct and concentrate one's attention on, to use and apply. It also means union or communion. It is the true union of our will with the will of God.[1]

This "yoking" of your personal will to something greater can take you beyond your normal edges, whether by way of a yoga asana, a physical pose that stretches and strengthens your body, or by way of contemplative practices that stretch and strengthen your powers of attention and insight. When I take a good yoga class, the teacher will guide me into physical positions that are sometimes extremely difficult to hold. Yet, if I can surrender into and through the discomfort, eventually a vibrancy will come into the stretch and I will find myself at home far beyond the boundary of what I thought was possible for my body to do. To me, this ease and the mental opening that invariably comes with it are intriguing. It seems that shaping my will and body to a pose that yogis have practiced for centuries sometimes opens a door between the worlds so that a flood of consciousness, passed down through the ages, pours into my cells.

This can happen with a poem. If you consciously choose one that you know will take you beyond your comfort zone, the yoga of joining your consciousness to the consciousness inherent in the words can stretch you from the inside out. As I said in Chapter 1 and will explore further in the next chapter, a poem is a physical event. It enters your body as well as your mind. It affects your lungs, your pulse, and the tones and textures of your voice.

One of my students, Hedda, chose to work with a poem by Sharon Olds for this reason. Hedda was born in Germany and her first language was German. In her 20s she "escaped" to the States to get away from her extremely authoritarian father and mother. Though she was a playful spirit at heart, decades later she still carried herself with a seriousness and rigidity reminiscent of the parents she had fled. She knew this and yearned to free herself from this legacy. But her professional life, as a teacher of English in a juvenile lockdown facility, required her to be quite regimented in both her appearance and her actions. While she chafed at the binding of this persona, she was also aware that something felt very safe and familiar about it.

Hedda was longing to be in a romantic relationship. She knew that her softer side was too successfully hidden by her almost military stiffness, which even her friends found difficult to permeate. How could a potential lover reach through such armor?

Sharon Olds's poetry is sensual. Whatever she's talking about—from laundry to mothering to dying to birthing to writing to sex (with many other subjects in between)—her words come from deep in her body. And many of her poems are indeed about sex. Hedda daringly chose one of these, a poem called "It," to bring to class.

"Sometimes we fit together like the creamy / speckled three-section body of the banana," she began. The whole class held its breath. It was a shock to associate this prim and proper schoolteacher with a banana, much less with sex. She went on, "And sometimes you have me bent over as thick paper / can be folded." Hedda was going for it, allowing the words to bring forth a voice none of us had ever heard from her. It came from somewhere in her belly. One moment there was a delicate edge of breathiness, almost a whisper, and the next her voice gushed out like a primary color slathered into sound for all to see. As if it were a powerful yoga pose, the poem was stretching her into a new shape. "And I feel you going down into me," she murmured. She was suddenly shy, blushing a little, but her eye contact with us did not waver. She was not "acting." She was letting the poem magnetize a real, sensual element of her true self that had been dormant for most of her life.

The class and I could see the poem's medicine taking its course through her body. First, it melted the hard encasement of her voice, permeating it with breath, with the darker tones of her deep belly, with sudden surgings and cracks that popped out without her volition. About halfway through the poem, the melting moved into her torso, which had, until then, been stiffly held in spite of the opening in her voice. We could see her spine loosening, beginning to move in a subtle wave motion, and with it, her hips took on an unexpected life.

In its final section, this poem takes a turn, as do so many of Sharon Olds's works. In the heart of the utterly private, a door opens into the heart of the world. Hedda, riding the waves of the exquisitely erotic imagery, found herself suddenly in the midst of these lines:

> *And sometimes it is sweet as the children we had*
> *thought were dead being brought to the shore in the*
> *narrow boats, boatload after boatload.*[2]

As often happens in a beautiful sexual experience, one moment she was drenched in sensual pleasure, the next she was weeping.

"Always I am stunned to remember it," Hedda spoke the final lines quietly, her cheeks still glistening. "I / sit on my bed the next day with my mouth open and think of it."

When she finished speaking, we, too, were stunned. There was silence. Hedda was glowing. Without needing to hear a word from us, she knew she had invoked a powerful medicine that was already igniting new sensations and impulses within her and there was no going back. She didn't know where it would lead her, but in that moment it was clear that a door had opened.

Stretching Through Taboos

I have frequently chosen poems that will stretch me into possibilities I cannot inhabit without them. At a turning point in my relationship with my parents, I chose several sections of Mary Oliver's book-length poem *The Leaf and the Cloud* to be my "yoga."

This was one of the poems I worked with during the period I spoke of earlier, when my mother and father were both recovering from their health crises, and I was driving the long ribbon of the Mass Pike between their home and mine. On the way home my mind was often tangled with reruns from the recent visit. I felt so helpless to do or say much at all to alleviate their suffering. Helpless to be the daughter I thought they wanted and be true to myself at the same time, and helpless to bring into my parents' home the spiritual clarity that I often felt outside of it. I couldn't accept these moments of helplessness. My mind kept trying to rewrite them so they would come out more to my liking. A good friend of mine called this a bad case of "the woulda-coulda-shouldas."

The day after she diagnosed my "condition," this same friend e-mailed me a few sections from *The Leaf and the Cloud*. Though I had the book in my library, I hadn't read it in a very long time. I took it out and immediately read it cover to cover. For me, this poem is a breathtaking meditation on mortality, largely seen in the mirror of the natural world. But in several pivotal sections, Oliver uncharacteristically talks about her mother and father. Not only does she speak of them, but in a few short stanzas she does an unflinching study of the agonies they carried and wove into the family psyche. Then she succinctly disentangles herself and turns away.

It was for this medicine that my friend sent me the poem, of course. And she was right. I needed a dose of Oliver's commitment to telling the truth, however uncomfortable, without fanfare or apology. I printed out the sections I wanted to work with and put them on the passenger seat. Each time I stopped at a stoplight or rest area, I would read a few more stanzas. As I drove on, I worked with the lines, speaking them out loud, working from memory or glancing quickly at the paper if I forgot a word.

This poem is subversive in a most potent way. Interspersed with exquisite portraits of the natural world are lines like buried knives, which wield truth that cuts right through the most tender lies. Oliver compares her mother to "the blue wisteria" and "the mossy stream out behind the house." This reminded me immediately of my own mother, who loves her garden and watching the changing light on the pond just beyond it. Then, with piercing precision, she describes her mother's life: "Heavier than iron it was / as she carried it in her arms, from room to room."[3] It was hard to speak these words out loud, to name so baldly a quality I had seen not only in my own mother but also, at times, in myself.

And the next lines were even harder. She puts her parents in a box, buries them, and walks away.

I could not bring myself to say those words. My own mother was still very much alive, our relationship was better than ever, and I was not ready to turn away. The very shock of the lines, compounded by the insight that I was nowhere near able to fully inhabit them, stopped me. I pulled over to the side of the road and rolled down the window, taking the icy air into my lungs.

It was a freezing gray afternoon. I was on a section of the highway that has no defining features—no curves or road signs or hills or bodies of water—just the turnpike going on and on, lined by a forest of elm and oak trees in their winter nakedness. The powerful gust of wind from each passing truck caused my little car to shudder rhythmically, as if it were breathing with me.

I held the poem against the steering wheel and read out loud. "It is not lack of love / nor lack of sorrow. / But the iron thing they carried, I will not carry."[4] Suddenly I knew that whether my parents were living or dead, this poem was asking me to put to rest a way of relating to them that had long outlived its time. It was not so much about how I interacted with them on the surface as it was about letting go of an invisible feeling of responsibility for their happiness or lack thereof.

I sat in my car on the side of the road for about 45 minutes, taking in the words of the poem and speaking them out loud. Each time I said certain lines, tears sprang to my eyes and my heart began to pound at the thought of such a radical change in my attitude. Some ancient voice in my psyche shouted: "Taboo!" How dare I "scatter [my] flowers over the graves and walk away"?[5]

Little by little the words sank into my cells. I won't say they completely replaced the taboo in that one afternoon. But I was able to feel them and allow them to coexist with my fear.

It took years to navigate the inner terrain between my "woulda-coulda-shoulda" self and the life offered in Oliver's poem. Indeed, I am still navigating it. The verses have lived inside me like a beacon, pointing the way. In the process, my relationship with both of my parents has become lighter and freer. Ironically, now that it does not weigh upon me like "the iron thing [they] carried," I seem to be able, every now and then, to truly contribute to their happiness.

Awakening to the Heart of the World

Since then, I have often called on a poem to help me bring out a voice from within me that I have been unable to access on my own. When my country invaded Iraq in 2003, for instance, an urgent need to speak out suddenly possessed me. But I had never been a politically engaged person. I didn't even read the papers or listen to the news. My focus had been completely on the inner world. I had poured myself into the navigation of unseen layers of consciousness, adventuring as far as psychology and spirituality could take me and guiding others in their inner excavations. Yet only rarely did my reach expand beyond those who, for the most part, were like me—relatively sheltered, materially comfortable, and white.

Some of the spiritual understandings I held at the time seemed to support my tendency to refrain from activism in the outer world. I felt strongly that peace, in the words of the famous song, had to "begin with me." It seemed to me that the greatest peacemaking I could offer was to "be peace," as the Vietnamese monk Thich Nhat Hanh has said: to heal the wars within myself and help others to do the same. I believed that, until this inner reckoning took place, I had no business meddling in the affairs of the world because my actions would be coming, at least in part, from projecting my own wounds, agendas, and private battles onto others.

Yet these concerns were only a part of what held me back.

Underneath them was a simpler cause: I was just plain shy. I was afraid to move beyond the radius of the people who were basically like me. I was afraid of going to places where suffering was more on the surface, opening my heart, and then being tongue-tied, judged, and helpless to make a difference in the face of more pain than I could bear.

By some genius of fate or fortune, it happens that my close friend Eve Ensler is one of the most engaged and effective activists in the world. Eve and I have been friends for years. I have watched her devote her whole life to speaking out against violence toward women and girls. She has written plays, poems, and books that have literally changed the way the world thinks about women. Through her organization, V-Day, and thousands of performances of her play *The Vagina Monologues* worldwide, she has been able to mobilize a network of support that helps and protects women everywhere.

Eve and I met the day I arrived at college as a freshman. She was a junior. We were an unlikely pair—me with my shyness, billowy long skirts, and intense introspection and her with her revolutionary zeal, skin-tight T-shirts, and wild, risk-everything lifestyle. In college, I watched her lead marches, direct radical plays, and give brilliant and politically edgy speeches. I remember sneaking into the back of the big tent where she was the student speaker at her class's graduation. She spoke about the role of a true teacher, which was to encourage students to find their own voices and stand up for what they believed. "We are not here, in this institution of higher education, to learn to be neutral and analytical." I remember the passion in her voice as she sent sparks through the crowd of graduates, parents, and professors. "A true teacher will teach us to take a stand and speak out."

Over the next three decades, I watched my friend speak out all over the world. I watched with love and awe and deep respect, but no inclination to participate. Until, in 2003, something changed in me. In part it was ignited by the depth of my horror at my own country's aggression and the ensuing devastation being wreaked upon innocent people. But the main spark came through Eve.

Our friendship was deepening. At the same time, V-Day's work was expanding exponentially and Eve's writing was becoming more prodigious and necessary than ever. I often had the good fortune to provide a late-night ear for a newly written scene or poem or chapter.

There was no way I could listen to such fierce, tender portraits of women's struggles without being profoundly changed. For the first time, I felt summoned from my focus on the inner life to move out into the world. Questions haunted me: Could I, too, go into prisons to connect with those inside? What would it be like to travel to the Rift Valley to help girls who were escaping female genital mutilation? Could I offer anything to people who had lost everything they knew to war or disaster?

For over 30 years, Eve had helped me free myself from strait-jacket of my fear. Now I turned to her again. I did not ask her to take me with her into her work, although I'm sure she would have. I turned to a poem she had written called "V-World." If I could speak this poem, if I could bring it into my body and breath, I might begin to give voice to all that was pressing for expression within me.

Like all the poems that have stretched me, "V-World" seemed at once deeply kindred and unfamiliar at the same time. It offers a vision of a world without violence by traveling to some of the most violent places on the planet and portraying women there who fiercely and tenderly choose life even in the face of horror.

"V-World is in the center of us," it begins. "It is longing, and it is remembering." I could thoroughly relate to that paradoxical tension. For me, it came with any powerful vision, as if I were at once reaching forward to an utterly new universe and back to a preincarnate paradise at the same time. But the next sentence of the poem challenged me into a world I didn't know.

V-World is what it smells like when they let you go,
when you're not waiting to be hit.
When you perspire from the sun instead of worry.

Suddenly there were women in prison camps, calloused hands

slicing the air, the anxiety of not knowing where the next viola-
tion would come from. The poem continues into new territory,
invoking "the 16-year-old suicide bomber who turns back," the
Afghan woman in a burqa secretly videotaping "the execution of a
woman accused of flirting," the aging "comfort women" who were
sexual slaves to the Japanese Army in World War II, the Bosnian
woman in the refugee camp who gives Eve her only egg as a good-
bye present. The poem gathers into its lines women from parts of
the world I knew only through the devastation that took place
there: Srebrenica, where the young girls wait for news of their men
"even though they know they have all been murdered"; Sarajevo,
where a woman wears lipstick and high heels "even though snip-
ers are firing on her city from above"; an Afghan refugee camp
in Pakistan where a baby sucks and sucks on empty breasts; the
Great Rift Valley of eastern Africa, where "V-World is the clitoral
cut that doesn't happen." Interspersed with these specific portraits
are glimpses of experiences I knew as intimately as my own body:
"V-World is unfolding between your legs. / It is urgent and slow";
or as close to me as my own most precious awakenings,

> *V-World is what lives after the pain has left*
> *and we sit in the utter emptiness*
> *and we stop creeping around the hole but fall into it.*
> *And it is not what we thought.*
> *It is the opposite.*

Women I had never met, from places I had never been, poured
into my heart. I began to speak "V-World" everywhere I could. The
cellist Jami Sieber wrote a powerful piece of music inspired by the
poem, and together we offered its message in concerts and prisons
and community gatherings. Often we would ask for a moment of
silence after the powerful final lines:

> *V-World is borderless and groundless.*
> *It is the armor we finally take off.*
> *There is nothing to defend.*

Again and again, in the wake of the words and music, it felt like the room was teeming with the invisible women who now lived inside me.

So much had they become a part of me that several years later, when Eve introduced me to some of the women she had written about from Afghanistan, Bosnia, and Kenya, I greeted them as if I had known them my entire life. I felt like I was reuniting with long-lost and dearly beloved friends. Still later, I traveled to Kenya to be with girls who are referred to in the poem. While my shyness never completely disappeared, it was nothing compared to the joy of finally meeting these people who had lived for so long in my heart.

Where I Do Not Wish to Go

When I really think about it, every time I embody a poem it stretches me in some way. Sometimes I consciously choose a poem because I want to stretch in a particular direction, as I did with *The Leaf and the Cloud* and "V-World" and Hedda did with "It." But sometimes the poem will give me a tug in a direction I never expected. Usually the process of embodying a poem is like stepping onto a magic carpet. You might think you know where you're going. But most likely you'll be wrong, and the most powerful lessons will surprise you, carrying you to places you hadn't imagined when you signed on for the ride.

One of my favorite quotes is the one at the beginning of this chapter, from the Gospel of John. Christ says to Peter, "Very truly, I tell you, when you were younger, you used to fasten your own belt and go wherever you wished. But when you grow old, you will stretch out your hands, and someone else will fasten a belt around you and take you where you do not wish to go."[6] What a reversal, to think of having independence when you are a child and being led around by the belt as an adult! Yet the statement holds a profound truth. It takes a long time to become mature enough to be led by another. So many people, myself included, seem to be focused much of the time on making sure they have their freedom, their personal power, their identity intact. Yet here Christ is saying that this kind of freedom is for children, not adults. This powerful statement will not win a lot of popularity, at least not in America, "the home of the free and the brave." In the United States there seems to be an unwritten law that everyone must strive to be a very independent "somebody."

Here Christ's words really address the developmental stages of a soul, not biological age. According to this definition, many people seem to be "children" much of the time, acting as if they and they alone are in control of their fate. Yet there are others, of all ages, cultures, races, and creeds, who are living in another way. They know how to surrender to the one Rumi might call "the Friend" or "the Beloved": a guide who leads them where they would not have chosen to go otherwise. Emily Dickinson says, probably referring to this passage, "He put the Belt around my life— / I heard the buckle snap—."

That belt can come in the form of the circumstances life brings—the needs of those you love, the limitations of age or illness, unexpected loss or good fortune, for instance—or it can appear from within, as an unusual impulse or inner knowing that points you in a new direction: a direction that may not initially make sense to the survival-oriented part of you, but is calling to your soul. Ironically, such surrender can lead you to a sense of inner peace and, yes, freedom.

The process of choosing a poem is a paradoxical one. It requires that you follow your own will and let it go at the same time. Your will, your desire, will lead you to the poem. Yet, once chosen, that poem may ask you to relinquish your personal desire and surrender to going where the process leads. Thus, for me, the poems I choose are the "someone else" I stretch my hands out to. They do indeed fasten a belt around me and take me where I do not wish to go.

What does it mean to go "where you do not wish to go"? The truth is, I do actually want to go wherever the poem takes me (or

I wouldn't have "stretched out my hands"). And at the same time, in spite of myself, I resist the journey. It seems I am hardwired to want to stay safe, to hold fast to the known, to avoid rocking the boat. Often a poem will take me into areas of myself that I have avoided, consciously or unconsciously, from fear. Sometimes it is simply the unknown that scares me. At other times, I'm afraid of pleasure, or of pain, or of losing control. The possibilities for fear are endless.

But when a poem has me by the belt and is pulling, I have learned to welcome the fear. It is a sign that I am following the call of my soul, even though on the surface it might seem to be exactly where I "do not wish to go." Fear always occurs at the interface between known territory and the unknown. If I'd been there already, I probably wouldn't be afraid. But then I wouldn't be so curious either.

The poet David Whyte once said, "Enlightenment is giving up all hope of immunity." To really offer yourself to the poem, to be "borrowed," as D. H. Lawrence says—body, breath, and voice—means letting go of the hope that the poem will give you only the feelings you want and will protect you from the ones you don't. Often I've seen someone choose a poem because the feeling or atmosphere or idea of it looks like a lovely place to be for a while. As with going on vacation to a beautiful Hawaiian island, the hope is that a sojourn inside this poem will provide a getaway from all the challenges of being human. Sometimes people choose mystical poems—by Rumi or Hafiz or Kabir, for instance—because they seem to promise an excursion to ecstasy. And often this does happen. But working with any affirmation—whether it is a poem affirming a longed-for state of being, or a mantra, or a simple phrase that expresses your desires—is more complex than meets the eye. I have found (to my great joy) that no affirmation will help me avoid the more difficult colors of what life brings. There is a difference between using a poem to avoid or suppress an unwanted experience and using the same words to actually invite the difficult terrain, carry you through it, and bring healing or wisdom in the process. Even on a Hawaiian island, the volcanic combustion under the surface of paradise can cause earthquakes, eruptions, and strange weather patterns. If you're headed for ecstasy, whatever obstructs it within you has to emerge one way or another.

When this starts to happen, people sometimes find themselves backing away from the poem. My students often discover, just as the work of getting to know their poem begins, that they don't like it after all, or that there is this line they never noticed before that they just can't stand, or that it could really use some serious editing. But when you have fallen in love with a poem enough to want to know it and give it voice or even learn it by heart, discomfort about any part of it is almost certainly arising because, in deepening intimacy with the poem, you are also deepening intimacy with yourself. And you may hit some rocky territory. Committing to a relationship with a poem is just that: a commitment. As in a relationship between two people, commitment can bring up a whole parade of challenges.

Have you ever had the experience of a friendship or a romance where it seemed like life had finally brought you the perfect person, whose tastes and beliefs and dreams matched yours, whom you were so connected with that you didn't even have to speak? And then, after a month or three of this Eden, you inevitably began to realize your differences. It turned out that when it came right down to it, he didn't actually share the same beliefs as you, and what mattered most to you made him very nervous. Maybe she seemed to like your kind of music in the beginning, but later she admitted it gave her the creeps. Suddenly one morning you wake up, look your beloved in the face and say, "Who are you? You weren't like this when we fell in love!"

At this point, the difference is sometimes too great to survive. You separate from each other. Or you deaden the aliveness of the relationship, relegating your togetherness to what small corner of the connection does not rock the boat.

If you hang in there without fleeing or numbing your heart, you may discover more about who you really are than you ever imagined. Your beliefs may be shaken and your masks may crumble. You might even discover a connection with your partner that is not contingent on harmony and agreement.

The same is true of a relationship with a poem. If you are willing to get curious about what is triggering your judgments instead of abandoning the poem or changing it to fit your comfort zone, you may find that the very lines that give you trouble hold the key to undiscovered layers of your own nature.

Gina's favorite poem was from Rilke's *Book of Hours*. She carried it on a tattered index card in her purse and often pulled it out to read to friends. She was excited about deepening her relationship with it and came to my workshop with the intention of doing so.

But as she began the process, she balked. Suddenly she decided she didn't like the poem anymore. Another poem, Robert Frost's "West-Running Brook," got very attractive to her. "The whole song of that poem is rushing through me," she said. "I can't concentrate on the Rilke." She felt torn, drawn to the Frost poem but trapped by her commitment to the Rilke, even though she was no longer in love with it.

She could have been describing a romantic struggle. She admitted that this feeling of being torn was a familiar refrain in her life, played out again and again in her relationships with men: as soon as the time came to do the work of going deeper, someone else showed up who became very compelling.

I asked Gina where she was stuck in the Rilke poem. She pointed to the lines "Each thing— / each stone, blossom, child— / is held in place."[7]

"Was that your experience as a child?" I asked.

"No." Gina closed her eyes tight, but the tears still spilled out. "No. I didn't feel held. Each stone, blossom, child is *not* held in place," she whimpered. "The poem is lying!" She and I both knew this was a deeply buried voice, drawn to the surface by the poem.

"Why did you originally love this poem?" I asked her.

"Because I so long to be held like that. I long for that feeling of being safe on the earth. But right now, I don't believe in it." She was choking back the sobs. "I was so alone as a child. My great-uncle had abused me and nobody knew. I felt like I was living behind an invisible shield. My mom didn't notice because she was so self-involved and distracted. I ended up taking care of her, hoping I could make her strong enough to take care of me."

Gina was rocking back and forth, her own arms wrapped tightly around her.

"To really make this poem your own," I said to her, "you may need to let yourself go through these feelings. Are you willing?"

Reluctantly Gina began to repeat the line over and over. At first we could barely hear her. But as she allowed the waves of pain to come to the surface, her voice became stronger.

"It's true, I have such a longing to be 'held in place' by something bigger than me," she whispered. "I want to know what Rilke felt when he wrote this line."

"So I invite you to be 'held in place' by your commitment to this poem. Don't get distracted like your mother did. Don't go off to another poem. Hold yourself right here, as a healing to the unheld one within you."

Even through her tears, Gina knew that this poem was the exact medicine she needed to heal the heartbroken child who was so disillusioned by what had happened to her. She had unconsciously prescribed it for herself. Now it was drawing out a trauma that had been buried since she was very young. And even as the poem opened Gina's wound, it gave her a perfect balm to heal it.

A Hunger for Ambiguity

Isn't it possible, you might ask, that a part of a poem actually *is* flawed? Or that it simply doesn't speak to me? Perhaps, but do you meet the poem as an editor meets a manuscript or do you meet it as a disciple meets a guru? Do you change the poem or do you let the poem change you?

As Leo worked with Naomi Shihab Nye's poem "Kindness," he found several places that really bothered him. Though he loved the poem, he was ambivalent about going deeper with it. He felt that if he could just change a few words or delete a verse, the poem would flow more smoothly.

I was first introduced to the poem (which you can find at the end of this chapter) in Roger Housden's book *Ten Poems to Open Your Heart.* An ode to the true and complex essence of kindness, the poem has completely changed my relationship to the word. Before I read Nye's lines, the word *kindness* was a cliché for me. It had a two-dimensional, pastel-pink, goody-two-shoes connotation. It was for old ladies with purple hair and cucumber sandwiches or Buddhist meditators who, I imagined, practiced "loving-kindness" in a tedious practice-makes-perfect way. It felt like an ideal state that I "should" aspire to, but one that did not particularly attract me.

In Nye's poem, kindness is not a state, but a natural grace that arises on its own when you have been intimate with the most painful of human experiences. When you have touched loss, desolation, death, and grief without shying away, "it is only kindness that makes any sense anymore." The word *kindness* comes from the same root as the word *kin,* which means "of the same family; related; akin" and "of the same kind or nature; having affinity."[8] Nye's poem is telling me that until I've felt my kinship with all of humanity, even and especially those whose losses are more shattering than I can imagine or bear, I will not know what kindness really is.

Leo had known of this poem and read it frequently for several years. Now he wanted to go deeper with it. He thought he might include it in a one-man performance piece he was planning for his 75th birthday, if he could change it to fit his needs.

Leo was a retired university professor. After leaving his position on campus, he had written a number of textbooks and had also become known as a fierce and brilliant editor by his friends and colleagues. This was one of his favorite poems and he saw no reason not to apply his gift to make it even better.

"What is it that disturbs you about the way it is written?" I asked.

"It's so irregular," he complained. "One stanza has 13 lines, the next 7, the next 6. I could easily make each stanza three lines long and it would be much more poetic."

Leo also felt it would be a good idea to cut out some lines in the middle of the poem. He was upset by the imagery where "the

Indian in a white poncho / lies dead by the side of the road." He wanted to cut that whole stanza. "The rest of the poem is so beautiful and gentle," he said. "Why put such an upsetting image right in the center of it? I think it is better without that stanza."

Even the last line was a problem for Leo. He wanted a clear resolution at the end of the poem, not the ambiguous duality between kindness as a shadow and kindness as a friend. Would it make that much difference, he asked, if he deleted the word "shadow"?

It was quite a challenge for me to even entertain Leo's questions. Not only was he carving up a perfectly good poem, but he wanted to amputate the lines and words that were closest to my own heart! Yet I was curious. I knew there was something very important underneath Leo's urgent need to reshape Nye's poem. I just didn't know what it was.

The German poet Gottfried Benn once said, "I don't write these poems to be understood, you understand. I write them to terrify and console." Ambiguity is the lifeblood of Nye's poem. It baffles "understanding," which wants to put the world in neat boxes. The friction between seemingly unlike experiences is at the heart of this poem's medicine. Kindness is a word that carries with it a sense of hope, gentleness, and compassion. Yet to paint its portrait, Nye leads the reader into loss and desolation. The future "dissolves," an Indian "lies dead by the side of the road," the vastness of the cloth of sorrow is spread out, and we are told to feel for its edges. Images and concepts rub against each other in unexpected ways until the mind bursts into flame and the true meaning of kindness is seen in that fire. In order to know kindness, Nye tells us clearly, you must know its opposite.

Nye herself has lived in the friction of opposites. Born to a Palestinian father and an American mother, she spent some of her childhood in Jerusalem and some in Texas. As an adult, she traveled widely. She wrote this poem while visiting Colombia in 1978.

Colombia itself was a world of opposites at that time. The beautiful land was wracked with guerrilla violence. The divisions between the rich and the poor were more and more volatile. In desperation many of the Indians turned to growing poppies, and the country became the world's primary producer of cocaine. Guerrillas were often known to murder the growers to get their crop. The image of the Indian dead on the side of the road holds the whole history of the ravaged country Nye rode through.

Leo and I researched the background of this poem together. When he realized the layers of meaning in the image of the Indian in the white poncho, he knew those lines could not be cut. But he was still uncomfortable with the poem's mix of beautifully poetic concepts and disturbing imagery. This kind of ambiguity was difficult for Leo. He felt a poem should be one or the other: beautiful or disturbing. Not both at the same time. He wanted clear understanding, order, and a sense of resolution at the end.

But ambiguity is one of the greatest gifts and challenges of good poetry: it unlocks the stronghold of the pragmatic mind so that the complexity of direct experience can rush in. A capacity to tolerate ambiguity is a rare treasure in this "information age," where—at least culturally, if not personally—there is an unspoken assumption that security depends on certainty, without any nuance or doubt. Though the language of good poetry unravels the seeming security of your grip on what you think you know, it opens you to another kind of security, another kind of knowing. Perhaps it could be called a knowing of the heart. As Eve Ensler said in her book *Insecure at Last,* "Real security is not only being able to tolerate mystery, complexity, ambiguity, but hungering for them and only trusting a situation when they are present."[9]

I remember delivering Stanley Kunitz's poem "King of the River" at a conference a few years ago. The poem begins,

> *If the water were clear enough*
> *if the water were still*
> *but the water is not clear*
> *the water is not still . . .* [10]

Each of the first three stanzas begins with this dialectic between a statement and its undoing: "If the knowledge were given you /

but it is not given," "If the power were granted you . . . / but the imagination fails," "If the heart were pure enough / but it is not pure." Later, one of the members of the audience took me aside and said he thought the poem would be much better without all those negative statements. Couldn't I just deliver the positive ones and drop the others?

"King of the River" is one of the most profoundly shamanic poems that I know. Everything about it points to a dissolving of ordinary consciousness. The rhythms, the line length, the curl of the tongue over the sounds of it, invoke a transformational journey. For me, the strongest mystical medicine in the poem occurs through these oppositional phrases, which stretch the mind, creating and erasing thoughts simultaneously, undoing ordinary reality and allowing another reality to penetrate. Naomi Shihab Nye sets up similar tensions throughout the poem "Kindness." The result is disorientation from analytical thought and a proliferation of ambiguity that only the right hemisphere of the brain can process. The result is holographic, direct insight that defies logic.

Though Leo was uncomfortable with the poem, his love of it and his curiosity about his own inner workings—why was he so disturbed by ambiguity?—inspired him to allow the poem to rattle his tight grip on reason and clarity. As he repeated the poem out loud, he could feel in his body how he was holding on for dear life.

I asked him what he feared if he were to let go.

"I'll lose my whole grip on reality. Everything will spin. I won't know what is up and what is down. I won't be able to even read these words or know what they mean." As he spoke, shakiness came into his usually emphatic voice. He realized he had felt this way before. Since he was a child he had struggled with dyslexia. He had also suffered from increasing hearing loss in recent years. We both wondered if, as an attempt to stabilize himself amidst the uncertainty of his perceptual challenges, he had developed a tendency to cling with a vise grip to order, form, and the way things "should" be.

Yet Leo had chosen a poem full of paradox and ambiguity, a poem that did not follow a rational agenda. The poem, essentially, was about the willingness to let boundaries shatter: between one-self and others, between knowing and not knowing, between what a word means and what it doesn't. Something deeper than Leo's habitual hold on control had drawn him to the poem.

As he worked with the poem, courageously restraining his almost irresistible impulses to edit it, Leo slowly realized that the disturbing images and the erratic rhythms and line lengths were indeed a medicine to shake up the rigid outline of his personality. Personalities can be so narrow. Yet to leave the comfort of the familiar is often more terrifying than confinement. "Perhaps," I said to Leo, "it's time to rock the boat a little."

"Well, a little rocking is okay, but I don't want to drown!"

"Drowning," I responded, "might be the best luck of all! What might you discover in those depths?" Recognizing that he had unwittingly chosen for himself the perfect poem to help him capsize the boat of his rational mind, Leo simply bowed in silence.

The Call of Kindness

Several years after I worked with Leo, the poem "Kindness" became an unexpected lifeline.

It was the fall of 2008, and the stock market was careening like a crazed, dying animal. I was in a transitional period. I had let go of a stable income as a therapist and was leaping into the unknown, trying to figure out how to make a living as an emissary of poetry's healing power. Dividends from stocks were supplementing my reduced income. So I felt I couldn't afford to gamble in the volatile market. Instead I took radical action: I sold all my stocks and invested just about everything I owned in a fund that promised stability based on a 40-year track record.

Two months later, a friend's message on my voice mail told me the fund had been a fraud. My savings were gone.

The minute I heard the message, all I could think of was this poem. I didn't choose it by design. The poem seemed to choose me. It was like the part in a movie where suddenly the noise of the scene fades into the background and all you hear is the thunderous throb of the protagonist's heartbeat over a kind of otherworldly hum. In my case the hum was there, but it was the lines of this poem that pulsed over it:

Before you know what kindness really is
you must lose things.

I hit replay on my voice mail. The message had been left by Geneen, one of my best friends, who had also invested with the fund. Her voice was a monotone. Clearly she was as flipped out as I was. She told me the man who ran the fund had just been arrested. Everything was lost. A ticker tape of fears about the future clicked across my mind.

Feel the future dissolve in a moment
like salt in a weakened broth.

Somewhere behind the pounding in my head I heard myself thinking, *Oh, I get it, "a weakened broth." You add salt to it because you don't have enough money for the real ingredients.* I had never understood that line before.

I stared at the phone in my hand. I did not know where to turn or whom to call. In a spooked state, I watched the next lines of the poem, like a karaoke crib sheet, unfurl behind my eyes:

What you held in your hand,
what you counted and carefully saved,
all this must go. . .

I remembered how carefully I had hoarded the money from selling my house several years earlier. I had chosen to live in a series of one-room cottages (one so small the fridge was on the front porch) rather than spend more than I had to on rent. Clothing came from discount stores or hand-me-downs from my wealthier friends. I turned the heat off whenever I could. Of course, there had been times when I dug into my savings—to make ends meet in the lean months, to send a contribution to a humanitarian organization, to do volunteer work in Kenya—but these were rare. I was too busy saving my money as insurance against some unnamed problem in some fictitious future.

As I hung up the phone, I was possessed by an overwhelming need to look up the next words of the poem. I tried to reason with myself: there was so much more to worry about than the second stanza of "Kindness"! And besides, I had never really loved that poem. Yes, Leo and many other students had brought it to my workshops, but I had never felt much of a personal connection with it. So it was all the more surprising to find a mysterious recording of it playing inside me now. I had no idea it was even living in my memory!

But I was desperate. I needed guidance, and I was in no position to be picky about how it arrived. The poem was the only voice talking to me. So I did the obvious: I searched my computer, found the poem, and printed it out. I sat on the floor and began to read aloud.

As if summoned by the sound of the words, the kindness began. Geneen called back to invite me to stay with her for a few days, until the first wave of shock and trauma passed for both of us. Her husband was away on a trip and we both felt the need for companionship. When I arrived at her house—toothbrush in one hand and "Kindness" in the other—she said that she had picked up exactly the same poem as soon as she heard the news. Just before my arrival, she'd been reading it aloud.

In the days that followed, we immersed ourselves in "Kindness." We read it to each other—sometimes several times a day. Meanings we'd never noticed before popped open in the terror of what we were living. The poem became my mainstay of sanity, reminding me that what seemed a tragedy on the outer level was indeed a gift in deeper and more essential ways.

Through the portal of this loss, the opposites in the poem, which had so troubled Leo, were revealed to be utterly accurate. I realized that in bringing together loss and generosity, tenderness and gravity, death and breath, sorrow and kindness, the murdered Colombian Indian on the side of the road and my own life, Nye was not calling on sophisticated poetic devices or being overly dramatic, she was simply telling it like it is. Until you lose enough to find yourself woven into the fabric of sorrow that touches most of the world, you won't feel your kinship—and therefore your kindness—to all beings.

I had never realized how my financial security separated me. Now a protective shield I didn't know I had been carrying was gone. Though my life was still relatively privileged, my loss connected me with people in a way that I didn't know I had been missing. I still had work I loved, a car, and enough money, at least for the moment, to buy organic vegetables and Earl Grey tea. But now I was one of the millions who didn't know if they would find enough work to pay the rent, who didn't have any savings, who faced the real possibility of not being able to care for themselves or their loved ones in times of need. There was a strange relief in suddenly finding myself in the same situation as so many friends and strangers.

Every night before going to bed on Geneen's couch, I worked on learning "Kindness" by heart. I repeated a few lines over and over like a mantra. Then I placed the now ragged piece of paper under my pillow as I slept. The next morning, I stretched my memory to recall the newly learned lines, saying them like a morning prayer before I rose, then again at breakfast with Geneen. I had the feeling we were in "kindness school": the poem was our text and this financial catastrophe was the teacher.

In all the years of reading and hearing this poem, it had never occurred to me that Nye might be writing about *receiving* kindness from others. I had always assumed she referred to *giving* kindness: the tragedies described were medicine to break open the heart so that kindness would flow out.

But now the kindness was flowing in. Almost every person who heard of my loss immediately offered help. People who had always been poorer than I were now richer, and many were reaching out. A couple who had little to spare took me out to dinner and told me they wanted to loan me money, interest-free and indefinitely. A recording engineer gave his skills and studio without charge so I could complete a CD I was about to abandon. A musician showed up and played for free. My hairdresser cut her rates. Friends invited me to come and live with them or offered frequent-flier miles so that I could travel to be with my loved ones. My landlord lowered my rent. Students in many corners of the world organized workshops for me to lead. After I mentioned that I'd given up Starbucks, a friend sent me a check, enough to cover my entire deficit for a year, with a note that said, "For lattes."

I began to realize that in the abundance and self-sufficiency of my previous life, there had been little opening for the kindness of others. "Where lowland is," Rumi counsels, "that's where the water goes." Kindness is drawn to you, it seems, when you are empty, when you need, when you are vulnerable, when you are lost.

I don't know how I would have navigated that fierce passage without "Kindness." I am forever grateful to Naomi Shihab Nye for knowing what I could not know until I lived it and, even then, might not have discovered without her poem to help me mine the jeweled depths of my loss.

An Autobiography in Poems

When I was in high school, my mother gave me a deep blue velvet-covered blank book, a gift to the blossoming poet in me. For years I kept it almost constantly by my side, filling it not only with my own poems but also with other pieces of poetry and prose that had touched and turned the course of my life: excerpts from John Steinbeck's *Of Mice and Men*, several of Dag Hammarskjöld's journal entries, the Prayer of Saint Francis, and, of course, several poems by E. E. Cummings, among many other treasures. Today it sits on my bookshelf among my poetry anthologies. To look through its pages is to see, in my loopy, self-conscious, teenage handwriting (in my favorite turquoise pen), the trajectory of my inner life of that time, which, it turns out, is not so different—minus the fancy pen and careful handwriting—from what I care most about today.

When I started my practice of learning poetry by heart back in 1994, I discovered that although I could remember the poems themselves, I could never remember the whole list of what I had learned. So on my computer I created a list of the names of the poems in the order I had learned them. To this day, unless I carry around a bedraggled copy of this list, I cannot for the life of me think of more than four or five of the dozens that I know.

In the back of my mind I always thought that I should organize them by author or title but I never did. Noting them in the order they came into my life was a quick and convenient, if haphazard, way of keeping track of what I had in my memory.

One day, after I had been working with poems for almost a decade and there were about a hundred on the list, I realized that I held in my hands an autobiography of the last ten years. I could see the chapters of my inner life, the great questions I had wrestled with, the contours of my soul journey. Only the names, places, and personal dramas were missing.

For instance, when I first started the practice of taking poems to heart, I was struggling with how to let go of my ambitious, achievement-oriented approach to life, which had left me feeling empty and depressed. I knew I needed to learn "to die and so to grow," as Goethe says in "The Holy Longing," which is the first poem on the list. A bit further down the page is a poem by Rilke where he puts it this way: "When we win it is with small things / And the triumph itself makes us small." This is followed by a poem by David Whyte that recalls when "you too saw, for the first time, / your own house turned to ashes. / Everything consumed so the road could open again." And several poems further down is my favorite, the fiercest teacher of that period of my life, Rumi's poem "Checkmate":

> *The soul is a newly skinned hide, bloody and gross.*
> *Work on it with manual discipline,*
> *and the bitter tanning acid of grief,*

and you will become lovely, and very strong.
And if you can't do this work yourself, don't worry.
You don't even have to make a decision,
one way or the other. The Friend, who knows
a lot more than you do, will bring difficulties,
and grief and sickness,

        as medicine, as happiness,
as the essence of the moment when you're beaten,
when you hear Checkmate, *and can finally say,*
with Hallaj's voice,

      I trust you to kill me.[11]

Of course, Emily Dickinson's "I'm Nobody! Who are you?" is among this first group of poems, as well as several of my own, including "Practice":

Not the high mountain monastery
I had hoped for, the real
face of my spiritual practice
is this:
the sweat that pearls on my cheek
when I tell you the truth, my silent
cry in the night when I think
I'm alone, the trembling
in my own hand as I reach out
through the years of overcoming
to touch what I had hoped
I would never need again.

Each of these poems had guided me, in its own particular voice, toward the same truth. "Leave everything you know behind," David Whyte writes in "Tillicho Lake," summing it up in a single commandment.

  The next group of poems on my list reveals how this surrender of my idealized image of myself plunged me into a world of chaotic feelings, memories, and longings. Most of the poetry in this phase is by Rumi, the great master of longing. His "Love Dogs" told me that "this longing / you express is the return message." The next poem I learned, "Cry Out in Your Weakness," demanded: "Cry out! Don't be stolid and silent / with your pain. Lament!" I completely identified with "The Reed Flute," where Rumi says, "Since I was cut from the reed bed / I have made this crying sound." Several poems later on the list, "Undressing" offers me a way to meet the pain: "The hurt you embrace / becomes joy."

Then, reading further down the list, there is a turning point in my path, where the poems of "seeking" give way to the poems of "finding." Somewhere between Rilke's "I am too alone in the world" and "I am not I" by Juan Ramón Jiménez, I can almost detect the moment when I first stumbled into the vast, silent ocean of emptiness that the mystics speak of. Now all my yearning was no longer relevant. I was already there, in the heart of longing's destination. Rumi says, "When I learned the name / and address of that, I went to where / you sell perfume. I begged you not / to trouble me so with longing." Miraculously I had found "the one who is silent when I talk, . . . the one who will remain standing when I die." One of my favorite portraits of the reality that opened for me in this period is in the words of Wallace Stevens when he describes a person in the snow, who, "nothing himself, beholds / Nothing that is not there and the nothing that is."

The list of poems goes on, charting a map from the mystical to the mundane and back again. It shows my first movements toward speaking out against violence that began with "V-World." It shows the blossom and fade of several relationships. It talks about writing, aging, and dying—poem by poem by poem. Perhaps no one else can see the weave of a life story spun upon the loom of these poems, but I can.

As you take poems into your life, keep a journal of them. This can become a mirror that, unlike the one on your wall, can show you yourself from the inside out.

How do you choose which poems to live by heart? Pleasure, curiosity, and love. Pleasure can draw you to choose poems as inspiration and refuge. Curiosity can compel you to choose poems that become your "yoga of poetry" by stretching you beyond your personality into new forms. And love can call you toward all sorts of poems without giving you a clue about why, until you discover they hold a key to a door you didn't even know was locked. And then, at some distant time, in a place you cannot even imagine, you may find yourself, as Rumi says, "helping people you don't know / and have never seen."[12]

Kindness

Before you know what kindness really is
you must lose things,
feel the future dissolve in a moment
like salt in a weakened broth.
What you held in your hand,
what you counted and carefully saved,
all this must go so you know
how desolate the landscape can be
between the regions of kindness.
How you ride and ride
thinking the bus will never stop,
the passengers eating maize and chicken
will stare out the window forever.

Before you learn the tender gravity of kindness,
you must travel where the Indian in a white poncho
lies dead by the side of the road.
You must see how this could be you,
how he too was someone
who journeyed through the night with plans
and the simple breath that kept him alive.

Before you know kindness as the deepest thing inside,
you must know sorrow as the other deepest thing.
You must wake up with sorrow.
You must speak to it till your voice
catches the thread of all sorrows
and you see the size of the cloth.

Then it is only kindness that makes sense anymore,
only kindness that ties your shoes
and sends you out into the day to mail letters and
purchase bread,
only kindness that raises its head

from the crowd of the world to say
It is I you have been looking for,
and then goes with you everywhere
like a shadow or a friend.

— Naomi Shihab Nye

Chapter 5

THE ANATOMY
OF A POEM

Words, after speech, reach
Into the silence. Only by the form, the pattern,
Can words or music reach
The stillness . . .

— T. S. Eliot

As in any romance, there are stages of intimacy when you fall in love with a poem. The first step is to get to know everything you can about the one you love. This shouldn't be too hard, since new love makes your hunger to learn unstoppable. You want to hear every thought and find the resonance within you. You want to explore every inch of this new body and discover how it touches and awakens your own.

What attracted you to this poem? What do you love about it? Where does it draw you into new territory in yourself and the world around you? How does it mirror the questions and know-ings in the heart of your life right here, right now? How does it affect your body? And how does it create the special "Aha!" that parts the veils of the mundane to allow some bright insight to shine through?

Many ingredients combine to work the poem's magic. One of the most powerful is the physical dimension of the poem. The rhythms and sounds, the visual shape on the page, and the way the poem affects your breathing and pulse have important consciousness-shifting effects, often without your awareness.

There have been many fantastic books published in recent years about prosody, which is the word for the study of the sounds of poetry. Masterful poets such as Mary Oliver, Jane Hirshfield, and Robert Pinsky have put their thoughts to the page, explaining the acoustic technology inside a poem in much greater detail than is my intention here.[1] In this chapter, I will not dwell on the technicalities of poetic forms, nor on the language that has developed for naming them. Instead I want to look at how these physical components of a poem can affect your particular body, mind, and feelings and how this awareness can be an aid to receiving the poem more deeply and letting its medicine work in you.

The body of a poem affects your body. Literally. At first you may only be conscious of the conceptual level: what the words mean to you. But whether you are aware of it or not, your breathing has changed. You are feeling the beat of the poem's rhythm in your blood. You are hearing the song of the words inside you. It is even affecting the subtler pulsations of your cerebrospinal fluid and the waters inside your cells.

For instance, as you read the poem, the length of the lines has a physical impact on your eye movements. The eyes are the only part of our bodies that literally touch the brain. Moving the eyes causes ripples in the cerebrospinal fluid that encases the brain and also flows down the center of the spine.[2] This can create biochemical changes that affect consciousness.

In the old Popeye shows, the cartoon character Bluto used to hypnotize Olive Oyl with a pocket watch on a chain. The slim heroine would become inexplicably fascinated with the pendulating object until she was entranced and oblivious, whereupon Bluto would proceed to beat up her beloved Popeye (again!) while Olive Oyl moved, her eyes closed and her arms stretched before her like a sleepwalker, through some treacherous landscape unscathed. A similar principle (though different motive!) informs a number of psychotherapeutic practices such as EMDR (Eye Movement Desensitization and Reprocessing) and Radix work. These processes work with eye movement to cause subtle changes in brain chemistry and activity so as to release trauma and effect healing.[3]

Thus reading Stanley Kunitz's regular, short lines:

If the water were clear enough,
if the water were still,
but the water is not clear,
the water is not still,[4]

will cause a different wave motion in the brain than reading Marie Howe's longer lines:

Someone or something is leaning close to me now
trying to tell me the one true story of my life[5]

In the movie *Sylvia,* the young Ted Hughes, already an accomplished poet, is courting Sylvia Plath, recently arrived on the Cambridge University poetry scene. "It's magic," he says, speaking of poetry. "It's not *about* magic. It's not *like* magic. It *is* magic . . . Incantations, spells, ceremonies, rituals, what are they? They're poems. So what is a poet? He's a shaman, that's what he is."

"Or she," Sylvia responds.

Regardless of the gender of the spell-maker, a good poem, like the shaman's drum, rattle, and song, changes consciousness. When you enter the world of a poem, whether through reading it, hearing it, or speaking it aloud, you make yourself available to its spell.

In the sense that it alters consciousness, it is a spell. But in another sense, it is quite the opposite of a spell. A poem alters consciousness back to its natural state, prior to patterning. Instead of a spell, it is a spell-breaker.

In some ways, we spend most of our lives under a spell. The habits of reaction woven into our cells by our responses to painful events in our history, as well as more general cultural and family mores, have been entrancing us since we were very young. A poem can pierce this familiar dream and ignite a quickening within. As the poet Pablo Neruda says:

> *and something started in my soul,*
> *fever or forgotten wings,*
> *and I made my own way,*
> *deciphering*
> *that fire*[6]

The Shamanic Anatomy of a Poem

A constellation of elements creates that quickening. I call this a poem's "shamanic anatomy." Poetry's task, like the shaman's, is to melt the veil that separates the visible from the invisible so that you can move back and forth between these worlds. The shaman journeys between the realms, even over the lip of death and back, to bring wisdom and healing from beyond the known. Sometimes she or he uses a drumbeat, a song or poem, or a certain way of breathing to thin the skin between ordinary and non-ordinary realities. Like a shaman's drum, the beat of the poem's rhythm can alter consciousness, opening it beyond its normal limitations. And like a shaman's song, the sounds of the words and the way they echo, rhyme, and chime to each other within the poem can soften the boundaries of ordinary perception, allowing in new levels of awareness and insight.

Not only sounds but also symbols and images play a part in working the poem's consciousness-altering magic. Just as the shaman crosses the threshold between worlds, metaphor carries us out of our ordinary world, where unlike things stay neatly inside their familiar definitions, to a more mysterious realm where opposites are miraculously recognized as one.

Each poem has its own "medicine bag" of tools that do their work inside the human mind and body. I think of them as breath, drumbeat, song, and image.

Breath

In an obscure corner of the August 2, 2004, issue of *Time* magazine, there is a short article entitled "Does Poetry Make the Heart Grow Stronger?" It tells the tale of a group of European researchers who taught volunteers to recite passages from Homer and discovered that "the result was an increase in the synchronization of cardiorespiratory patterns that are believed to be favorable to the long-term prognosis of cardiac patients."[7] Apparently speaking lines from *The Iliad* was much more beneficial than ordinary breathing exercises.

A poem changes the patterns of your breathing with its rhythm, line length, and phrasing. This changes the density of oxygen in your blood, which affects your heartbeat as well, heightening the sensations of aliveness in your cells. Together these effects produce subtle shifts in your biochemistry, which lead to inner states of relaxation or agitation. These states change consciousness, bringing new experience that would be impossible within the confines of habit.

For millennia, healers and spiritual teachers in many different cultures have known that to change the breath is not only to change the body but also to change consciousness. Yogis practice the "breath of fire" to awaken the mind and energize the body. Buddhist meditators count their breaths. Hindu chants, Jewish davening, and Wiccan songs cause the breath—and thus the mind—to open to new possibilities. Even the Bible is written in such a way that your breath changes as you read it. Different sections of the scripture have different breaths, different rhythmic phenomena, and different sentence lengths. Some phrases are quite short: "Then God said, / 'Let there be light'; / and there was light. / And God saw the light, / that *it was* good; / and God divided the light from the darkness. / God called the light Day, / and the darkness He called Night."[8] These lines ask for a shorter, faster breath, like the yogi's "breath of fire." Some phrases are extraordinarily long, like at the beginning of Deuteronomy: "These be the words which Moses spake unto all Israel on this side of the Jordan in the wilderness, in the plain over against the Red Sea . . ."[9] And it continues on and on for quite some time before finally resting, for only a moment, in a period. To speak this sentence requires a great wave of breath to carry your voice all the way to the end.

One of the most challenging and thrilling poems I have ever spoken aloud is Stanley Kunitz's "King of the River," which you can find at the end of this chapter. The short lines and long sentences take such powerful possession of my breath that I often find myself almost gasping as I struggle upstream like the salmon in the poem. At times, while I am delivering the poem, I become flushed with heat and even feel a tingling in my fingertips from the increase of oxygen in my blood due to the rapidity of my breathing. I feel my breath shape-shifting into the wheezing gills of the fish on its mission of death and rebirth.

Here are the lines we looked at earlier in this chapter, followed by the rest of the first long, action-packed sentence.

> *If the water were clear enough,*
> *if the water were still,*
> *but the water is not clear,*
> *the water is not still,*
> *you would see yourself,*
> *slipped out of your skin,*
> *nosing upstream,*
> *slapping, thrashing,*
> *tumbling over the rocks*
> *till you paint them*
> *with your belly's blood:*
> *Finned Ego,*
> *yard of muscle that coils,*
> *uncoils.*[10]

Notice what happens to your breath as you read these lines aloud. Perhaps, like me, you may find that the shorter, quicker breaths required to follow Kunitz's salmon over the rocks have an effect on your thinking and your sensations. Like the volunteers who recited Homer for their health, you may find this infusion of extra breath has far-reaching effects. Habitual tightness and control dissolve. The body becomes charged with new electricity. Through the oxygen-filled physiology, spontaneity and insight erupt like the passion of the salmon itself.

Drumbeat

I remember it well. It was eighth-period English class. Outside the sky was frozen white, pregnant with snow. Inside the radiators shrieked and wheezed, and I could hear each tick of the big clock on the back wall in its unbearably slow waltz toward the final bell. The itch of my fishnet stockings under my new kilt was almost unbearable. Miss Eidelstein, in her blue wool suit and sensible shoes, was at the chalkboard pointing at a line from *Romeo and Juliet,* "But, soft! What light through yonder window breaks?" Each syllable had a chalk mark over it, a little smile shape or its fiercer brother, the downward accent line that looked like a cartoon person's angry eyebrow. Below the line was written "iambic pentameter."

We were supposed to be learning about rhythm in poetry. I was learning nothing at all, except that I hated poetry and wished I had worn different stockings to school that day.

If Miss Eidelstein had communicated even the tiniest spark of passion for the power and beauty of rhythm in a poem, I would have forgotten my itchy fishnets instantly. But the lesson was so dry and mechanical that I never learned about the meter of a poem—the drumbeat that happens in the play between emphasized syllables, softer syllables, and pauses. And I certainly didn't learn about the magical power immanent within it.

It wasn't until three decades later that I put together what I knew about inducing altered states of consciousness through musical rhythm with what I knew about rhythm in a poem. As a therapist and healer, I had explored many portals to non-ordinary consciousness. I had traveled far and wide leading workshops where I guided students in deep breathing exercises that could release memories, emotions, and a cascade of inner visions. To support the process, I had accrued a large collection of music from all over the world, which I used to create environments that helped people let go of their habitual control.

The rhythm of music is known as a force of healing and transformation in many cultures. The shaman's wordless chant sings throughout the night in the Achuar longhouse in the heart of the Ecuadorian rainforest. It carries those gathered on a healing journey between the worlds. The pulse of the Native American's rattle melts the veil between the sacred and the profane so that the circle in the sweat lodge is transported. The particular beat of a kirtan, a hymn, or a bhajan carries the seeker across the threshold of an interior sanctuary and steeps her in devotion. Even the throb of the drum track at the all-night rave enthralls a hundred heartbeats into one so that the blood, breath, brain, and fingertips of everyone in the room all pulse together.

So I already knew how rhythm, drumbeat, and breath dissolve the walls between the conscious and the unconscious. I also recognized the healing possible in those altered states. But I had never before realized that the pulse of language itself could enter and change consciousness. Now I saw that rhythm in a poem is like the drumbeat under a piece of music. Just as different drumbeats cause the boundaries of the daily mind to melt, a poem has its own rhythm that changes the consciousness of the reader, listener, and speaker.

Human beings are creatures of rhythm. The fluids within our bodies pulse, our hearts throb, our breath comes in rhythmic patterns that change with our emotions. In the womb, we are rocked rhythmically by the cadence of our mother's walk and the throb of her heart. We come out craving a rocking, pulsing, singing world that will carry us into our dreams, or swaddle us close to a beating heart, or teach us the alphabet in rhythm and rhyme.

So rhythm is a powerful force. It can be entrancing. It has been used throughout human history to awaken us or lull us to sleep. At times it has been used to possess us. The poet Robert Hass has said, "Because rhythm has direct access to the unconscious, because it can hypnotize us, enter our bodies and make us move, it is a power. And power is political."[11] Hitler knew this. I have been moved to tears when I heard what I later realized was a Nazi anthem. If you give people enough rhythm, they will feel passion. They don't even have to notice what they're feeling passion about. Rhythm creates entrainment. Entrainment creates passion and movement. And we're not alone in this movement. All of a sudden everyone within earshot is riding a wave together. Sometimes we don't even bother to notice where the wave is going. How many times have I felt the gooseflesh rise and the heart surge with some unnamable, irrational allegiance as a marching band spouting Sousa passed amidst flocks of Independence Day floats? "What," I had to ask myself, "am I being moved by? What am I being moved *to?* Do I really care about this cause? Or is this music moving me on its own agenda?" Something in the undiscriminating organism of me wells up to join the rhythm and yearns toward the fusion it seems to promise.

Think, for a moment, about the lullaby "Rock-a-Bye Baby." The beginning is benign enough:

Rock-a-bye baby
In the treetop
When the wind blows
The cradle will rock

This regular rhythm and singsong melody soothed millions of us to sleep when we were small. We fell so deeply asleep that we may never have noticed the danger lurking in the second verse, camouflaged by the same apparently harmless beat:

When the bough breaks
The cradle will fall
And down will come baby
Cradle and all!

So what is the difference between a rhythm that serves to awaken us and one that "puts us to sleep?" Beyond the obvious components of motive and purpose, there are clues in the rhythm itself.

I pick up a greeting card at the drugstore and read,

If you knew how many hearts are touched
by everything you do,
you'd know the gratitude and love
that's always felt for you.

Even though it says "many hearts are touched," I'm not touched at all by this little verse. Why is that? The rhythm is unbroken, utterly predictable. There are no surprises. And, as Brother David Steindl-Rast has said, "If it's not surprising, it's not a good poem."

A rhythm wakes us up when a pattern is established and then broken. The unpredictable enters. We sit up and listen.

Emily Dickinson says,

I'm Nobody! Who are you?
Are you—Nobody—Too?
Then there's a pair of us!
Don't tell! they'd advertise—you know!

How dreary—to be—Somebody!
How public—like a Frog—
To tell one's name—the livelong June—
To an admiring Bog![12]

This poem splits open the seams of the rhythm and spills out into the silences, into the unpredictable. The first time I really heard this poem was in 1994 as I was grappling with my depression. I'd known of it for as long as I can remember, but it became a teacher during that painful period of my life. It came to me by way of a wise friend from whom I'd sought help.

"You are always in groups where you are a big fish in a little pond," he said to me, referring to the loneliness I was feeling. "You're too used to being special. I think you need to be a nobody for a while!" And he took a pad of paper and wrote down the lines of this poem. "Learn it by heart, and recite it every morning like a mantra," he suggested. "Pretend it is a holy phrase given to you by some enlightened guru. I think you'll see some changes begin to happen."

As I followed his guidance, I discovered that this little poem began to have a powerful effect on me. It got me to question why I wanted to be "somebody" and was afraid of being "nobody." And it wasn't just the meaning that was working this magic. The rhythm of this poem worked in a very particular way to convey its message directly into my body.

My friend was right. I had spent most of my life magnetized by wanting to be "somebody," thinking that was the key to life. The stereotype of being nobody was boring and empty. Yet the energy of this poem is exactly the opposite. The rhythm of the stanza about being "nobody" is wildly innovative and unexpected while in the second stanza about being "somebody," the beat is as predictable as the greeting card. Clearly within the world of this poem, if you're "nobody," each time you enter yourself it is a new experience, like the rhythm of the lines. "Nobody" is free, unconfined by a name or even by a rhythm. Being "Somebody," on the other hand, is as predictable as a rhyme on a greeting card: "How DREARy—TO be—SOMEbodY / How PUBlic—LIKE a FROG—"

What exactly is the difference between the rhythm in Dickinson's poem and in the greeting card? Why does one wake us up and the other lull us into unconsciousness?

A steady rhythm runs underneath Dickinson's lines, like the drummer's rhythmic tap on the high hat during the trumpet solo. But her words dance in and out of the meter, a jazz musician's riff. They cannot be contained.

It is often the friction between two unlike things happening at the same time that creates a moment of surprise, allowing space for new insight and creativity. In this case, it is the friction between the expected rhythm and the actual beat of the language of the poem.

In the poem on the card, I find none of this friction. The rhythm of the lines proceeds as expected: four strong, regularly spaced beats in one line and three in the next: "you'd KNOW the GRA-ti-TUDE and LOVE / that's AL-ways FELT for YOU." It is the same rhythm that runs under Dickinson's lines, but there it rubs against the fitful, almost chaotic beats in the actual words: "I'M NObody—WHO are YOU / are YOU NObody TOO?"

As I returned to the poem each day, an ancient and compulsive striving to be "somebody" started to unclench within me, and I began to taste the possibility of simple being, without definition or goal.

Song

Friction works its magic in a poem through the song in the sounds of the words as well as through the drumbeat. Words rub together, chiming back and forth to each other across the lines. The sound of a word hangs in the air and resonates with the subsequent words that contain a similar sound.

There is a plethora of ways that words can sing to one another. The most obvious of these are repetition and rhyme. For instance, the mesmerizing power of Kunitz's poem "King of the River" comes, in part, through the repeated variations on the first lines of each stanza. The themes change from stanza to stanza, moving from "If the water were clear enough" to "If the knowledge were given you" to "If the power were granted you" to "If the heart were pure enough." But each stanza opens with a line that repeats some of the words, sentence structure, and rhythm of the first lines of previous stanzas. So each new version has the others singing inside it and expanding the meaning. We come to know these lines like the refrain of a song.

There are subtler symphonies, too, going on in most poems. A sound in one word may be echoed in several others. For example, consider the repeated *ing* sounds as Kunitz's salmon fights his way upstream "slapping, thrashing, / tumbling." Can you hear their momentum building to splash full force into the phrase "over the rocks"—through the two *o* sounds and smack into the final harsh *k?* Or try following music of the *s* sounds as they slide and surge through that first stanza with the struggling fish: ". . . See yourSelf / Slipped out of your Skin / noSing upStream . . ."

Perhaps, like me, you learned about alliteration, consonance, and assonance in that same eighth-grade English class that drilled you on the names of the different meters. What I didn't learn there was that these tools are actually alchemical implements of consciousness, weaving the body and mind together and affecting both in ways beyond cognitive control.

When the sound of one word echoes, or "chimes" with, a previous word, we are semiconsciously hearing both words at once in the friction and resonance between the sounds. For instance, listen to the repeated *r* sounds at the ends of words in these lines from the last stanza of "King of the River":

If the heart were pure enough,
but it is not pure,
you would admit
that nothing compels you
anymore, nothing
at all abides,
but nostalgia and desire
that two-way ladder
between heaven and hell.
On the threshold
of the last mystery,
at the brute absolute hour,
you have looked into the eyes
of your creature self,
which are glazed with madness,

and you say
he is not broken but endures,
limber and firm
in the state of his shining,
forever inheriting his salt kingdom,
from which he is banished
forever.[13]

Can you hear the *r* sounds echoing down through the lines of the stanza? *Pure* in the first line sings to the *not pure* in the second. Both are echoing inside the word *anymore* in the fifth line. The word *desire* in the seventh line takes up the song of the *r*'s, which courses on through the rest of the poem through the words *ladder, mystery, hour, your, creature, are, endures, limber, firm, forever,* and again *forever.* Can you sense how these repeated sounds amplify and complexify the power of each subsequent word, as if they were infusing them not only with the tumult of sound, but with all the accumulating meanings as well? Unconsciously you hear the word *pure* inside the word *anymore,* and the whole river of resonating words inside the final *forever.* Some cumulative, inarticulate experience is conveyed, more like the felt knowing that comes from music than the pragmatic meanings we usually ascribe to language.

If you decide to learn a poem by heart, noticing the sound-play laced through it can help you weave the lines into your memory. And when you forget words and phrases, discovering exactly why they are placed where they are in the symphony of the poem can help you to retrieve them, as I will explore further in Chapter 5.

Image

"The image," poet Jane Hirshfield says, "summons the body into a poem."[14] Neruda's "fever or forgotten wings" beat inside my own chest, connecting me with his moment of poetic discovery. Dickinson's frog telling its name "To an admiring Bog" instills in my body a sense of her repulsion at being a public "somebody." I can graphically sense Kunitz's king salmon inside my very cells when I know myself as a "yard of muscle that coils / uncoils."

It is the body that feels the images in a poem. Try tracking the sensations that arise as you speak the short Dickinson poem quoted above. Notice that you are feeling more than the rhythms and sounds. You are also being moved by the images: without that frog, the sensate experience of the poem would be a very different one!

An image, especially one that surprises with its capacity to evoke rich and unexpected connections, defies your patterns of perception. It undoes them through a simple, startling rightness that invokes your whole being into a moment of pure experience: "This morning the green fists of the peonies are getting ready / to break my heart." Mary Oliver's image moves into my body. I not only see the peonies, I feel the clenched fists of them in my own fingers. I can't help but viscerally connect the words *fist, break,* and *heart* in a vector that catches my breath in an exquisite confusion of beauty and pain.

This happens not only because the image is from the world of flesh, rock, and tree, but also because, in the convergence of two unlike things, the brain simply cannot sustain its tendency toward either/or thinking. Peonies, frogs, and bogs are raw matter. Yet each is connected with a rather heady concept: the peonies are "breaking [the poet's] heart," the frog is "public," and the bog is "admiring." The mind cannot make sense of these pairings in a linear way. A delicious ambiguity is born.

This can be a challenge, particularly in the Western world, where ambiguity is often avoided and there seems to be a premium on rational analysis and knowing exactly where we stand. One person wants to stay safely in the mind and avoid the wet underworld of feelings. Another wants to only swim in a sea of emotion, never touching the dry shores of reason. We want to divide everything into black or white, good or bad, right or wrong. As George W. Bush told the world in a news conference in November 2001, "You're either with us or against us."

But by its very nature, an image unifies the polarities. Neruda's "forgotten wings" asks the listener to think and feel at the same time. It is neither right nor wrong that in our salmon selves, we are a "yard of muscle," in Kunitz's words. Even the right brain and the left brain are woven together when an image appears in a poem, for it is the right brain that receives forms and the left brain that processes language. When a form arrives in language, the whole brain is summoned into the movement.

An additional alchemy takes place when images appear as metaphors—figures of speech in which a word or phrase usually designating one thing is used to represent another. Metaphors are the koans of poetry. A koan is a paradoxical question used in Zen Buddhism as a tool for attaining enlightenment. Like the famous koan "What is the sound of one hand clapping?" a metaphor is a logical impossibility designed to shatter the limitations of the mind. It brings together two experiences that cannot coexist or be made to fit into the mind's habitual categories.

Many other mystical practices call on the power of converging opposites to open the mind's circuitry. Kabbalistic scholar Jason Shulman says, "When we are capable of vividly holding opposites within our body, which is to say not only as a mental construct, but as a sensation or sense of physical knowing within the body, the 'third thing' that frees us appears as a gift . . . Our work is not finished until the moment we say, 'Life and death are One in God,' and bring these two poles closer and closer within our mind and body until they merge. Then a new freedom, palpable and alive, is born."[15] In Yoga Nidra, a practice derived from the ancient Tantric wisdom of the East, a similar process of holding opposites is found. Richard Miller explains:

> The ego-mind moves linearly. It focuses in one direction or it focuses in another direction, but it cannot move simultaneously in two directions at once. For instance, in this moment be aware of the space out in front of your body. You probably take yourself as a "someone" who is attending in this linear direction. But watch what happens to your sense of being a doer if I ask you to be simultaneously aware of the space out in front of and behind the

back of your body. The mind becomes silent and the sense of being a doer drops away while you experience yourself expanding in a multidimensional spaciousness. The thinking mind has to stop when we invite it to be simultaneously open in different directions. And when the mind is quiet we taste our spacious, non-linear nature.[16]

In Kunitz's poem "King of the River," the tension between images is constant. There is layer upon layer of metaphor: "You would see yourself / slipped out of your skin / nosing upstream . . ." Surely I, the reader, am a person. Yet I am being addressed as a salmon within the first lines of the poem. Human and fish collide, and both disappear in the torrent of experience. My favorite phrase, the one that startles my mind every time I speak or hear it, is "finned ego." The joining of the wild, water-bound fins of the fish with that which is driest and least primitive in a human dumbfounds and excites me. I cannot contain both, and, at least for a moment, I break open—perhaps into a state more akin to the salmon the poet has dared me to become.

As in Naomi Shihab Nye's poem "Kindness," this is a direct confrontation with the power of ambiguity. At a panel discussion at the Dodge Poetry Festival in 2002, aptly entitled "Poetry as Disruptive Seed, Poetry as Centering Force," Robert Hass, then America's poet laureate, said, "Poems must move in two directions at once: enchantment and disenchantment, life and death, knowing and having no idea." The poet Mark Doty added, "Yes, a good poem is the yoking of polarities. A poem that doesn't move us is usually a poem that does not feel as complicated as life." Kunitz's words challenge the pragmatic mind, flooding awareness with many layers of sense that flow in all directions like the rushing current the salmon swims.

I remember arriving at my poetry group one rainy winter morning, still bleary-eyed in spite of having infused myself with two cups of Earl Grey tea. Our host's apartment smelled a little of mold. The stuffing from the armchair I was curled into was seeping out of the ratty fabric and attaching itself to my new black pants. I was wondering if I could make up some excuse to climb into my car and head back to bed.

The meeting began with a member of the circle reading that week's poem from *The New Yorker*. To this day, I don't remember what the poem was about. But toward the end I heard through my fog, "A whole bouquet of crows came apart outside the window."[17] Suddenly, I was shocked awake, completely present and energized. The extraordinary blending of images had completely stopped my mind. I had to drop my toxic load of compulsive thoughts, sit up, and listen. Who ever heard those words put together? A "bouquet" cannot be "crows." But I knew exactly what the poet Sharon Olds experienced when she saw that. For at least a moment, logical thought had stopped and I was one harmonious wave where sensing was feeling, was knowing, was being in this magic show of bursting blacknesses on sky.

King of the River

If the water were clear enough,
if the water were still,
but the water is not clear,
the water is not still,
you would see yourself,
slipped out of your skin,
nosing upstream,
slapping, thrashing,
tumbling over the rocks
till you paint them
with your belly's blood:
Finned Ego,
yard of muscle that coils,
uncoils.

If the knowledge were given you,
but it is not given,
for the membrane is clouded
with self-deceptions
and the iridescent image swims
through a mirror that flows,
you would surprise yourself
in that other flesh,
heavy with milt,
bruised, battering toward the dam
that lips the orgiastic pool.

Come. Bathe in these waters.
Increase and die.

If the power were granted you
to break out of your cells,
but the imagination fails
and the doors of the senses close

on the child within,
you would dare to be changed,
as you are changing now,
into the shape you dread
beyond the merely human.
A dry fire eats you.
Fat drips from your bones.
The flutes of your gills discolor.
You have become a ship for parasites.

The great clock of your life
is slowing down,
and the small clocks run wild.
For this you were born.
You have cried to the wind
and heard the wind's reply:
"I did not choose the way,
the way chose me."
You have tasted the fire on your tongue
till it is swollen black
with a prophetic joy:
"Burn with me!
The only music is time,
The only dance is love."

If the heart were pure enough,
but it is not pure,
you would admit
that nothing compels you
anymore, nothing
at all abides,
but nostalgia and desire,
that two-way ladder
between heaven and hell.
On the threshold
of the last mystery,

at the brute absolute hour,
you have looked into the eyes
of your creature self,
which are glazed with madness,
and you say
he is not broken but endures,
limber and firm
in the state of his shining,
forever inheriting his salt kingdom,
from which he is banished
forever.

— Stanley Kunitz

Chapter 6

WRITING POEMS
ON YOUR BONES

Give back your heart
to itself, to the stranger who has loved you

all your life, whom you ignored
for another, who knows you by heart.

— Derek Walcott

Nine times out of ten, when I tell people that I love to learn poems by heart, they say, "I wish I could join you. I've always wanted to be able to remember a poem. But I have a terrible memory. I can't even remember where I left the car keys!"

Neither can I. Nor can I remember the name of my neighbor's Shih Tzu or if the plural of *fish* is *fish* or *fishes*. And, of course, it's getting worse. As the passage of time seems to corrode the edges of my brain, street names, multisyllabic words, and what I was going to say just before the phone rang are all dissolving in the brine.

Luckily, these inevitable little lapses have nothing to do with remembering a poem. Because learning by heart is different from memorization. It doesn't require fierce discipline, concentration exercises, or even a good memory. All it requires is the love of a poem, the curiosity to get to know it intimately, and the willingness to let it help you know yourself.

You might have noticed by now that I try to avoid the word *memorize.* For me and many others I have met, the word reeks of all sorts of horrific moments from childhood—compulsory conjugations of Spanish verbs and rote recitations of the Gettysburg Address. This approach seems more like conquering a poem than entering into a relationship with it. Even the suffix *-ize,* which means "to make," gives a sense of enforcing one's will over something: privatize, computerize, terrorize, memorize.

Learning by heart is a partnership, not a conquest. It is about entering into a relationship with a poem in which, as in any real relationship, you are changed by the other and the other is changed by you. If anyone is conquered in this partnership, it is you, as you surrender to the poem's guidance and allow it to lead you into unknown territory. Ultimately, it is not as much about the achievement of having the poem in your memory as it is about where the process of learning takes you.

"Learning by heart" is a wonderful phrase because it holds within it the invitation to receive something with your whole self, not just your mind, and to take it into your body with your breath. To learn it with your feelings and the insights that spring not from your head, but from your very core.

The ancient Greeks believed that memory actually resided in the physical heart, along with intelligence and feelings. Our word *record,* usually used in reference to some sophisticated piece of technology, echoes back to that wisdom. It is built of the prefix *re-,* meaning "again," and the word *cor,* which means "heart." A mechanical recording device is actually an artificial replica of that organic chalice of memory we all have: the heart.[1]

Even after history books took the place of epic poetry as the memory bank of the community, learning and delivering poems by heart was standard practice among poets and laypeople alike. This was not only because there were few in poetry's early audience who could read but also because it went without saying that poems were devised to be spoken by heart. Only then could the full life of the creation be breathed into being. As poet and essayist David Barber tells us, "Poetry was memory's darling. In ways we now can scarcely imagine, memory breathed life into poetry and poetry in turn made memory something truly memorable."[2]

The art of memory was seen as a sacred endeavor until at least the late 16th century, especially among poets. Simonides of Ceos, a poet who lived around 550 B.C., is said to have originated the art of memory by developing a way of housing veritably unlimited information in what he called a Memory Palace. This is one of several highly sophisticated techniques developed in the ancient world and taught in schools of philosophy, rhetoric, and meditation. "Ancient and medieval people reserved their awe for memory," says Mary Carruthers, author of *The Book of Memory*. "Their greatest geniuses they describe as people of superior memories."[3] Among these are Cicero, Saint Thomas Aquinas, and Aristotle. For Plato, the art of memory was a mystical pursuit in which the memory of the material world interacts with the memory of "the realities which the soul knew before its descent here below. True knowledge consists in fitting the imprints from sense impressions on to the mould or imprint of the higher reality of which the things here below are reflections."[4]

In ancient Greece, individuals known as *rhapsodes* learned Homer's *Odyssey* and *Iliad* by heart. Not only did they perform these epic poems as part of the Olympic Games and other competitions, they were held as oracles among the people. For a fee, you could ask the rhapsode a question and receive a personal recitation of a passage from Homer as a form of guidance or divination.

Through the work of Italian philosopher Giordano Bruno in the Renaissance, classical techniques of memory became the intense, magical, religious core of the Hermetic tradition. Bruno, who was burned at the stake for his occult teachings, tells how the god Hermes gave him a book containing the secrets of the art.[5] Through these practices, it was said, one could learn the roads to Heaven and transform the stuff of the material plane. This equation of the art of memory with the wisdom of the soul is essential to the practice of "learning by heart."

The mystical component of the art of memory has been woven into all of the major religions of the world. Monks and mystics who memorize the Bible, Muslims who learn the Koran from cover to cover, rabbis who cantillate (sing) the Torah, like ancient bards and modern-day griots,[6] may be gleaning some ineffable, alchemical benefit from holding these tracts of truth within them, even beyond the practical reward of remembering and reciting such wisdom.

For the Buddha's first students, too, remembering was a transformative, whole-body experience. They could neither read nor write, so they recorded the Buddha's utterances by learning them by heart. Years later, this practice of committing key phrases to memory became known in Tibetan Buddhism as "writing on the bones." What a perfect phrase to describe the power of taking in a text so deeply that it seems to reside in the cells of your body. Yongey Mingyur Rinpoche, a modern Buddhist master who combines spiritual teachings with neuroscience, speaks of how focused attention has been shown to contribute to the creation of "new connections between brain cells, which in turn determine how other nerve, organ, and muscle cells respond to thoughts, feelings, and sensations."[7] So a holy text or your favorite poem, when "written on your bones," may even reroute your bioelectric circuitry, *literally* transforming the way you respond to life.

This has been my experience. When I learned my first few poems by heart on that long, straight highway back in 1994, I had no idea I would end up with over a hundred poems in my memory. I thought I'd learn six or eight of my favorites and that would be that. But then I got a taste of the fruits of my labor. Of course there was the thrill of being able to speak a poem to a friend or to myself at a crucial time. But even more compelling was a subtle, pervasive shift in my whole way of meeting the world.

This was quite obvious because most of my poem-learning was done en route to visit my parents in the home where I grew up, a place where some of my least appealing behaviors tended to run rampant. Patterns of childish reaction seemed to be inscribed in the very air inside that house: my withdrawn silence at the dinner table or the way I could become as petulant as a four-year-old whenever I felt criticism coming my way. Now, instead of clamming up and giving whoever seemed to be threatening me "the look," I sometimes found a poem blossoming into my consciousness with a perfect medicine for me. "You do not have to be good," Mary Oliver would whisper in my inner ear. Or, "so long as you have not experienced / this: to die and so to grow, / you are only a troubled guest / on this dark earth," Goethe would warn my prideful temper. It was as if I had a throng of guides within me, calibrated to show up at the perfect moment, 24 hours a day.

A poem remembered is a powerful thing. For what is poetry but the language of the true self, the self that unstoppably sings its note under all the encrustations of confusion and contrivance, under all the costumes of culture, family drama, and creed? To "write it on your bones" is, as Mingyur Rinpoche confirms, to rewire the synaptic circuitry of your nervous system into alignment with your deepest nature.

What Is Memory?

While an ancient Greek would tell you that your memories live in your beating heart and an early Buddhist could read to you from scriptures written on his bones, a modern scientist can't tell you much with certainty about what memory is or how it works. It is quite remarkable that with all the information we humans have accrued by studying our own bodies, no one has conclusively cracked the mystery of memory. Of course there are throngs of techniques and even surgical procedures—not to mention medications, vitamins, herbal concoctions, and foods—whose purpose it is to enhance memory. But no one can tell you for sure its size or shape or capacity or exactly why it behaves the way it does. As British memory researcher Martin Conway says, "We just don't know . . . But there have to be some unanswered things left in research, otherwise it's not worth doing!"[8]

Though they may not have found a way to measure the capacity of your memory, scientists have discovered in recent years that exercising it can be as important as exercising the body. It turns out that memory exercises stave off dementia and other forms of mental loss. Books, flash cards, and classes in the field of "Neurobics" have flooded the market with do-it-yourself memory workout programs for the aging brain.

You may be muttering under your breath by now that this is all well and good for some people, the ones who actually have an innate proclivity for memory, but you are not one of them, never have been, and never will be. I have heard this, or versions of it, from a startlingly high percentage of people. When I do, I feel the kind of heartbreak that a singing teacher must feel when, once again, she encounters a music lover who was told in sixth grade, as I was, to "just mouth the words." I spent three decades believing I couldn't sing—until Chloe Goodchild, a vocalist whose work is appropriately called *Your Naked Voice,*[9] unlocked the cage of my history and set my voice flying into the present moment. Now I'll blurt, bellow, and serenade at the least provocation. And, though I'm not always singing the expected notes, it turns out I am definitely not tone-deaf.

Anyone can learn a poem by heart. Perhaps your natural capacity is obscured by memories of painful attempts in your past and projected failures in your future. But I've never met anyone who couldn't eventually learn poems with ease. One of my best friends, Hannah, was certain that she had been born with some basic piece missing where the capacity to remember words was supposed to be. She often bemoaned the irony that she, The Woman with the Worst Memory in the World, was friends with me, whose passion and profession was learning poems by heart. It was all the more painful for her because she had loved poetry since she was a child and longed to be able to speak it from memory. Hannah's father, an immigrant from Germany, had dozens of poems committed to memory. He would recite every night at the dinner table. He was a difficult man, and there had been painful conflicts between him and Hannah throughout her childhood. But when he spoke poetry, Hannah melted. In fact, the whole family was transformed. To the young girl, it felt as if the perpetual harshness between them miraculously dissolved, and for the short duration of the poem, the family shared a kind of Holy Communion.

But her father's gift had a dark side. Whenever anyone else attempted to deliver a poem, the whip of his criticism and contempt lashed out instantaneously. Hannah had seen him mortify her mother on many occasions. Her favorite aunt, his sister, actually knew many more poems than he, but rarely spoke them for this reason, and never when her brother was in the house. So even though Hannah was magnetized by the beauty of his recitations and would have loved to try it herself, she froze in fear before she even started. Imagining the humiliation of her own failure was enough for her. She didn't even want to try.

This fear stayed with her through school and college. Every time she was asked to commit something to memory, she found an excuse to opt out of the experience. As an English major, this was sometimes a problem, separating her from her peers. But it seemed a small price compared to the certain humiliation of her inevitable failure. She came to truly believe that there was a defect in her brain that made it impossible for her to learn anything by heart.

It was no accident that she and I became friends. Part of what drew us together was our kindred craving for the soul language of poetry and our love of how it took us below the surface of our lives. Hannah introduced me to some of the poems that would become my greatest teachers—from T. S. Eliot, Rumi, and Rilke. I found in her a listener whose hunger for hearing the poems I knew by heart was almost as great as my love of speaking them.

It wasn't easy for her to tell me that she believed she had a disability in exactly the area that was one of my greatest strengths. It was even harder for her to begin to admit, to herself and to me, the pain and longing that still roiled underneath this belief. Of course, I instantly offered to walk with her through her fear, to do whatever it took to help her reclaim what I knew was her innate capacity. But for years she refused my offer.

I don't remember if it was she or I who discovered the tale of Caedmon, the first known poet of the English language. The story, which is part history and part legend, is that Caedmon was an extremely shy laborer who lived around A.D. 660. Some say he had a stutter and was ashamed to speak. When all the workers gathered to pass the harp and recite poems to entertain each other at the end of the day, Caedmon would flee, mumbling something about the cows in the barn needing to be tended.

One night, as he lay in the straw among the beasts he trusted, an angel came to him in a dream and ordered him to recite a poem. He refused, explaining that he had a handicap and was unable to remember or speak verse. The angel responded, "However that may be, you shall recite to me." When Caedmon asked what he should recite, he was told to "sing of the beginning of created things."

Thereupon Caedmon began to spontaneously speak verses praising God and creation. He woke with perfect memory of his poem, which he shared with his fellow workers. They celebrated, exclaiming to the abbess of the local monastery about his gift. She challenged him to recite more poems, based on passages from holy texts. Soon he became known far and wide for his gift of reciting poems in praise of God. The Anglo-Saxon scholar Bede, considered the "father of English history," says of Caedmon, "He never could compose any trivial or idle song, but, as he recognized that it was God who had opened his lips, therefore, till his dying day, did his mouth show forth his praise."[10]

My friend Hannah identified with the stuttering Caedmon. She knew that in his story was a message pointing right at her. Like him, she fled when it came her turn to recite. Like him, she felt safer with the animals than with a circle of humans jockeying to impress others with a poem. And, like him, she had a profound reverence for the invisible unknown, which Caedmon called God and she herself had no name for but "the Mystery." Her whole life had been devoted to listening for that vast reality beyond the tangible world. This devotion infused all her relationships and her work as a spiritual guide to others.

But when she thought about learning a poem by heart, her ancient terrors crowded out the memory of what really mattered to her. Suddenly she was a child again at her father's table. From that perspective, speaking poetry was not about communicating what she cared most about, or, as in Caedmon's case, praising God. It was about survival. It was about personal mastery or personal defeat: either she would be successful and conquer the poem and whoever might be listening, or, more probably, she would sink into panic and a veritable quicksand of horrific memories.

Caedmon's example gave her the fire to face her demons. She asked me to help her learn a poem by heart. She chose a few lines from T. S. Eliot's *Four Quartets,* lines she had loved since high school.

At first, she panicked each time she was unable to remember the next word, "You see! I can't do this. I was right!" But with each stumbling I assured her that anyone would go through the same process of forgetting a word, searching for it, finding it, losing it again, and so on. She wasn't special. She didn't have a unique handicap. The only difference between her and others was that she got terrified when she forgot a word and they didn't. While others saw their faltering as an invitation to get to know the poem and themselves a little better, she found herself gasping for breath in a wave of painful memories and self-annihilating assumptions.

Slowly, with each forgotten word, Hannah's panic lessened. She began to realize that she had unconsciously chosen a passage from Eliot that had, at its heart, the same lesson that Caedmon had taught her. Eliot writes:

> *You are not here to verify,*
> *Instruct yourself, or inform curiosity*
> *Or carry report. You are here to kneel*
> *Where prayer has been valid.*

For Hannah, the art of remembering and speaking a poem had to come from her devotion to something greater than herself, the same devotion from which Caedmon's words were finally ignited, otherwise she would indeed fail. She had to "kneel / where prayer has been valid." She was simply unable to learn a poem from her ego's need to prove that she could, or from the little child's longing to impress her father. Or from the vise grip of a conquering mind that wanted to "verify, / Instruct yourself, or inform curiosity / or carry report." For Hannah, learning a poem by heart had to be an act of prayer. As she appreciated this, the tyranny of her perfectionism began to melt away and with it her terror of making a mistake. She actually began to enjoy the process.

Bit by bit, she worked the poem into her memory. In reality, it took only about 40 minutes, though she felt as if it were a lifetime. When she finally had it, she was giddy as a little girl, dancing through the house reciting the lines to the mirror, to me, and to Rumi, the cat.

But early the next morning she called me in dismay. "I've forgotten it! I woke up this morning, and I cannot even remember the first line! See? I'll never be able to learn a poem by heart." She was truly upset, on the edge of tears. For her, this failure had all sorts of meanings: that there was indeed something wrong with her, that she would never be able to know a poem by heart, that she couldn't heal the wounds left by her father's contempt, which were made more painful because of the longing he instilled in her for the communion of poetry.

When I told her that the same thing happens to me the morning after I learn a poem, she was silent. "You? You, who know so many poems? What do you mean?" I explained that I forget a new poem several times a day until it is firmly embedded in what I call the "Third Chamber of Memory." It usually takes me a week, or, with a longer poem, several weeks, before I have the lines dependably in my inner archive. But every day the process gets easier and easier, more and more enjoyable. I begin to actually look forward to the breakdowns because over the years I've learned that forgetting a line or a word can be the most valuable part of the process. Each time I forget, the poem is calling me beyond myself, inviting me to some experience that is new and unfamiliar. If the words had fit in with my habitual self, they would have been easily absorbed into my memory. The places I forget chart a map showing where the poem is calling me into a new territory. They offer me the Gift of Forgetting, which I will explore further in the next chapter.

Hannah's adventurous spirit was ignited by this prospect. As her curiosity grew, the voltage of her panic dimmed. Within a week, she knew her chosen lines by heart and had even spoken them as part of a lecture before a large gathering. Her tenacious belief in her defective mind was crumbling. Eagerly she picked the next poem to learn, this time a bit longer: "Why Mira Can't Come Back to Her Old House'" by the 16th-century Hindu mystical poet Mirabai.

Her fear did resurrect periodically through the years, usually after she hadn't thought of a poem for a few months. Reaching into her memory and not finding it there, she would panic again. But once she realized how quickly these seemingly lost poems could be reinscribed "on her bones," even this last vestige of her painful history dissolved.

Whatever beliefs you hold about the limitations of your own memory, I urge you to question them. As scientists and mystics will concur, memory is a great mystery and whatever you believe to be true about it could as easily be fiction. Who knows how vast your memory is or what it can hold? Science's latest theory is that a memory is a pattern of synaptic connections in the brain. There are about a thousand trillion such connections possible. That means there is the potential for 30 times as much to be stored in your brain as is stored in the entire Library of Congress.

In the pages that follow, you will find no techniques for remembering poems or anything else. Throughout history people have memorized gargantuan amounts of information by using all manner of memory tricks. You can associate words with colors or visualize them in specific locations or connect them with random images or make acronyms of their first letters. There are even annual World Memory Championships in which people win recognition and lots of money by remembering unbelievably long lists of numbers or names by way of one technique or another.

Learning a poem by heart is different. Just as you need no technique to remember a really great kiss, a list of your favorite foods, or a mystical experience, you need no tricks of memory to recall a poem you love. It happens through allowing yourself to be touched and changed by the creative relationship. As Plato might say, when the words on the page are connected with the wisdom of the soul, memory happens.

I invite you to learn a poem by heart. Write it on your bones, plant it in your synapses, give it a home in your memory palace. The question of exactly what memory is and why it behaves as it does can remain unanswered, swathed in the wonder that the ancient Greeks may have felt when they worshipped it as a goddess: Mnemosyne, the great mother of the Muses.

The Four Chambers of Memory

Researchers tend to break memory into two parts, short-term and long-term. While I do not know what is scientifically true, when learning a poem I have found it much more useful to think of memory in four increments, not just two. I call these the Four Chambers of Memory.

The word *chamber* has resonance with the anatomy of the human heart: the four cavities through which the blood passes on its way to and from nourishing the cells of the body. But unlike the chambers of the heart, which follow a circular path, the chambers of memory are more like the caverns of an underground temple. Each is deeper in the earth of memory; each is further along the path of relationship with a poem. And each is a different world, offering its own particular gifts and challenges. The final chamber has a quality of everlastingness about it, like the inner sanctum of an underground temple where the remains of the dead are laid to rest for eternity. Like your ABC's and the nursery rhymes you've never forgotten, a poem that makes it all the way to the Fourth Chamber will probably be with you forever.

It was one such underground temple that became the inspiration for my understanding of these realms of memory. On an island in the middle of the Pacific Ocean, there is an ancient burial cave cut by hot lava. When you drop down through the secret hole in an overgrown pasture, you find yourself in a huge cavern whose mouth opens out wide to the sea. Often you can see spinner dolphins in the distance leaping and twirling above the waves or, in the winter months, the spouting of whales. Threading from this open chamber back into the darkness there is a network of tunnels. By flashlight, you can navigate into the blackest, most silent spaces imaginable. Sometimes you have to crawl on your belly, slithering between huge rocks. Then, suddenly, the tube opens into one of several large chambers. Each is further underground. Each seems to have its own purpose and character. One has three large cairns, which are piles of stones signifying a holy place. One is empty but for the petroglyphs carved by someone who lived at least six centuries ago. The innermost sanctum is so far inside the earth you have to crawl through the pitch-black tunnels for almost a mile to get there.

I fell in love with this cave. It gave me an outer experience of what I had found to be the interior terrain of memory. The four phases of learning a poem were the cave's four chambers. Just as each chamber of the cave was deeper in the earth and required a deeper commitment to get to it, each of these inner chambers was deeper in my heart.

The First Chamber of Memory: The Vestibule

The First Chamber is commonly called short-term memory. It is one of the brilliant features included in the basic package of the human mind. Like a vestibule between the outer world and the deeper recesses of the inner life, short-term memory is where everything lands for a moment before being either taken in or dropped out of your awareness. Through short-term memory, you can look at a poem and, looking away, remember a few words or phrases for a brief period of time before they either disappear into thin air or are taken more deeply into your heart.

Thanks to short-term memory, I can safely learn poems in my favorite study hall, the car. My car is often littered with poems—strewn on the passenger seat or stuffed alongside it, pressed between the sun visor and the roof or blowing around in the back seat. Holding a tattered piece of paper curled around the steering wheel, I can snatch a line or phrase when I am stopped at a light or in traffic and return my eyes to the road in a split second. That short, quick, superficial memory holds the words for me just long enough to let me taste them, roll them around in my mouth, speak them out loud or silently.

I repeat them, noticing everything I can about my own response, as if I were a scientist dropping the words into the alchemical test tube of my inner state. I watch for any reaction from within. What rises to greet them? What is my gut response—feelings, insights, physical sensations? As I do this, I am naturally noticing elements of the poem I had not been aware of before, deeper levels of meaning, details of rhythm, song, and breath—in other words, the poem's "shamanic anatomy."

The Second Chamber of Memory: Precious Difficulty

As soon as any visceral, personal connection is made with the line—shazam!—it lands solidly in the Second Chamber of Memory. The connection might be an insight or emotion evoked by the words. Or it may be a reaction to some aspect of the shamanic anatomy of the poem—the rhythm, breath, music, or imagery. And the response doesn't have to be pleasurable. Sometimes it is actually my discomfort that carries the phrase through the portal and drops it into the next chamber. For instance, in a piercing poem called "Thanks," W. S. Merwin writes, "With the crooks in office with the rich and fashionable / unchanged we go on saying thank you thank you." His unabashed political rant startled me. Even though I agreed with his sentiments, the bald truthfulness of Merwin's feelings felt like a punch in the stomach. I had never heard him speak with such overt outrage. The very shock of the encounter locked the lines into my memory.

The Second Chamber of Memory is a precious, difficult territory. It is precious because the poem will never again be so new, so fresh and full of undiscovered treasures. It is difficult because you will stumble and make mistakes. Like a baby just coming upon words, you have to find each one anew.

When you don't remember the words, you have the opportunity to tumble through a crack in your mind's control. Whatever you find through that crack is sure to be much more interesting and vibrant than the bland success of "getting it right." Because the places you forget are inviting you beyond your familiar patterns into a new experience of yourself and the poem. This is the Gift of Forgetting, one of the greatest treasures of the process, which I will explore in depth in the next chapter.

The work in the Second Chamber is challenging at times. The poem can look like it is 3,000 miles long. Later, you may marvel at how short it actually is. Often I have no idea how I will ever develop a relationship with all of that mileage, much less learn it by heart. Yet this is also the gift of the practice: The poem seems to go on forever because there is so much to discover within every phrase. World after world may be opening inside each line as you dig into the earth of your heart to plant the poem.

Here is the period (perhaps a phase in any partnership, whether with a poem or a person) when "falling in love" is transmuted into real relationship. The "young love," the immediate gratification, the sudden rushes of affection, the unexpected delights and insights, all must give way to the conscious navigation of the connection between you and your partner. Rilke expresses it this way:

Just as the winged energy of delight
carried you over many chasms early on,
now raise the daringly imagined arch
holding up the astounding bridges.[11]

Perhaps the "winged energy of delight" is a portrait of Eros, that wild child Cupid whose love-dipped arrow sends its "victim" into a swoon of infatuation. The serum lasts just long enough to get you over the threshold of a relationship, but not longer. Have you ever watched the life drain out of a romantic connection after the initial "falling in love" phase? To take the next step, to foster an enduring relationship, seems to require the effort of bridge build-ing.[12] Rilke goes on to say that this is not willful striving; it is the necessary, hard work of building a soul connection. Most of this work takes place in the Second Chamber.

Notice everything you can about the lines that defy easy entry into your memory, and everything you can about what they call forth in you. Mary Oliver, in her poem "The Summer Day," talks about this quality of focus: "I don't know exactly what a prayer is. / I do know how to pay attention." The "prayer" of the Second Chamber is paying attention.

It's a bit like grafting the poem into your memory. I've watched a gardener, when grafting a branch of one apple tree to the trunk of another, scrape at both surfaces to make them porous to each other. So, too, I scratch at the surface of the poem by digging into the particulars of its sounds and meaning. And at the same time I scratch at the surface of my own psyche by seeking personal con-nections with each phrase. It is as if, through this "gardening," the poem and I become open to each other. In reality, though, it is only about me opening to the poem; the poem has always been open to me.

I remember learning one of my favorite poems of all time, Pablo Neruda's "Poetry," which you can find following Chapter 1. The beginning slipped easily into my memory. But every time I said the poem, I unconsciously skipped the lines "and I made my own way, / deciphering / that fire . . . " When I finally noticed my omission, I realized it was because these words made me very uncomfortable.

In the last chapter I spoke about the "yoga of poetry" and how a poem can stretch you beyond the limitations you draw around your sense of who you are. Sometimes you sign on consciously for this stretching, and sometimes the poem can surprise you by "taking you where you do not wish to go." This can happen at any point in your relationship with a poem—as you first begin to read it, as you take it into your memory, or as you speak it aloud. For me, the Second Chamber is usually where I encounter the most opportunities to stretch. This was certainly the case with Neruda's poem.

At times like this, curiosity is a valuable asset. When curiosity overrides discomfort, my greatest learning happens. Through curiosity I can consciously turn toward what is unsettling me instead of unconsciously turning away. And when I do, my world is instantly bigger. I uncover new dimensions of myself and the poem. Not only that, but the very discomfort I am feeling becomes the grafting compound that cleaves the lines to my memory.

This part of Neruda's poem points directly at one of my life's greatest struggles: writing. Though I treasure every aspect of taking already written poems to heart, writing them does not come easily. When I was a child, a steady stream of poetry poured out of me unselfconsciously. But in my adult years I have toiled to "decipher that fire," frozen between my longing to articulate the ineffable and my perfectionism.

As I meditated on the words, I noticed that even the rhythm, in this beautiful translation by Alastair Reid, reflects the uncertainty and effort of the task. The first few lines have a lilting, regular rhythm, a beautiful loping stride: "and SOMEthing STARTed IN my SOUL, / FEver OR forGOTten WINGS . . ." Then suddenly the rhythm staggers, stumbles, becomes complex and chaotic: "and I MADE my OWN WAY, / deCIPHering / that FIRE." This is an example of how the sound of a poem can carry emotional meanings that bypass the mind. The drumbeats of the line are jostling each other inside my body, conveying messages that could never be put into words.

In these lines, Neruda guides me down a path I have only walked unsteadily. It is the path of writing that "first, faint line," no matter how nonsensical it might be, and seeing "the heavens unfastened and open" in celebration. It is as if the poet takes my broken, uncertain "forgotten wing" under his own and reminds me how to fly. This is one of the most generous medicines a poem has to offer: the chance to enter its particular stream and let it carry you beyond the circumference of your individual reach.

In spite of the way my mind bucks and frets against the discipline of the Second Chamber, the actual time spent there is only a small part of the whole spectrum of my relationship with a poem. Working with about 14 lines—a sonnet, for instance—may take an hour or less. Sometimes in my workshops we'll take 20 minutes to go outdoors and learn as much of a chosen poem as possible. I've been stupefied when some students have returned with a two-page poem well ensconced in the Third Chamber of Memory. Although such a feat is not within everyone's reach, most people are quite startled when they discover how quickly they can plant a poem firmly in their memory.

But it will not stay there, however well planted, unless you feed and water it. Like a seedling, it needs special attention in the first few days. If I work with a poem tonight and don't reconnect with it tomorrow morning, it will surely disappear from my memory bank. I need to speak it first thing in the morning, even before getting out of bed. I need to remember it last thing at night as I fall asleep. I need to say it while I'm driving, while I'm brushing my teeth, taking a shower, going for a hike. I need to say the poem several times a day over several days before it is firmly rooted within me.

The moments before you fall asleep and when you first wake up are excellent times to invoke the poem you are learning. It seems that when the brain is less cohered, the poem floats into awareness with more ease. Some memory researchers think that sleep is an essential component of memory. Indeed, I have sometimes found a poem inexplicably more whole and sure upon waking than it was the night before. More often, the opposite is true, as it was with my friend Hannah. Even so, it is always relatively easy to reinstall it on my "hard drive" the next day.

You'll find that parts of your poem slide between the Second and Third Chambers for the first few days. How can you tell the difference? When a line is in the Second Chamber, remembering it can feel, in the words of Rilke, like "pushing through solid rock." In the Third Chamber, even though you may not know if the next phrase will show up, there is a sense of flow, of being carried by the poem. You don't have to consciously plumb the layers of your psyche for the connection to each word. It arises on its own.

The Third Chamber of Memory: The Wave

Now that the poem is learned by heart, it is flowing. This can be a wonderful time in your relationship. The poem is rising to meet you. You are diving to find it. Nothing is taken for granted. Like a young romance, there is no certainty, no routine, no habitual way of being together. Insights blossom spontaneously each time you and the poem meet.

Here, even though you know the words, you have to find them again every time you say them. You cannot rest in the known for long. The next phrase does not arise unless you live toward it completely, igniting it from your direct, personal experience of the line before. There is a sense of living on the edge because you don't know if the next line will emerge from your memory or leave you stranded. And it doesn't come unless you're completely present.

But the poem's wave motion is in you—the flow of the language, the cadence, the contours of the terrain. Like knowing almost all of a song, the rhythm and sense continue even when memory fails to come up with the words. How many times have I found myself singing with gusto, "I've been working on the railroad all the livelong day, I've been working on the railroad da di-da da da da da!"

In this phase, I like to work with the poem when I'm in motion. One of my favorite practices is to speak the freshly learned poems while walking or working out, often to music. You might think that this would make it more difficult to concentrate. However, there is some surprising benefit to distracting the busy mind. The sound and the movement so overwhelm the mind that it lets go, relaxes, and allows the poem to slip in and take root. At times I'll even work with fairly loud dance music. The rhythms within the music help me to hear drumbeats in the poem I might not have noticed. And the centrality of the music grips my attention so the poem can slip in, free of the hypervigilant surveillance of my mind. When I decided to learn Dr. Seuss's *Happy Birthday to You*, my friends at the gym used to get a kick out of seeing me arrange the pages on the magazine rack of the step machine, put in my earphones, and begin climbing, my lips moving a mile a minute with words like, "And the Drummers who drum and the Strummers who strum / Are followed by Zummers who come as they zum!"

Some of the most ecstatic moments I've known have come when I am alone in nature speaking a poem that is in the Third Chamber of Memory. "The Thunder: Perfect Mind" is a Gnostic gospel, written around A.D. 300 in the voice of the divine feminine. In a translation by Jane Hirshfield, it is one of the most powerful pieces of writing I have ever encountered. Many lines of the long poem bring together two opposites, resulting in a scripture that defies duality and seems to be the very voice of the One behind the many:

> I am the first, and the last.
> I am the honored one, and the scorned.
> I am the whore and the holy one.
> I am the wife and the virgin.[13]

It seemed only right to learn this vast and sacred poem in a place that reflected equal glory. I chose the expanse of Kehoe Beach, near where I was living in Northern California. On many afternoons in the spring of 2002, I would follow the sandy path through lupine-scented air to where the sea exploded onto the shore. The cries of the gulls were barely audible over the ocean's drumroll. I tossed my voice to the wind and waves: "I am strength and I am fear. I am war and I am peace." If I did not make an absolutely personal connection with each phrase, the words would disappear from my mind. That connection might be as simple as the rush of heat in my chest that comes when I hear a fierce truth:

"Why, you who love me, do you hate me / and hate those who love me?" Or as complex as the memory of seeing a loved one convicted of a crime: "I am the condemnation and the acquittal." To this day, when I return to Kehoe, I can still hear fragments of *The Thunder* whispering in the wind.

Sometimes, even when the poem has been in the Third Chamber for a long time, you might forget a word. Out of the blue, it can disappear. Even after months of saying the poem by heart, these unexpectedly dropped words show you that there are still mysteries to unfold between you and this poem.

The most important practice for rooting your poem in the Third Chamber is speaking it to other people. You can know it perfectly in the shower. You can sing it to the trees on your favorite path through the woods. You can speak it in the car no matter what kind of music is playing on the radio. Yet when you go to offer it to another human being, whole chunks of it flee. For this reason it is very important that you find as many occasions as possible to speak it to others. Offer it to your friends at lunch, share it with colleagues at work, find unexpected moments to slip it into conversations over the phone. Discover how the poem lives in the space between you and another person.

A poem is a conduit of relationship. It gives language to dimensions of our inner lives that most of us rarely talk about. To speak Rilke's line "I am too alone in the world, and not alone enough" can plunge you and your listener into a potent, shared knowing of a private and yet universal experience. Saying these words aloud to another person can feel unexpectedly vulnerable. But it is a vulnerability to be celebrated (a subject I explore further in Chapters 7 and 8).

The Fourth Chamber of Memory: Surrender

In the Fourth Chamber the poem starts singing to you. Now that it is a part of you, its words and rhythms unfurl effortlessly—and sometimes even mindlessly—with every breath. This often gives rise to both wonder and dismay. It can be alarming to hear your own voice reciting Rilke's magnificent "First Elegy" as if it were "Twinkle, Twinkle, Little Star." But it can also be wondrous in a tense moment to go into that chamber and find the perfect lines telling you exactly what you most need to hear. "For us there is only the trying," T. S. Eliot reminds me as I worry over how my new CD will be reviewed. "The rest is not our business."

The Fourth Chamber is where "rote" memory dwells. This is where your ABC's, nursery rhymes, and the Pledge of Allegiance all came to rest, in most cases indelibly. There are poems that are so deeply engraved in my Fourth Chamber that I can speak them out loud while writing an e-mail or thinking about what I want for dinner without even listening to what my own voice is saying. It is very different from the Third Chamber, where I have no choice but to be awake to every line. There, I can't remember the next line if I'm not finding the connection inside me, feeling specifically how these words move me emotionally, physically, and mentally.

The Fourth Chamber offers another task. Here I have to *choose* to wake myself up. I have to *choose* to listen to the words, because they show up whether I am present or not. Actors often confront the challenge of saying the same lines over and over, sometimes eight or nine times a week for months on end. There are myriad books and acting techniques that speak of how to keep lines fresh night after night. Often they suggest some kind of creative invention: actively giving the words different inflections, making up a new subtext for the scene, or imagining different circumstances preceding it.

While you could use these approaches with a poem in the Fourth Chamber, my approach is very different. Learning and speaking a poem is not acting. It is less about invention than about surrender.

Surrender is the deepest teaching of the Fourth Chamber. Trust that all the active learning of the previous Chambers has instilled layer upon layer of rich and personal relationship with the poem. Now allow yourself to be carried by it. In the words of

D. H. Lawrence, "If only, most lovely of all, I yield myself and am borrowed / By that fine, fine wind." Let yourself be borrowed by the poem. Or, perhaps more accurately, by the voice within you that the poem calls forth.

So rather than making an effort to invent a new tone of voice, or working to find new layers of meaning, let the poem simply wash over you. Lean back and ride the waves of its rhythms, let your voice sink into the textures of the words. Open your inner and outer ears and let the poem sing to you. Listen to your own voice and the sounds of your surroundings. Every moment is fresh if you are awake and listening. Even if you've spoken the exact same words a thousand times, this moment has never happened before. You have never been exactly who you are right now. You have never spoken to this listener (whether that listener is you or someone else). You've never brought this poem into this particular circumstance. New layers of meaning and inspiration can open on their own every time you say the words. There is no need to create newness. Newness is constantly creating itself.

The beauty of this phase is that your poem has really become a part of your body. Think, for instance, of your hands. They automatically hit the computer keys, brush a hair from your eye, or lift the fork without your thinking about them. Then one day, you happen to notice the extraordinary miracles on the ends of your arms—the intricacy of veins, an age spot you never saw before, the grace of the fingers tapping out the letters.

When a poem is flowing out of you without conscious effort, a miracle can occur. The poem may start talking to you in your own voice. You may be less the speaker than the listener. You may hear the poem say new things. You may hear your own voice do things you've never known it to do. "Borrowed" by the poem, your voice can move in ways that completely surprise you.

The poems you have in the Fourth Chamber of your memory provide a natural home entertainment system. Stuck in traffic, waiting in the checkout line, or driving long distances, you can go into your archive and lose yourself in the words of your favorite poets. During the years of her childhood when she was mute,

Maya Angelou worked dozens of poems into the Fourth Chamber of her memory. "I don't say I understood them, but I had them," she reported in an interview. "I just put them all in the machine. And then when I was walking down the dirt roads of this little hamlet in Arkansas, it was like I had a computer. I could punch up, say, Rudyard Kipling, and just have it recite itself to me in my brain!"[14]

As the poems "recite themselves," they may touch you in new ways every time you reconnect with them, even after many years. I remember inadvertently rediscovering a poem by Rilke that I had learned by heart at least five years earlier. Though it had lived in the Fourth Chamber of my memory and I had spoken it frequently, I suddenly heard the words, summoned by a crisis in my life, in a completely fresh way.

I was in the throes of a new relationship. My partner and I had been carried by the ease and free play of infatuation for about three months. But now this was quickly changing. Disagreements and conflicting needs were snagging the flow of our communications. Each of us was feeling hurt and unseen by the other. Every other day I fantasized about storming out, my pride in my teeth, and slamming some invisible door.

In a moment of pure synchronicity, one of my students arrived for her session holding an index card with a sonnet on it. She had carried the poem around in her wallet for years, frequently reading it to herself or any companion who seemed in need of its wisdom. Now she wanted to learn it by heart.

The poem, which I quoted earlier in the description of the Second Chamber, was a sonnet by Rilke, translated by Robert Bly, which begins, "Just as the winged energy of delight." Until then, I had thought this work described the creative process. It speaks of the transition point when the initial rush of inspiration turns into the conscious work of creation. Now I heard it soundly confronting me about my love relationship. I blushed like a scolded child.

Pushing my feelings aside, I focused on teaching. I asked her to read the poem to me over and over, allowing her voice to change with whatever feelings, sensations, or impulses arose. Then I took the card she was reading from and told her to continue. Of course she froze instantly, as if I had suddenly taken the training wheels off her first bicycle. But soon she found she actually remembered much of the poem. Each time she forgot a line we looked together to find out how those words were stretching her into a deeper knowledge of both herself and the poem. Within about 15 minutes she was able to remember without stumbling. As often happens when I am teaching, at that point we started alternating: she spoke the poem to me, and then I spoke it to her, and so on.

As I listened to my own voice carrying the familiar words, I heard them in an entirely new way. I couldn't avoid hearing the poem's message to me. "Denser and denser the pattern becomes—" I heard my voice say. "Being carried along is not enough." I was flooded by a stream of images. Painful scenes in my current relationship and a veritable slide show of similar struggles from the past filled my inner screen. These conflicts I was facing were not new. They were the deep grooves of patterns I had repeated since childhood. After realizing this, there was no way I could continue to blame my partner for our difficulties. The veil of my pride was pierced. The poem was challenging me: "Now raise the daringly imagined arch / holding up the astounding bridges." It was time to do the hard work of bridge building across the seemingly impossible chasm between us.

Even though I was supposed to be the "teacher," my eyes brimmed with tears. I fell silent, stunned by the impact of the message. My student sensed the power of the moment and continued to repeat the poem softly. A deep tenderness and wisdom filled her voice.

Even after she too became silent, the last stanza kept reverberating inside me:

Take your well-disciplined strengths
and stretch them between two
opposing poles. Because inside human beings
is where God learns.[15]

I knew this poem so well I could almost recite it backwards. But I had no idea it had a hidden door that could open into an entirely new country of meaning when I most needed it.

This is my experience with every poem that lives in the Fourth Chamber of my memory, yet each time that door opens it seems like a miracle. Recently, as I prepared for a series of public events celebrating the release of my CD *Only Breath,* I was horrified to realize that each night of the tour I would need to speak exactly the same poems. Usually, during these public offerings I vary the program each night. I even leave some of it unplanned to make room for spontaneity. But for this series, my collaborator, Jami Sieber, and I felt it was important to introduce audiences to the poems featured on the CD. So not only would I have to limit myself to only those 12 poems, but they happened to be poems that I had just spent over a year repeating incessantly in the process of making the recording!

At first I balked. I love the surprise element that goes with not knowing what poem is coming next. I missed the way the musicians and I had to listen to each other when we were working with an unfamiliar poem. I missed choosing the poems to fit the audience, or my mood, or whatever Jami might spontaneously improvise on her cello.

But then the poems started taking me places I had never been. In concert after concert, my voice found new nooks and crannies of sound; my breath discovered new rhythms. My whole body began to surrender to being carried on the currents of the poems. I had never experienced such freedom from inhibition. And it was a freedom born from confinement. Speaking the same words over and over. Going deeper instead of wider. Surrendering instead of innovating. Letting the poems carry me.

The Hidden Tape Recorder

As I've said before, a poem lodged in the Fourth Chamber will probably be yours for life. Although a few words and phrases may crumble with time and lack of use, they usually are easy to return to memory.

In fact, it turns out that whatever is stored in the Fourth Chamber is the last to dissolve as the mind falls away, even in the face of extreme brain trauma, stroke, and dementia. Medical research has documented that, as the functions of the brain deteriorate or are interrupted by aging, illness, or injury, this domain of memory persists. Many are the stories of patients who cannot talk but are able to recite poems and nursery rhymes. Dr. Bonnie Gintis tells of caring for a patient who was mute because of a severe stroke. He had been in the hospital for weeks, barely able to point at an alphabet board to get his needs met. One day a new patient moved into the next room with a portable tape player. Soundtracks from Broadway musicals began to blare through the wall. The nursing staff was concerned for the mute patient and asked him if the music was disturbing him. Instead of pointing at the alphabet board, he burst into song, articulating perfectly the words of "Bali Ha'i," which was wafting into his room from the tape of *South Pacific* playing next door.

The nurses were shocked. One of them paged Dr. Gintis. By the time she reached her patient's bedside, he had finished singing "Bali Ha'i" without missing a word and had started in on the next song coming through the wall, "I'm Gonna Wash That Man Right Outta My Hair!" A small crowd of hospital staff had gathered around him in glee, celebrating his newfound ability to express himself. Later that day, he startled the nursing staff even more when his neighbor put on the tape of *South Pacific* again and they heard him singing loudly, "Can I have . . . some water!" to the tune of the chorus of "Bali Ha'i." It turned out his brain could deliver new words as long as they fit in the well-worn tracks of the patterns of the song.

In Tillie Olsen's famous short story "Tell Me a Riddle," Eva, who has become embittered and monosyllabic in her old age, undergoes a transformation in the final stages of her cancer. Poems, famous speeches, and songs begin to bubble out of her irrepressibly, a continuous stream. Her husband is jealous of these words she never shared with him:

"It helps, Mrs. Philosopher, words from books? It helps?" And it seemed to him that for seventy years she had hidden a tape recorder, infinitely microscopic, within her, that it had coiled infinite mile on mile, trapping every song, every melody, every word read, heard, or spoken.

We all have that hidden tape recorder within us. Dr. Raymond Moody, known for his research on near-death experiences, has documented several hundred cases in which people have been heard to recite poetry just before they die. Often these are people, like Eva, who have never shown an interest in poetry before. Yet somewhere in the Fourth Chamber of their memory, poems that may have been learned many decades earlier are waiting to be called forth at that most crucial moment.

Moody has dubbed this "The Swan Song Phenomenon," an analogy that originated with Socrates. According to an ancient Greek folk belief, a swan sings its most beautiful song just before it dies. Socrates, who had been known for his disparagement of poets during his lifetime, began writing and reciting poetry as he waited for his execution. He likened his impulse to that of the swan: an outburst of poetry in anticipation of a beautiful afterlife.

"The ancients thought that swan songs attuned the souls of the dying to the higher states of existence they were about to enter," Moody relates.[16] He cites how Pythagoras's students, as well as members of at least one Gnostic sect, were instructed to write poems that they called "passwords," which they would recite at the moment of death to ease the transition. He also compares the phenomenon to the shaman songs of many indigenous traditions, in which lengthy verses carry the practitioner to and from the spirit world.

As my friend Hannah's mother was dying, a stream of exquisite German poetry, as well as lyrics from many of Wagner's operas, poured almost constantly from her lips. Finally, her husband's judgment no longer mattered and the poems welled to the surface unchecked. It seemed to Hannah, as she sat by her mother's bedside, that the verses emerging from the "hidden tape recorder" made up a path of words that her mother was walking, poem by poem, to the other side.

Thanks to this phenomenon, when my grandmother was dying, I had many tender moments with her. I had never been very good at generating conversation between us. Though she was always interested in my adventures, we didn't seem to have a lot in common. But as she lost the capacity to talk, our relationship bloomed. Others felt awkward with her, not knowing how to make contact. But I was finally able to converse in a language I was comfortable with: I talked with her through touch, rhythm, and rhyme. As I stroked her arms or massaged her feet, she would recite numbers: 1 to 6, then 17, 18, 19, then repeat them like a chant. Sometimes we'd sing together:

Row, row, row your boat
Gently down the stream
Merrily, merrily, merrily, merrily
Life is but a dream.

Until I sang this song with my 98-year-old grandmother, her body pumping as if paddling toward the veil between the worlds, I'd never heard its wisdom. "It's true, isn't it, Nana?" I would ask her. "Life is the dream. Where you're going, maybe that's the reality." She didn't answer, but I felt her press her cheek into my hand as we began the song again.

Sometimes, when I think of my own death, I like to imagine a few lines of T. S. Eliot or Emily Dickinson trickling out of the side of my mouth as I go.

My Nana Like the Trees

My Nana, like the trees,
was well-dressed in her time.
Now she barely wears her skin;
arms and feet and fluids caving in
and breath so thin you can see
to the other side.
Ancient fingers curl at her chin
and tumble off the edge of vagrant words
into the season, like the leaves,
retiring from green
to blaze a naked moment then careen
to earth.

My Nana counts at the edge of time
as thoughts melt into numbers: one to six,
seventeen, eighteen, nineteen, then begin again
like the ancient monk
whose measured chant
at once keeps time
and shatters it.

My Nana chants in the autumn light,
numbers pumped from a distant past
fall from her breath, like leaves
from the tree of a branching soul
that reaches wider, higher still

even as the stuff of time
is strewn below or hangs
translucent from the bone
with no wish but to journey down
on gravity's verging tide

and something brilliant,
barely known,
rises through the naked trees—

— Kim Rosen

Chapter 7

THE GIFT OF FORGETTING

The art of losing isn't hard to master:
so many things seem filled with the intent
to be lost that their loss is no disaster.

— from "One Art" by Elizabeth Bishop

Everyone forgets. Names, telephone numbers, the combination to your locker at the gym, the next line of the poem you are delivering by heart. What goes on inside of you when you forget? Does your mind scramble to get a grip? Do you furrow your brow and squeeze your brain tight in hopes that the lost word will be pressed onto your tongue like a drop of orange juice? Do you frantically try to cover the sudden silence by distracting whoever is listening, or make up a story to fill the hole, or wring your hands in self-flagellation?

My hairdresser, for instance, forgets how I like my hair cut every time I see her. She fakes it desperately, making up conversations we've never had about this or that style I never asked for.

Eventually, through trial and error, the information is retrieved and the hair is cut. I am always awed by the amount of anxiety and frantic creativity that goes into hiding her forgetfulness. Yet I have to admit that I know the feeling. When I can't remember an intimate conversation that a friend is referring to or the name of her husband or son or dog, I have watched myself do that same desperate dance.

I invite you to join me in a new approach to forgetting. There are so many gifts just waiting to be opened in the moment you forget. I know that might seem like Pollyanna's "glad game" in the face of inevitable embarrassment, but it's not. Forgetting has been one of my greatest teachers.

A few years ago, I had a life-changing dream. I am standing at the front of a hall churning with people, about to give a performance of spoken poetry with a group of musicians. I don't know what time the performance is supposed to be. I can't find any of the musicians anywhere. A radio station is coming through the sound system, riddling the air with a mix of static and some '60s song like "My Way." There are not enough seats for the audience. People are annoyed, restless. I begin frantically setting up folding chairs.

Finally everyone is seated. There is still no sign of the musicians, but at least someone has turned off the radio. I stand on the stage, knowing I must begin alone. I cannot remember what poems I was going to deliver. In fact, I cannot remember the words to any of the poems I know. There is a lump in my throat, and I'm holding back tears. The audience looks at me, ticking with irritation.

At last the words to Rilke's "First Elegy" come to me. With relief I begin, "Who, if I cried out, would hear me among the angel's / hierarchies?"[1] But there my memory shuts down completely. The steady stream of poems always available to me is nowhere to be found. The audience growls, whispers to one another, titters. Some people start pushing their way past the others in an effort to storm out.

I've had versions of this dream dozens of times since I was a child. When I was little, I found myself in a classroom where I helplessly tried to remember how to spell *Constantinople* in front of evil Miss Kaplan, who threw chalk at you when you made a mistake. As a teenager, I was at a horse show where I forgot my clothes and, arriving in my pajamas, was prohibited from entering the ring. Later I was in a theater, with a script I had failed to memorize flaking to ash in my hand. Or at a workshop I was supposed to be leading where I forgot to bring my notes, or the participants refused to sit down, or the waves of the ocean poured in through all the windows. In all these dreams, I am desperately struggling to hide my failure and appear in control.

But in this dream it is different. I don't fight it.

I say to the audience, "I'm sorry, I cannot remember the poems." People start to mock me and walk out. I watch, helplessly exposed. Soon everyone is gone except a huge police officer and a tiny, wizened Peruvian grandmother. Her braids swing to her waist and the colors of her wool poncho seem to vibrate with the ancestry of her indigenous wisdom. The man's height of almost seven feet would be imposing, but his whole body is reverently bowed toward his tiny companion as he follows her to the front of the hall. They timidly approach the stage, where I am frozen in mortification. I move to offer my apologies. "No, no," they say, "you just gave us the greatest gift we could have hoped for. You let us see you naked, undefended. You did not cover up the fact that you didn't know what to do. You have changed our lives forever. We do not know how to thank you."

We come to poetry for moments of truth. We share it with others for moments of communion. We are following the scent of something that can take us closer to ourselves than daily conversations or the routine thought patterns we buy into again and again. We want something more real, more immediate. As Rumi says, we want "the fabric torn and drawn away."

In the moment of forgetting, you can almost hear the fabric tearing if you pause long enough to listen. Yet, until I had that dream, my response had always been to flee.

Now there was another choice. I saw that the most powerful medicine of learning a poem by heart might, paradoxically, be what happened in the moment I forgot. I began to learn poems not only to have them in my internal archive but also to become a student of my own forgetting. Gradually I learned to slip through that tear in the fabric of the predictable and welcome the gifts to be found there.

And the gifts are many. Forgetting happens at the border between the familiar and the unknown. So the places I forget in a poem chart an exact map of where I am called beyond my ordinary limits. Each time I honor my forgetting instead of covering it up, I have the opportunity to explore a new territory.

Die Before You Die: The Willingness to Stop

In order to enter this rich inquiry, the first step is to consciously welcome the moment of forgetting. This is not the usual response to a breakdown of memory. Usually people run from it, "faking it" like my hairdresser or in some way trying to hide what is really going on, because we want to get it "right" and have a feeling of resolution.

However, when I really think about it, the greatest peace I have ever known had nothing to do with resolution. I remember hearing Pema Chödrön, the Buddhist teacher and author of *When Things Fall Apart*, exploring the idea of resolution:

> The truth is "you can't get no satisfaction." All the time we're motivated to get some resolution, get ground under our feet . . . Then we don't have to touch that shakiness, that vulnerability. But this work is about giving up all the old ways we protected against feeling anything unpleasant or unwanted. Finally we're willing to relate with it as honestly and as gently as we can. Stepping more and more into groundlessness.[2]

Like Pema's Buddhist practice, the practice of stopping at the moment the mind ceases to remember can train you to develop the capacity to tolerate groundlessness. Even to dive into it.

John Keats, one of the principal English poets of the 19th century, speaks to the heart of this practice and the need for it in the creative process:

> At once it struck me what quality went to form a Man of Achievement . . . I mean Negative Capability, that is, when a man is capable of being in uncertainties, Mysteries, doubts, without any irritable reaching after fact and reason.[3]

Keats's "Negative Capability," like Pema Chödrön's "groundlessness," is a prerequisite to true inquiry. It is a key that unlocks the mind's repetitious patterns, allowing something new to appear from beyond the borders of the known.

To pause in the midst of forgetting is a simple act and may take less than a second. But it is quietly profound because it represents a disengagement from your hardwiring for survival. Each moment of forgetting is like a little death. The momentary loss of the capacity to remember portends other losses that may be yours someday. You may find yourself unable to walk or hear or lift a spoon to your lips. Loss is preprogrammed in these bodies you and I are wearing. And when that time comes, if it hasn't already, we can either fight the inevitable or find the capacity to embrace our incapacity and all the challenges and, yes, gifts that come with it.

In French, *la petite mort*, "the little death," refers to a sexual orgasm. As the French seem to know, there is pleasure in the loss of control. Yes, it is a momentary death of who I thought I was and what I thought I was doing (reciting the poem), but, at the same time, it is an opening. If I don't push my forgetting away, I have the opportunity "to step through that door full of curiosity," as Mary Oliver says in her poem "When Death Comes."

In one way or another, every spiritual path I've ever studied teaches the practice of "dying before you die." For instance, from Buddhist wisdom I have learned that meeting the myriad "everyday little deaths"[4] that life brings me is a profound practice, which can prepare me to gracefully meet my physical death when the time comes. From Christian wisdom I have learned that opening to these daily opportunities to practice "dying" is the only way to fully embrace every moment of my life. The symbolism of the Jewish Passover story shows me the courage required to leave Egypt, which in Hebrew means "the narrow place," and face my death again and again on a journey into the unknown in order to reach the "promised land" of true freedom.

So when you come to that place in the poem where the words disappear and memory crumbles, release the rodent-like scurrying of your mind in its attempt to get the "cheese" of the right word or phrase. Pause. In that space, wonderful things can happen. Some people tell me that just by stopping and relaxing into the moment, they see the lost words come floating up from wherever they hide in the stress and scramble of a driven mind. This is not the point of stopping—to trick memory into behaving the way you want it to—but it is delicious when it happens. The point of stopping is, in Mary Oliver's words, to "notice / something you have never noticed before."

Speak the poem you are learning to yourself, internally or aloud. When you come to a point where you can't remember the words, stop and breathe. You might even say to yourself, *I can't remember the words.*

Once you acknowledge this, the poem can open more fully to you and, in turn, open you more fully to yourself. At that point, I have found four different inquiries to be quite valuable. Often I will pursue one or two of them, which is all I need to firmly lodge the forgotten text in my memory along with some rich insight. But sometimes I use all four. One takes me deeper into intimacy with the poem: how is that particular phrase in that specific place working some magic in the poem's "shamanic anatomy"? Another takes me into deeper intimacy with myself: what is it about that particular line that is stretching me beyond my normal way of being? A third leads me into the stillness that arrives in the moment thinking stops: who am I in the space between my thoughts, and what is that silent, boundless presence? And the fourth is the path I unwittingly lived in my dream. It takes me into deeper intimacy with those around me: can I allow myself to be visible and vulnerable even in this moment of incapacity?

Intimacy with the Poem

You can begin with any question. Usually I start by asking myself how the forgotten words are inviting me to notice something new about the poem. My inquiry might take me into any aspect of the poem, including its anatomy. Remember the poem's body is composed of many elements: including rhythm, breath, shape, song, and meaning. The delicate interplay of these elements creates its particular magic. The words I cannot remember are essential to this "shamanic anatomy." They must appear at that exact moment. No other words will do.

Mary Oliver's poem "The Summer Day" is an exquisite and startling invitation, one that has been singing me toward a more authentic life for many years. Because I had read the poem hundreds of times, I learned it by heart easily, except for one phrase. In the middle of the poem, Oliver admits that though she doesn't know "exactly what a prayer is," she does know "how to kneel down in the grass, / how to be idle and blessed . . ." The words "idle and blessed" refused to root in my memory. Each time I arrived at that point in the poem, either I would stutter into silence or I would unknowingly continue, skipping the phrase. But something within me felt the absence. I worried the hole like a tongue looking for a lost tooth.

What was it that I was missing? Something in the fabric of the poem needed those words in that way at that moment. What hadn't I noticed and appreciated about the way the poem works its magic? How were those words essential to the music and meaning of "The Summer Day"?

Doing this kind of detective work in a good poem can be as rewarding as reading a Sherlock Holmes novel. You know your curiosity is going to yield wondrous and satisfying answers. Nothing lands where it does by accident.

In "The Summer Day," Oliver's brilliance as an orchestrator is at its finest. She is weaving melodies and sub-melodies through a symphony of language. Some are connected to the music of the words. Some are connected to the different layers of meanings that run like contrapuntal themes beneath and through them.

I began by listening to the sounds of the words I had forgotten and their placement within the music of the poem. I let the words "idle and blessed" play over my tongue, listening to the song of the vowels and consonants and feeling the shapes they made in my mouth. As I repeated them, I became increasingly aware that I had heard a kindred "melody" elsewhere in the poem. Suddenly I realized it was in the final stunning lines, "Tell me, what is it you plan to do / with your one wild and precious life?"

The words "idle and blessed" and the words "wild and precious" are singing to each other! The *i* sound in "idle" chimes to the *i* sound in "wild." The *d* and *l* sounds in "idle" find their mirror reflection in the *l* and *d* sounds in "wild." The *eh-sed* sound in "blessed" (if you say the word in two syllables) finds its echo inside the word "precious." This is what is called assonance, in which the vowel sounds of the two words match but the consonants do not, creating an internal rhyme-like music. Assonance works subliminally to weave acoustic and conceptual connections. In Oliver's poem, these phrases toll back and forth within the body of the poem, like bells we barely know we hear. An alchemical mixing occurs so that the later phrase, "wild and precious," actually has the earlier phrase, "idle and blessed," singing inside it, subtly infusing it with new meaning. And the earlier phrase, upon subsequent readings of the poem, delicately portends the final, searing question.

As I continued to work with the words I had forgotten, additional gifts were revealed. Certain words and phrases have what I call a "trance" attached to them. It is as if they come trailing a veil of feelings, memories, and intimations spun from the other contexts in which we are used to hearing them. *Idle* and *blessed* are words that pulse with biblical associations, though Oliver makes no direct reference to religion. Earlier she speaks of prayer and kneeling. But her church is the grass, her communion is the sugar she shares with a grasshopper, and her prayer is to be found in the attention she pays to the scripture of nature. In the case of the phrase I forgot, the word *idle* reverberates with a moralistic back-story like "idleness teacheth much evil."[5] But Oliver says that she is at once idle and blessed. As I said earlier in relation to the power of metaphors, whenever we bring two very different experiences into the same moment, this sudden "Aha!" occurs. The mind can't contain them both; it has to open.

Hearing the complex music of the paradoxes, I realized that the phrase had escaped me because in my own life there was no possibility of those two words living anywhere near each other. To be idle is bad, not blessed! To dare to admit—even celebrate—being idle requires a rerouting of some of my most entrenched belief systems. With this realization, I found myself engaged in the next layer of inquiry: how is my forgetting calling me into deeper intimacy with myself?

Intimacy with Yourself

Perhaps you are forgetting particular words because they are asking you to experience and express something that is outside the circumference of your familiar personality. Here is where the poem becomes the "Friend," as Rumi puts it, the most loyal and fierce of allies, who unflinchingly points to the edge of your known self and invites you to jump.

Like that juncture in an intimate relationship after the first flush of new love when you begin to realize that there are aspects of your partner that make you really nervous, the poem is tugging you into experience that is not your norm. On the 50th anniversary of his marriage, Wendell Berry wrote:

One faith is bondage. Two
are free. In the trust
of old love, cultivation shows

a dark and graceful wilderness
at its heart. Wild
in that wilderness, we roam
the distance of our faith,
safe beyond the bounds
of what we know. O love,
open. Show me
my country. Take me home.[6]

Though Berry wrote these lines about his marriage, it also describes what is possible in relationship to a poem. When I cannot remember the line or the word, the poem carries me "beyond the bounds / of what [I] know," showing me who I really am outside of my comfort zone, taking me to my true home—beyond my boundaries, beliefs, and narrow definitions.

In Coleman Barks's translation of Rumi's poem "Love Dogs," there is a section that, for years, I consistently misquoted. The actual stanza reads: "In your pure sadness that wants help / is the secret cup." I invariably deliver it: "In your pure sadness / is the secret cup." The difference might seem small, but the truth is, the experience of "wanting help" is one I have tried to avoid for most of my life. This line is asking me to reckon with it.

How can I find the experience of these words within myself? To some extent I try to be so self-sufficient that I live in the illusion I don't need help, let alone want it. To find this phrase within me, I must travel into my own history, to a time before wanting help was hidden beneath my pride.

I was a painfully timid child. I clung to my mother's skirts, frightened of leaving her side. I remember my panic as I followed her through the jungle of the supermarket aisles. Her purse dangled at exactly the perfect height to thump me in the forehead every now and then as I struggled to stay glued to her. Finally, in a panic, I reached for its strap as a lifeline amidst the chaotic colors and shapes. I grabbed and missed and grabbed and missed. Boxes of Cocoa Puffs and Fruit Loops leered from the shelves. I was terrified.

Forgetting Rumi's words about wanting help points me unquestionably in the direction of that frightened, needy little girl. It is not that Rumi speaks of childish feelings. Rather it is that I have not consciously allowed myself to fully feel such feelings since I was a child. This forgotten line asks me to reconnect with the whole experience of wanting help, physically, emotionally, and mentally: to remember the sensations in those outstretched arms, the feeling of helplessness, the belief that I will be lost if I can't grab onto that purse strap. In the process I realize how I have numbed myself to my need throughout most of my life. Rumi is even telling me that reaching out could be my salvation. My "pure sadness that wants help," he says, "is the secret cup."

One of my students, Christopher, also chose to learn "Love Dogs." An actor in his early 30s, he was a perfect Prince Charming: blond, lithe, and bursting with energy. He had many years of training in movement and voice and drove his body like a fine little sports car. Every move was calibrated and intentional. His singing coach had suggested he take my class to help him overcome some of the stiffness that plagued his work onstage.

As an actor, Christopher was undaunted by the challenge of learning words by heart, and he already knew a number of poems. At the first meeting, I invited everyone to share their hopes and fears about the class. Some revealed the vulnerability of not trusting their own memory; others spoke of their love of the intimacy and truth-telling that poetry brings. Instead of talking about himself, Christopher chose to speak a poem, Rudyard Kipling's "If," which was long and impressive. I remember the audible gasp of admiration from other class members as he finished.

Because Christopher had read "Love Dogs" many times over the years, he easily absorbed it into his memory, except one line. Barks's translation reads: "The grief you cry out from / draws you toward union." But each time Christopher delivered the line, he said, "The grief from which you cry / draws you toward union."

When I asked him about it, Christopher criticized the way Barks had translated the line. He liked his version better. It felt more natural to him. And his version changed only a word or two.

It seemed like a small difference. And besides, his was grammatically correct, and Barks's version wasn't. Never end a phrase with a preposition, remember?

Coleman Barks could have chosen to be grammatically correct, but he didn't. There is something more compelling than grammar moving the line: the sense, the momentum, the way the energy travels through the body as it is spoken.

Try saying the line both ways, and notice the difference in the sensations in your body and the movement of your breath. Notice how you feel as you speak each version.

The grief from which you cry . . .
The grief you cry out from . . .

Can you feel how the first line shuts tight at the end? It has a kind of closure, as if it were sealed. As Christopher spoke his version of the line, everyone in class could feel how his voice and body energy were cut off and contained. One of the reasons this happens is because of the meter. "The grief from which you cry," has a simple, regular iambic pattern: Da-DUH, da-DUH, da-DUH. ("The GRIEF from WHICH you CRY.") The rhythmic unit completes itself predictably at the end of the line. Not so in the line as Barks translated it. This line tumbles over itself. Its rhythm is irregular. It scatters in all directions and ends on a weak beat which hangs vulnerably in the air. Da-DUH da-da-DUH da. ("The GRIEF you cry OUT from.")

When he finally spoke the line as the translation is written, Christopher's voice suddenly broke and he choked back a sob. Unable to go on, his face became red and he held his breath. I suggested that he continue reading the poem, even if his voice cracked with emotion. Simply loosening his hold on his breath caused the suppressed tears to spill out uncontrollably. The power of the feelings scared and embarrassed him at first. But as he continued to speak the poem, he began to let go and enjoy the way his voice lost its predictable tightness as it became soaked in his feelings—a gravelly whisper in one moment, a prolonged note of longing the next. A sense of freedom and joy began to pervade the room. This is the message at the heart of "Love Dogs": the expression of your pain and longing will become its own fulfillment. Even the "anatomy" of this poem infuses speaker and listener with its message.

What was it that broke the lock on Christopher's feelings? It was not the *meaning* of the line, as it had been in my case. He had no trouble remembering the sense of the words. The impact was from the nonconceptual elements of the poem. It was the *rhythm* and *syntax*—the broken-open meter, the imperfect and uncontrolled turn of phrase—that shattered his habit of slick, contained expression.

From our earliest moments, we unconsciously shape the organic movements of our breath, musculature, and speech into patterns. Some of these patterns are the necessary effect of learning a particular language in a particular family at a particular time in history. Others come from our reactions to the circumstances around us as we are first learning to use words: an attempt to protect ourselves from the experiences we don't want and get the ones we do.

When we are infants, the play of sounds and facial movements is infinite.[7] As we learn a particular language, the spectrum narrows. Our muscles are sculpted into the patterns of our native tongue. Our lips forget the freedom of baby babble. Our mouths lose the capacity to let sound swim in all directions. My friend Judi tells the story of her daughter, Emilia, at 14 months, playing with a Dutch toddler of the same age. Though neither child had spoken her first word, their babbling was already destined for different languages. The Dutch baby talk was full of rolled r's and throaty discourse. Emilia's voice trilled with the wide vowels and consonants of English-to-be.

Have you ever found that you could say something in a foreign language that you were too shy to say in your native tongue? Or that by pretending to have an accent or speaking in baby talk, you could express tendernesses that would otherwise embarrass you? When you learn a foreign language, you are loosening patterns that are embedded in your lips, facial muscles, tongue, and breathing. Your speaking apparatus—and therefore your whole body—is coaxed into a new rhythm. This can open up emotional places that you might be too defended to allow through ordinary conversation.

Poetry is like a foreign language in that it can loosen the patterns of habitual speech so that an original vulnerability can well up to the surface. As you take a poem more and more fully into your body, as you "write it on your bones," the rhythms and unique ways of weaving words can open places within you that you may not have known were closed. This was what happened for Christopher when he finally allowed the rhythm of the line to move through his body without trying to reshape it into a more familiar pattern.

Most of us learned to speak just as we were coming to know ourselves as separate beings. We were crawling, beginning to teeter upright on our new legs, careening into our first steps. Those first steps toward independence are often fraught with emotional challenges. One school of developmental psychology calls this period of life our "second birth" because we are negotiating once again the poignant journey from the bliss of oneness to the separateness of an individual self.[8] Many of Rumi's lines echo this transition: "Since I was cut from the reed-bed, / I have made this crying sound." Kabir says, "The truth is you turned away yourself / and decided to go into the dark alone." The way we reconcile the need for independence with the yearning for oneness can imprint not only our subsequent relationships but also—because we are just learning words—our capacity to communicate. Many of us dissociate from our hearts, our bodies, and our feelings to protect against the pain of the transition. So words get split off from the heart as well, becoming a tool of the intellect alone.

Some poems speak an original language, a true "mother tongue" that comes from the wholeness before the schism between mind and heart. To allow such words to move through you can be profoundly healing and empowering.

148

Intimacy with Silence

A few years ago I discovered that forgetting the words to a poem gives me direct access to the vast silence of mind that the spiritual teachers of all faiths describe. Any moment of forgetting can provide such an opening. Forget where you put your keys, or what you had for lunch yesterday, or the name of the person walking toward you on the street, and there you are: You've reached the end of where the mind can take you. You are at the brink of a great silence.

Many of us have spent decades sitting on meditation cushions waiting for the thoughts to stop. But when it actually happens? We scramble for dear life! We seem to be hardwired to keep our thoughts going. It's true that our survival once depended on that vigilance, in a time when human life was much more vulnerable than it is now and the perpetuation of the species was tantamount. Apparently our hardwiring has not been updated recently, even though you are more likely to be reading this in the safety of your own home than out on the savannah where a lion could eat you at any moment. Our animal body's habit is to keep returning to the gotta-keep-thinking, gotta-stay-aware, gotta-keep-on-top-of-things mind. To be confronted with a hole in the mind and jump into it is completely counterintuitive.

Yet, with a little practice, we can get curious enough to leap.

Losing a poem midstream presents a great opportunity to let the mind stop and see what that silence is like. When I am alone, I often recite a poem to myself until I cannot remember the words. Then, for a second or a minute or even longer if possible, I open myself to the absence of thought. Speaking the poem like this may feel like walking down the gangplank. You know that place you always forget is coming. And then, inevitably, there you are: no words, no poem, no thoughts. Don't try to remember. Fall into the emptiness.

Begin by trying to remember a meaningless detail instead of a poem. It could be what you had for lunch yesterday, or where you were last Wednesday night, or the author of a favorite novel.

In the moment when you can't remember, don't work to reconstruct the circumstances or come up with clues to find the right answer. Instead, become extremely curious about what happens when the mind fails, when the thoughts stop. Consciously scan your awareness. What exactly is the experience? Do not be satisfied with a label, like "blankness." Go inside the experience, open it up. Probe into the very nature of blankness. What does it feel like? How big is it? Can you find its edges? Is it bright or dark or without qualities? Is it thick or thin? As if in a meditation, let this silence permeate your awareness. Relax into it. Who are you in the space between your thoughts?[9] Explore this until the mind starts up its thinking again, which can happen within seconds.

This practice can be done anywhere, under any circumstances. Sometimes when I'm driving and my mind is addicted to racing stories, I try to remember what I had for lunch yesterday just to get a breather from its constant muttering. I invariably fail to come up with the answer. I intentionally let myself fall through that "failure" into an expansive quiet, a pulsating nothingness. In one of my favorite poems, "Just Now," W. S. Merwin describes this experience:

> *The clear sky appears for a moment and it seems to me*
> *that there has been something simpler than I could ever believe*
> *simpler than I could have begun to find words for*
> *not patient not even waiting no more hidden*
> *than the air itself . . .*[10]

Even if it only lasts for a moment, there is a deep breath in that respite, a touch of the presence that goes beyond the little life-or-death urgencies that compel the thinking mind.

After you practice this a few times intentionally, try practicing it whenever your memory fails. The woman walking toward you smiles and waves. You know that you've met her, even shared a meaningful experience with her, but you cannot remember her name. Don't try. Welcome the blank of your mind. In the seconds before she arrives, drink of its silence. Then take the opportunity to practice the transparency I will explore in the next section.

Intimacy with Others

Now I invite you to step through the gap of forgetting and reveal your most human self. Openly embrace your inability in the presence of others. For me, this is the most difficult practice of all.

To do this, you simply expand the initial pause you experience when you fail to remember the next line. Until now, that pause was making a space for the next inquiry—into the poem, or into yourself, or into the silence between your thoughts. Now the invitation is to stay with the pause in connection with others and be open with them about your inability to complete the poem. Simple as it sounds, this is an act of great courage.

In the poem called "Dying," Rumi says:

Remember there is a Great Incapacitator.

God gave you this inability for some reason.
Ask why. Say, "I have tried,
but I'm in a losing business.

I did what you warned me not to.
I claimed not to love the world's images,
but I've been worshipping them."[11]

One of my "losing businesses" is the perpetuation of an idealized image of myself. I still have an unconscious habit of covering up my failings. I project to the world that I'm in control, I don't have breakdowns, I don't need help (as we've already seen!), I don't forget poems, and I certainly don't do it in public.

But my inability—in this case, to remember the line of a poem—can be a doorway to freedom. As in my dream that began this chapter, forgetting the next word is an opportunity to meet another "little death," this time of my idealized self.

Elizabeth Bishop coaxes us toward this edge with a deceptively playful voice in the poem that provides the epigraph for this chapter, "One Art." After enticing us to master the "art of losing," she tells us:

Lose something every day. Accept the fluster
of lost door keys, the hour badly spent.
The art of losing isn't hard to master.

Then practice losing farther, losing faster:
places, and names, and where it was you meant
to travel. None of these will bring disaster.

My friend Judith learned this poem by heart while she sat at the bedside of her dying husband. As the words worked their way more and more deeply into her memory, they opened her—to the grief and, yes, even the humor of being with her partner of 40 years as he lost his capacities, one by one. She told me she clung to this poem for solace during the days just before and after John's death. "You know, underneath those seemingly lighthearted words there is unspoken pain," she said. "That is what made it so powerful for me." And the beauty of the villanelle form of the poem, with its particular music of rhymes and repetitions, carried her as she lived, day by day, the poignant truth of the last stanza:

—Even losing you (the joking voice, a gesture
I love) I shan't have lied. It's evident
the art of losing's not too hard to master
though it may look like (Write it!) like disaster.

Can you open to the experience of your inability? Does your mind stand in the corner, poised to scurry back to the archives of memory and get the answer? Can you allow the reality of "I can't" without pushing through or avoiding it? Can you be honest about it with whoever happens to be listening? Can you, first and foremost, be honest with yourself?

Years ago I worked with an artist named Ellie, who traveled to the former Soviet Union every summer to teach art to a group of orphaned children. The kids and counselors, many of whom lived in extreme poverty, came to this subsidized camp from all over the region. She developed deep relationships with the other counselors, many of whom lived, for the rest of the year, in extreme poverty. Her closest friend was also an artist who barely had money for basics such as dish soap and envelopes. Access to art supplies was an impossibility. Each year Ellie would pack an entire suitcase full of paints, brushes, paper, and other essentials to give to her friend. Each year, somehow, her friend would make the supplies last until the next summer, when she would wait with great anticipation for Ellie's return.

Ellie lived for her trips to Russia. The work she did with the children was at the core of her identity. The friends she made were the most important she had ever had in her life.

One year, a week or so before she was to leave for her annual pilgrimage, she had a dream. In the dream she arrived at Domodedovo Airport in Moscow and got in a cab. She was carrying two suitcases, one full of art supplies for her friend and the other packed with her personal belongings. Under her arm she carried a canvas, a portrait of her friend that she had painted as a gift. When the cab dropped her on the curb in front of her hotel and sped away into the city, she realized that she had left the two suitcases and the canvas in the back seat. Even her purse was gone and with it all evidence of her identity.

Ellie's despair was overwhelming. She wanted to die. She could not face her friend without the suitcase full of gifts. She could not face the world without her identity as an artist. Screaming and sobbing, she rushed into the hotel, climbed the stairs to the sixth floor, and prepared to fling herself out of the window. At that point she woke up.

Even when Ellie told me the dream, it seemed to her that there was no reason to live if she was stripped of her professional identity and what she had to give. The dream made her anxious about her trip. How could she protect herself from this terrifying possibility? Her only waking alternative to the suicide in the dream was to hold onto her suitcases tighter, literally for dear life.

I know the feeling of having my fists clenched around those suitcases till my knuckles are white and my fingers are paralyzed with stress. But this practice is about letting go of the suitcases and seeing who or what I am without them. It is about arriving empty-handed, having lost the words of the poem I intended to give, yet alive and present in the connection with myself and others none-theless. In a poem called "A Zero Circle," Rumi says it this way:

> *Be helpless, dumbfounded,*
> *unable to say yes or no.*
>
> *Then a stretcher will come from grace*
> *to gather us up.*[12]

When you stop at the moment of forgetting a word in the poem, this helplessness, this empty-handedness, arrives. It is not a choice. For this reason, it is one of the most subtle and challenging gifts. The only choice is whether you let yourself show it or push through and hide what is happening.

The purpose of this practice is not to empower your self-image but to release you from it. Sometimes it is indeed important to strengthen your self-image, to know yourself as a unique, capable, and valuable human being. At other times, your path takes you beyond the confines of any idea of yourself. In the wreckage of your idealized image, new possibilities quicken that you might never have imagined.[13] The paradox and the punch line is that as you allow your self-constructed identity to dissolve, you often find out who you really are.

Julie experienced this directly in class one evening when she was working with her favorite poem, "Wild Geese" by Mary Oliver. Julie was the grandmother of six, but you'd never have known it from her appearance. She wore bell-bottoms and a billowy, embroidered top in the "retro" style that had just become the rage with college students.

Julie was in my advanced class. The members of this group had hung in there with each other for several years as each member stuttered through the poems he or she loved most. Their commit-ment to the intimate spaces invoked by the poetry had borne them through tears and laughter together. The quiet ones had learned to bellow. The strident ones had found moments of melting.

Julie had been working with "Wild Geese" for several months and spoke it perfectly in the car, the shower, before sleep at night. But when she spoke it to the class, she stumbled. Partway through the poem, the words slowed, then disappeared completely from her memory.

"So just hang out here for a second," I said. "This is the moment of truth. Here you are at the point where you can't remember any more. Can you be in the simple, human vulnerability of it? Can you be open about it?"

"Are you kidding? I'd rather fake it!" Julie exclaimed.

"I think it would be a precious experience to be willing to mess up openly right now."

"But I knew this poem perfectly on the way here!" she whimpered. "Just let me look at it for a second, and I'll be fine."

"See what happens if you don't go back to the words to get it right," I suggested. "Don't cover up. Be with that unsettled feeling of knowing you didn't get it. See what happens if you just hang out there. With yourself and us."

"My brain is completely confused by what you're suggesting," Julie whimpered.

"Could that be a good thing? Can you let your brain be disoriented?"

"This could be precious? To be visible in my failure? No way!" Though she was laughing, there was a frantic look in her eye, as if she might bolt or lash out at any moment.

"Listen, my dear." I spoke to the wild animal in front of me. "We are all going to have to face the 'failures' of our body and mind at some point. The time will come when you can't feed yourself or climb the stairs or remember the name of the person standing next to you. You might as well practice now."

With a deep breath, Julie began the poem again. Again, halfway through, the words failed her. There was silence. Julie breathed and looked at the ground. She closed her eyes and opened them again. She looked quickly at several members of the class, then away.

"Can you give us a commentary on what's happening?" I asked after several pregnant minutes.

"My mind is blank. I don't have any idea what the next line is. I feel shy," she said. "Very shy."

"Can you look at us with that shyness alive in you?"

Julie looked up. One by one, she met the eyes of the people witnessing her. Tears welled up and spilled down her cheeks, making watercolor rivulets as they melted her makeup and landed among the crocheted roses on her shirt.

"For me, the whole reason for sharing a poem is the sweetness of the real connection that is happening right now," I said. "Perhaps in this moment, the poem is no longer necessary. It has done its work. It has brought you into this intimacy and dropped you here. Can you allow yourself to rest in this," I asked Julie, "without ever going back to find the right words to complete the poem?"

"That feels good. I like the shyness. It feels like my heart is alive and connected with you. It's really me."

When I am speaking a poem to you and I forget the next word, there it is: a moment of real contact between us. There is nothing in the space between us, not even the poem. When I am lucky and awake, I can open to the experience, allowing the wave of my humanness to wash my pretense away. I am more naked and present with you and myself—in the heart of the communion I was hoping for all along.

The Summer Day

Who made the world?
Who made the swan, and the black bear?
Who made the grasshopper?
This grasshopper, I mean—
the one who has flung herself out of the grass,
the one who is eating sugar out of my hand,
who is moving her jaws back and forth instead of up and down—
who is gazing around with her enormous and complicated eyes.
Now she lifts her pale forearms and thoroughly washes her face.
Now she snaps her wings open, and floats away.
I don't know exactly what a prayer is.
I do know how to pay attention, how to fall down
into the grass, how to kneel down in the grass,
how to be idle and blessed, how to stroll through the fields,
which is what I have been doing all day.
Tell me, what else should I have done?
Doesn't everything die at last, and too soon?
Tell me, what is it you plan to do
with your one wild and precious life?

— Mary Oliver

Chapter 8

UNDRESSING YOUR VOICE

The shape of what is open inside you
trembles on invisible strings,
presses with fingers of sound
into the soft clay of me—

— Kim Rosen

A wise teacher once told me that each person turns and leaves a gift for their loved ones as she or he dies. It may be delivered in the way that person dies, or something that happens just before or just after. It may not be recognized as a gift until years later, when you discover the strength of the muscle you made as you helped in the dying process. Or it may pour through the very rhythm of the parting, as with my friend Melanie, who gave me the gift of dying in my arms, letting me row with her, breath by breath, so close to the edge between life and death that I could almost see to the other side. Or it can come right after the death, like the fox that appeared out of nowhere and walked up the steps to my house half an hour after my beloved cat of 20 years passed away.

Stanley Kunitz, one of America's great poets, died May 14, 2006, at the age of 100. In the wake of his passing, many "had the sense of receiving from Stanley some last gift, felt as blessing or revelation," the poet Jane Hirshfield reflected. "Generosity to others ran so deep in the currents of his life, how could it not be so? Even a meteor showers out sparks before disappearance."[1] Though I had met him only twice, Stanley gave me, too, a great gift as he passed. Several days after he died, Jane shared with me a recording of Stanley reading her poem "Against Certainty." It was made on his last day of full consciousness. In that recording Stanley taught me, beyond the shadow of a doubt, that one can find a portrait of a person's life in the sound of his voice.

Kunitz was not just the father of a generation of American poets as their teacher and mentor; he was also what Rumi called "a true human being." Several months before he died, I visited him for tea in his apartment in New York. I will never forget reciting "King of the River" in chorus with him and his assistant, Genine Lentine. Even though our time together was brief, I recognized in him a quality of presence and compassion that I had felt only a few times before and then only with someone considered to be an awakened master or guru. I imagine Kunitz didn't see himself that way. My guess is that his focus was on being as truly and truthfully human as possible. The poet Marie Howe, who was his close friend, expressed it in these words:

> To be human, he used to say, was to know yourself to be living and dying at the same time. But it always seemed to me that he lived at the intersection of time and eternity.[2]

Listening to Stanley read felt like a direct transmission from his soul to yours. You could hear the wisdom of a great being encrypted into the very sound of his voice. I remember thinking to myself the first time I heard him read that I might have been almost as inspired had he been reading a shopping list. "He read in what felt like the voice of a time before microphones," Jane Hirshfield said, "when amplification came from the body alone, and perhaps from the soul."[3]

The day after Stanley's death I received an e-mail from Jane. She had attached the MP3 of Stanley reading "Against Certainty."[4] That reading and her response to it are stunning testimonies to the power of speaking a poem. She wrote:

> His voice was so strongly, recognizably his; though hesitant, wavering, still his. And now, for me, it is very strange—the poem is entirely changed. It's as if being dipped through his life . . . altered it forever, alchemized it by the strength and depth of what he put there by choosing to read it. It seems to me that he found in it a poem I had not known I was writing, a poem to hold open the door of death.[5]

It was true. I had read "Against Certainty" many times. I have gratefully turned to it when my need to speak a paradoxical truth defies my capacity to find my own words. Yet in hearing the poem "dipped through [Stanley's] life," I experienced dimensions I had not imagined. There seemed to be no attempt to hide or control the sound of his physical frailty or the many currents of feeling that swirled at the threshold of his dying. It felt to me like tragedy, exaltation, dying, and living were merged in a single sound. As in a Zen koan or a Kabbalistic riddle, it was as if this convergence of opposites opened a door to "the great vanishing" that Hirshfield speaks of in the poem.

Such vulnerability turns into a beautiful strength when it is not hidden. The great power of Stanley's reading was hewn of all that trembled in his voice at that turning point in his life. "In his last year, reading aloud assumed a central role," Genine related shortly after his death. As he read a poem, she said, he would become more vitalized with each word. He would sit up straighter and his breathing would clear. However diffused he may have been when he began, the reading seemed to mobilize his energy and bring him back to himself. "I don't know what the physiological process was," Genine wrote later, "but I imagine the brittled synapses restored to their suppleness in the act of reading. I picture the sparks leaping across the axons as he found his rhythm."[6]

The Sound of Your Own Voice

Whenever you read a poem aloud, you too can awaken and change it. This is not a talent reserved for great poets. It is true of absolutely everyone. The French philosopher Gaston Bachelard writes that when we speak a poem aloud, "we begin to have the impression that we could have created it, that we should have created it. It becomes a new being in our language, expressing us by making us what it expresses; in other words, it is at once a becoming of expression, and a becoming of our being. Here expression creates being."[7]

The sound of your voice is the sound of the life you have led, which brought you to this moment. All your accrued experience—the losses, the joys, the successes, the agonies—are inscribed in your voice. When who you are merges with a poem, a new creation occurs. You don't need to work to make it happen. You don't need to practice. It cannot be otherwise.

There is an old saying, "She loves to listen to the sound of her own voice." Usually it is meant derogatorily. Yet most people never really listen, intimately and meticulously, to the sound of their own voices. You may listen avidly to the words you are saying and the ideas you are trying to convey, but have you really heard the flood of sound you utter? Try reading a poem aloud, as if you were sending your voice directly into your own ears. Imagine that the sound of your voice is like a viscous liquid, a vibrational medicine pouring back into you. Perhaps it is exactly the sound that can best heal and nourish you out of all the sounds of creation. Notice the texture, timbre, tone, and music of your voice. Feel how the sound coming out of and back into you is quenching some thirst you may not have noticed before. Let yourself develop a love of listening to this sound. It is a well you can drink from endlessly.

When you speak a poem, the resonance of your being meets the resonance of the poem. The words *resonance* and *being* can seem like disincarnate ideas, but I mean them graphically: Your voice, which emerges out of the interaction of breath with the shapes, tensions, and textures inside your body, has a particular tone and timbre. Your body, as actors often say, is an instrument. Just as a note vibrating within the particular hollow shape of a cello sounds different from the same note emerging from the contours of a violin, so too the voice that emerges from your interior sounds different than the one that emerges from mine. The metal body of a flute sings one song, the olivewood recorder another, and the Aborigine's termite-bored eucalyptus didgeridoo sings in yet a different voice.

When your voice connects with a poem, an original creation is born, made of the convergence of your particular life story and the poem. This is why a poem that you've heard a thousand times before can break open with fresh meaning when you hear it spoken by someone new, as "Against Certainty" did for me, and indeed for its own author, when Stanley Kunitz read it.

Of course, there are ways that your voice may be obscured by habits and defenses that costume your authentic sound, and the rest of this chapter will explore these, as well as the process of "undressing" your voice. But your true sound, however veiled, can never be completely hidden. You can hear it right now, when you really listen.

Becoming the Poem's Wind Chime

Sometimes your real voice is cloaked by defenses or tensions that you've unconsciously built into your body. Listen to the voices of people around you. You'll hear some that only resonate in the head while the rest of the body seems to be "off limits." You'll hear some that have resonant chambers from the waist up, but the pelvis is locked out of sounding range. You'll hear voices that come from the gut but will not permit the vulnerable flutter of a breast full of feelings. Perhaps you'll hear a voice that is dressed in happy tones and hides all traces of sorrow. Just today I heard a newscaster reporting on a heartbreaking surge of tribal violence in Kenya using a bouncy voice that sounded like she was announcing the winner of Pin the Tail on the Donkey at a children's party. Or perhaps you'll notice a voice that wears a cloak of gentleness and will not reveal the power that comes with rage or conflict. Leonard Cohen sings, "I smile when I'm angry / I cheat and I lie / I do what I have to do to get by."

A child often subtly and unconsciously costumes her voice to do exactly that: "get by." Whether you have the most caring of parents or grow up in circumstances of negligence and abuse, you mold yourself in whatever form seems necessary to survive. You learn to adjust the tone of your voice ("Talk like a big girl!"), hide your feelings ("Boys don't cry!"), force your impulses into submission ("Keep your voice down!"), and sublimate your needs ("Children should be seen and not heard!"). The very neurological firings that underlie the movements of your vocal cords, inhales, and exhales are patterned in ways that seem necessary to your survival. Over time, the possibilities of expression available to the infant turn into the narrower repertoire of the adult, and as Christopher discovered when working with the poem "Love Dogs," these patterns can become a disguise for your true voice.

The first time I fell in love, I remember making the disturbing discovery that everything I said to my lover sounded like a lawyer dictating a corporate contract. I had modeled my tone on the intellectual distance of my father, an attorney. My vocabulary was restricted to the language of reason. This was not only because of the proclivity for imitation that I share with all primates. I could have imitated the voice of my mother, who gave passionate expression to her feelings. But I didn't. A voice shrouded in the muted tones of intelligence and devoid of the wild colors of emotion seemed to me like the key to survival in my childhood. For many years, my voice felt dressed in a suit and tie. I found the only way I could be true to my heart's language was to give up on words and communicate through silence and touch. I began working as a masseuse and a healer. For a while, I lived largely in a world of physical contact, breath, and music. It wasn't until years later that I was able to open myself to the feelings that I'd fled as a child. As I did, my voice shed its tight business suit and began to recover an earthy vulnerability.

The inflections and textures learned in childhood are reinforced over and over by repetition. Your voice moves through your growing body like a river carving its path through earth. All of your musculature grows around these habits of sound. The 40 or so muscles of your face are meticulously trained to work with the muscles inside your mouth and throat. Together they mold the breath that emanates from your lungs into sound. Your body falls into habitual patterns of speaking, leaving behind many possibilities of sound and feeling.

I like to think of my voice as a hanging chime and the poem as the wind, which plays whatever notes it needs in order to sound itself into being. So I want all my notes available—the many tones of my body, my feelings, and any thought the poem might call forth. If I fear or prohibit certain feelings, thoughts, or parts of my body, the full range of my notes will be narrowed. For instance, if areas of my anatomy have been "out of bounds" since childhood—that is, if I was told directly or indirectly that it was forbidden or dangerous to experience them—these notes will be muffled or unavailable. How can a sound, carried on my breath, resonate within my pelvis if the musculature inside it is clenched against allowing some forbidden pleasure or sorrow?

The same is true of feelings. If the free flow of certain feelings has been inhibited, this can affect my voice. Perhaps you welcome the movement of your tears easily but you never let yourself express anger. Even if your poem is not an angry diatribe, certain lines may call for a powerful voice. In the process of retrieving that power, you may encounter your banished rage.

If I have been taught to avoid certain thoughts, this too can curtail the range of expression in my voice. Perhaps I revel in pure insight and clarity, but I won't touch the messy corners where doubts and contradictions gather. Or the opposite may be true: I may identify myself as a person who is constantly confused and needy, so statements of wisdom and authority are a stretch for me. When I speak such lines in a poem, they may sound contrived or pushed.

The lost notes of your voice usually come knocking at your door as soon as you invite them back. When I acknowledged that

I had never allowed myself to feel grief, suddenly the delicate edge of tears started creeping into my conversations at the most unexpected moments. Remembering to welcome them counteracted my autonomic habit of pushing them back down under my voice.

Rumi's poem "The Guest House" has been a great friend to me in this practice of opening myself to feelings and thoughts that I have unconsciously pushed away. Its guidance on the subject has become known far and wide—an Internet search yields over 28,000 Websites quoting its lines! The poem's injunction is to open the door to every feeling or thought that knocks—whether it's "a joy, a depression, a meanness" or "the dark thought, the shame, the malice." Rumi goes on to enjoin the reader:

> *Welcome and entertain them all!*
> *Even if they're a crowd of sorrows,*
> *who violently sweep your house*
> *empty of its furniture.*[8]

This practice can feel counterintuitive for many of us when our internal systems, both physical and psychological, have been calibrated to avoid certain emotions, sensations, and thoughts. Waltzing to the door and letting them all in when they knock can set off the internal fire alarm. Yet Rumi gives two really good reasons to reroute those systems and welcome the whole spectrum of feelings that comes with being human. First, there is the reminder that you are the Guest House, not the feelings that come and go, no matter how violently they sweep through you. Second, the promise that each "guest," from the most troubling to the happiest, "has been sent / as a guide from beyond."

I suggest that you take some time to reflect on the range of your own voice. You can simply begin by reading these words out loud and listening to the sound. From where in your body does your voice seem to emanate? Are there areas where your breath cannot penetrate? What are the primary feelings you hear in your voice? Is there any particular feeling that your voice wears most of the time, like a costume? Do you notice that there are tones and textures of feeling that you don't allow into your expression? For instance, do you confine your voice within a boundary of "niceness" or "intelligence" or "toughness" or "softness"? Sometimes it can be helpful to ask a trusted friend to reflect on these questions with you. (If you'd like to explore further, there is a more in-depth inquiry into these questions in the section called "Practices" at the back of this book.)

Retrieving the Lost Notes

Joan's voice sounded as if it came from a faraway region of her mind, arriving wrapped in some cellophane skin. Everything she said seemed distant.

One evening she arrived at class with "The Journey" by Mary Oliver. It was a very unlikely choice for her. Until now, every poem she'd worked with had a similar dreamy, contemplative tone. This poem was emphatic and stormy. It was the voice of someone breaking out of a life of pleasing others and taking a stand. This was why she chose the poem. She knew she needed to find that voice within her.

"One day you finally knew what you had to do," it begins. There is a determination in the poem, a necessary force. The lines are short, much shorter than those found in most of Oliver's poetry. There is a thrust to it. It pulses with the strength necessary to push through the cervix between the known and the new and then fight one's way down the birth canal. It is not a gentle poem.

Joan, however, had a very gentle voice. When she first read the poem it had the flavor of a distant lullaby.

I urged her toward the poem's force. I asked her to yell the poem, to punch it out with her voice and her fists at the same time. At first she was timid, so I offered to do it with her. I stood facing her on the other side of the room, so she could safely direct her energy toward me. With each word, we punched out at the air. First I belted "One!" with a fist from the right, then she belted "day!" with a fist from the left. I shouted "you!" with a hook from the left, she bellowed "finally!" with a jab from the right. Soon we were doing it together, exuberantly and anarchically. A heat surged through Joan; the power that had been hidden behind her mild exterior burst into flames.

When the last line ended, before she could withdraw, I asked her to begin the poem again, this time facing the rest of the class who had been watching our "duel" and cheering from the sidelines. She immediately launched into it, punches and all, in the direction of the whole group. Their enthusiasm egged her on and she gave the words even more wild energy than before. When Joan finished she was panting and flushed.

She turned to me, "That was fantastic! But that's no way to do the poem, is it? There are so many delicate currents in this poem. It isn't only about bashing my way out of bondage."

I told her that this was only one layer. But it was the layer that was missing in her voice. So it was important for her to exercise that muscle, to consciously invite it.

I suggested that she speak the poem again naturally, simply connecting with the words and the people listening. As she spoke, it seemed as if all the shouting had undone some corset around her voice and it fell open. The sound had depth and strength, color and subtlety. In the middle of the poem, tears came to her eyes as the words carried her away from all the other voices with their eternal demands, into the night where "there was a new voice": her own. As the poem came to a close, there was a rich quietness that poured into the room, a sense of completion.

"Maybe that sheath around your voice was a protective wrapper," I said to Joan, who had sat down on the floor and was leaning into the knees of a friend. I had never seen her make physical contact with anyone before. "Maybe now that you've found this powerful voice in you, you can take off that sheath. It was a stand-in for your power."

Months later Joan told me that the poem had ignited huge changes in her life. She had had no idea, when choosing to speak it to the class, what lay ahead. By the time the poem had done its work in her, she had left her accounting job and told her grown son, her daughter-in-law, and their three kids that they had to move out of her apartment. She was happily living alone for the first time in her life.

Jordi had a different challenge. Her voice was present and strong. But the softer notes were nowhere to be found. A neurologist at the top of her field, Jordi moved through the world with an authoritative stride and an unwavering voice. She had grown up in the '60s and '70s—the heyday of women's liberation. Independence, strength, and courage were the qualities that counted for her. When she was a girl of eight or nine years old, her father would tell her and her sisters to stop speaking in such high voices or no one would ever take them seriously. "Talk like a man!" he used to say, as he did what he felt was necessary to prepare them to succeed.

Jordi loved Edna St. Vincent Millay's poem "Renascence," with its intricate story of death and rebirth. But as she began to learn it by heart, the particular style of speaking used in the poem began to drive her crazy, irritating her when she read it to herself and embarrassing her in the rare moments she spoke it to others. She complained that there was a quality of prissiness, an affected femininity that she couldn't relate to. The contrived inversions of subject and verb ("And so beneath the weight lay I") made her feel ashamed and exposed. The exclamations ("I screamed and—lo!—Infinity / Came down and settled over me") seemed naïve. She said she felt as if the lines were wearing coquettish petticoats. For instance:

> But, sure, the sky is big, I said:
> Miles and miles above my head.
> So here upon my back I'll lie
> And look my fill into the sky.
> And so I looked and after all
> The sky was not so very tall.
> The sky, I said, must somewhere stop . . .
> And—sure enough!—I see the top!
> The sky, I thought, is not so grand;

I 'most could touch it with my hand!
And reaching up my hand to try,
I screamed, to feel it touch the sky![9]

"Renascence" was published in 1912. Millay was 18 when she wrote it. Though it relates a journey of tremendous courage and ecstatic awakening, Millay's voice is that of a young woman, shaking with questions, prayers, and wonder. The poem is about an experience of being overtaken by a powerful experience, not controlling it. If Jordi allowed this poem to live in her, she would have to undress her voice of its strong, independent, Modern Woman costume. She would have to allow a delicacy, an innocence, a surrender. This was threatening to the very essence of who she presented herself to be.

It was hard for her to allow any softness into her voice at first. After all, this was the tone her father had rejected. So much in her was geared to abolish it. But not everything. Even more powerful than her animal response of pleasing her father (and, she extrapolated, the world) was the research scientist in her. She was curious. Why on earth had this poem been her favorite since she had discovered it in her early 20s? She knew there was something drawing her into "Renascence" and was fascinated to find out where it would take her.

The voice of the young girl emerged from her shyly at first. But as the poem lived within her, it began to melt her tough edges and magnetize a part of her that had never been allowed out. Each time she spoke the poem she discovered she could open a bit more to this innocent, wise, and very female texture of her being. Soon she was begging friends to allow her to recite it to them (it took 12 minutes to deliver) so that she could hear the sound of that feminine self, which she had never before dared to express.

How Aren't You?

"Reach your long hand out to another door," Rumi says, "beyond where you go / on the street, the street where everyone says, 'How are you?' / And no one says, 'How aren't you?'"[10] Rumi's "How aren't you?" is the unplayed note in the wind chime of your voice. It is how you sound when your voice is undressed of any attitude you chose to put on in order to survive as a child. "How aren't you?" is the place in your body that your breath hasn't touched since you were five. It is the sound of the grief that knocks at the Guest House door for welcome. "How aren't you?" is the voice you have not allowed yourself to express. Until suddenly, without realizing where you are headed, a poem you love carries you into the heart of it.

As you invite more and more notes into your voice that don't fit with your normal "personality," a remarkable and possibly startling phenomenon begins to occur. You may become unsure of who you actually are. Characteristics that once defined you— your quietness or your buoyancy or your even-temperedness, for instance—may fall away. T. S. Eliot said that poetry asks of the artist "a continual surrender of himself as he is at the moment to something which is more valuable . . . a continual self-sacrifice, a continual extinction of personality."[11] I have found this to be true whether you are writing the poetry, or learning it by heart, or reading it aloud. This is another place in the path of living a poem fully where, if you are very lucky, the borders of your tightly defined self-image may begin to dissolve. You will never lose the essence that is you, but the false boundaries you have drawn around yourself may disappear. And then you may taste the vaster "How aren't you?" that Rumi points to: the presence that remains when all the stories of how and who you are fall away. Then you can truly become the poem's wind chime, with every note of being human available to you.

Against Certainty

*There is something out in the dark that wants to
    correct us.
Each time I think "this," it answers "that."
Answers hard, in the heart-grammar's strictness.*

If I then say "that," it too is taken away.

*Between certainty and the real, an ancient enmity.
When the cat waits in the path-hedge,
no cell of her body is not waiting.
This is how she is able so completely to disappear.*

I would like to enter the silence portion as she does.

*To live amid the great vanishing as a cat must live,
one shadow fully at ease inside another.*

— Jane Hirshfield

Chapter 9

BORROWED
BY THE WIND

If only, most lovely of all, I yield myself and am borrowed
By the fine, fine wind that takes its course through the
chaos of the world . . .

— D. H. Lawrence

The first time I ever spoke poetry to an audience turned out to be the most ecstatic and unexpected experience I had ever had. I had never really wanted to be a performer, at least not since playing Little Jake in *Annie Get Your Gun* at age ten. I simply had a love for speaking poetry aloud and the good fortune to meet some truly gifted musicians who agreed to try something new.

We called the event a "Poetry Concert." It was the fulfillment of a vision I had had several years earlier in the Teatro Colón in Buenos Aires. My friend and I were listening to a recital by the Argentine pianist Martha Argerich. The Teatro has some of the best acoustics in the world, so even though we were on the highest balcony, the air around us was almost shimmering with the reverberations of Mozart, then Prokofiev, then Chopin. The domed ceiling, which was only about ten feet above us, was painted with filigreed ballerinas, opera singers, actors, and musicians. I could sense the artistic legacy inscribed in the very structure of the place by the hundreds of performances that had unfolded there for over a century. Looking down on the matchbox-sized piano and the tiny virtuoso pounding out masterpiece after masterpiece was dizzying. Yet even from that distance, every note was crystalline.

As I listened, poetry began pouring through my mind—great, classical poems by Goethe, Dickinson, Eliot—matching the majesty of the music and the place. In my imagination, the piano and its player began to fade and I saw a lone person in the formal black-and-white garb of a concert musician walk to the center of the stage far below. In my vision, every seat in the theater was full. I imagined the hum of 3,000 listeners fading into a long, potent silence as the figure on the stage began to speak poems, filling that magnificent theater with words and silences that electrified the air.

I could not help but ask myself: Why do we so rarely, if ever, fill theaters and concert halls to bask in the beauty of great poems? Why are there piano recitals, opera performances, and theatrical events—but no poetry concerts? Why were no poets painted into the ceiling of this historical building when every other kind of embodied artistic form was represented? After all, poetry began as performance art: the earliest poets spoke their work, often with musical accompaniment. As an opera singer brings Isolde to life for audience after audience, as an actor's voice carries Lady Macbeth to the uppermost balcony, as Martha Argerich ignited my imagination with Chopin and Prokofiev, why not fill that great domed space and awaken thousands of listeners with the poetry of Rumi, Neruda, and Sappho?

Several years later, I was able to create my first Poetry Concert. Our little 80-seat performance space certainly wasn't the Teatro Colón, but it was a beginning. I had audaciously invited two musicians to join me, without even knowing if we could work together. Several months earlier, I had heard a CD of Jami Sieber playing her electric cello. I felt as if her unique rhythms and melodies were singing the unspoken layers of the poems I had been learning by heart for years. When I finally tracked her down in person, I proposed to her that we experiment together: she would create spontaneous improvisations while I delivered poetry. To my surprise, she agreed. Michaelle Goerlitz joined us on percussion. The three of us could only find time for a single rehearsal one week before the event.

Luckily we felt a connection among us instantaneously. Without warming up, getting to know each other, or even discussing what on earth we were doing, we found ourselves carried by a powerful creative current. In that rehearsal, each of Jami's cello improvisations seemed to call forth a particular poem that I knew by heart. As she and Michaelle played, I felt as if the poems I had been gathering into my memory for ten years were lining up inside, jostling each other in their enthusiasm to be spoken with the melodies and rhythms.

A week later we walked onto the stage with no plan other than to be present with each other, the poems, and the spontaneity of the moment. The performance space was packed. I picked up my microphone, which I barely knew how to use. Jami positioned her bow and Michaelle readied her cymbals and shakers.

I felt as if I were hooked up to some great poetry faucet. Poem after poem poured out of me. I didn't know which would be next or how it would fit with the music. My own voice drew colors from its palette I had never heard before. As I looked into the eyes of the audience members, many lines that I had known for years revealed utterly new meanings to me. At moments tears ran down my cheeks when some phrase, like an unexpected wind, shook through me: "Doesn't everything die at last, and too soon?" At other times I found myself in a sudden intimacy with a listener I'd never met, speaking as if I had known him or her forever: "Give back your heart / to itself, to the stranger who has loved you / all your life." I had never felt such pure joy in all my life.

Four hours later the poems and music were still streaming out of us and the audience was still riveted. I thought of the Sufi practice of *Sama*, an outpouring of mystical poetry and music that sometimes lasts until dawn. Only the blisters on the fingers of the musicians and my own voice growing hoarse compelled us to bring the evening to a close. As we finished, a deep silence descended over the hall. There was no applause to break the sudden peace. For a moment, we all fell into the intimacy of those who have experienced an unexpected wonder together.

Nothing Left to Lose

In that first Poetry Concert, I felt as if I were indeed "borrowed by the wind." The phrase comes from the poem by D. H. Lawrence from which the epigraph and title of this chapter are drawn. The wind in the poem is not just any wind, but one that is "blowing the new direction of time." My own prayer, like Lawrence's, has always been to serve such an evolutionary force. I want to be carried by a purpose greater than my own will, greater than my personal love of sharing poetry, greater even than my wish to awaken and inspire others. I want to be used by that wind of change.

But sometimes it is not as easy as it was on that miraculous night. There are occasions when I am not able to let that "fine, fine wind" carry me at all. Either I'm clinging to the steering wheel so tight that no wind could possibly lift me, or I feel as if a wall stands between me and the immediacy of the moment, separating me from myself, the poem, and the listener. Often the wall is built of my fears of being judged. Sometimes it is made of my investment in delivering the poem in a certain way with a particular result. At other times it is simply because of my discomfort with the intimacy with whoever is listening. Almost always, beneath all these fears and strivings, I am afraid of losing myself to the poem, of becoming "not I, but the wind that blows through me," as D. H. Lawrence writes. Yet that fear is also my greatest longing.

I was terrified, for instance, at my second Poetry Concert. There was very little fear the first time, perhaps because my identity had not yet coagulated around being a speaker of poems. The first concert was a complete surprise to everyone—musicians, audience, and especially me. But now that the word had spread, I had something to live up to. I fearfully imagined the audience members would arrive bristling with expectation and ready criticism. "Who does she think she is to be the voice of the great poets? What arrogance!"

Feeling frightened, I tried to control whatever I could. I bought a new outfit: eccentric, but not too flashy. I put on my makeup carefully, as if by applying my eyeliner perfectly I could ensure success. I went over and over the poems I wanted to speak until I was literally saying them in my dreams. I even found the perfect poem from Rilke's *Book of Hours* to begin the evening. It expressed exactly what I was feeling about the evening—both my longing and my fear. This is how it begins:

I have faith in all that is not yet spoken.
I want to set free my most holy feelings.
What no one has dared to long for
will spring through me spontaneously.

If that is presumptuous, then, my God, forgive me.
But I want to say just this to you:
my true power should come like a shoot, a force of nature,
no pushing, no holding back,
the way the children love you.

I walked onto the stage with my heart pounding in my ears. The little performance space was packed. As I took the microphone, I looked out over the faces. I have no idea what was actually in the eyes of those gathered. What I saw was a swarm of critics, all with their arms crossed, their jaws set, their brows knitted.

Jami began to play her cello. With a few strokes of her bow, she sliced open the tense atmosphere of the room, and every person there seemed to fall gratefully into a sacred space where breath deepened and the mind finally relaxed.

Except me. My thoughts were going a mile a minute. As I spoke the first words of the poem, I was sure everyone was wishing

I would be quiet so they could listen to the beautiful music. I was sure they knew I had no right to speak the poems of a mystical master—I couldn't even get it together to meditate regularly! And I was sure they hated my new silk tunic.

The poem ends with these lines:

And if this is arrogance, then let me be arrogant
for this, my prayer
that stands so sincere and alone
before the clouds that shroud your face.

But I was lying. I was not willing to stand, "sincere and alone," in the face of whatever might come in response to my outpouring. I wanted to hide, to duck behind the congas, to disappear between the strings of the cello. I didn't have Rilke's courage or commitment. I couldn't honestly say, "Let me be arrogant / for this, my prayer." In that moment, my fear of being judged and rejected by the audience was so consuming that I forgot every prayer I had ever made.

The chatter in my head didn't stop for a long time. Though I recited poem after poem aloud, silently my mind was reciting its litany of terrors. On top of that, because of the cacophony of my thoughts I couldn't hear my voice. So I spoke louder. I pushed harder. The faces of the audience seemed to be turning gray. I was pushing for some color, some reaction. It looked like one man in the front row might even be drifting off to sleep. So I put more expression into the lines. I tried to be more lively and interesting, anything to get a spark of response from at least one of the concrete faces before me.

In his essay "How to Speak Poetry," Leonard Cohen begins, "Take the word butterfly. To use this word it is not necessary to make the voice weigh less than an ounce or equip it with small, dusty wings." He goes on, with scathing brilliance, to enumerate all the ways someone should not act out the word *butterfly:* "It is not necessary to invent a sunny day or a field of daffodils . . . It is not an opportunity for you to hover, soar, befriend flowers, symbolize beauty and frailty, or in any way impersonate a butterfly." Further down the page, it becomes clear that Cohen is not railing against overacting, not even against *bad* acting, but against manipulating the listener. He pulls back the skin of our apparently benign intentions, as he often does, to reveal an epidemic of self-promotion. "The poem is not a slogan. It cannot advertise you. It cannot promote your reputation for sensitivity."[1]

In the intermission of the concert, while I sat alone in the little green room behind the stage, I thought of this essay and blushed. I was busted. Cohen had my number.

It was actually a relief to realize what I was doing, to confront my egocentric motives so completely. Until that moment they had been hidden, even from me. I wasn't consciously manipulating the audience. I wasn't consciously trying to promote myself. But in truth, my egotistical need for recognition had almost completely usurped my real reason for being there.

When we returned to the stage after intermission, half the seats in the audience had been vacated. Seeing the empty chairs, something broke inside me. My worst fear had happened. People didn't want what I was offering. Maybe they even judged me as arrogant. I had been. I had unconsciously tried to use the poems for my private agenda: to fortify my own image in the eyes of others. Not only had I been unsuccessful, but I had also completely missed out on the beauty inside the poems and music by pouring all my energy into winning over the audience.

Luckily, I had failed. I looked at the empty chairs and took a deep breath. I didn't fight the pang of shame and disappointment that welled up in my throat. I felt my face become hot and red. I felt my skin prickle, and tears momentarily sprang to my eyes. But as the feelings moved through me, something relaxed. The grip of my compulsion to try to be a "somebody" released. It was a moment of "holy defeat." There was a little pain and embarrassment, but underneath was a sense of excitement. I had nothing left to lose. I invited the remaining stalwart listeners to fill in the rows nearest the stage and, in simple communion with them and the musicians, let myself be borrowed by the poetry of, in Rilke's words, "my most holy feelings."

In Search of Spontaneity

Even when you know it well and have spoken it aloud hundreds of times, a poem lives in a new way each time it is delivered. The secret is to aim for the spontaneity that waits in the heart of every moment.

I have always hungered for spontaneity. When I was in college, I was obsessed with it, no doubt because I was less spontaneous than anyone I knew.

I went to college at 16, having skipped my senior year of high school. I hid my self-consciousness about being younger than everyone else under a feigned nonchalance and a sharp wit. Instantly upon arrival, I made a beeline for the theater, where I met a flock of creative young actors and directors. Like a band of refugees from the '60s, when experimental theater was in its heyday, my new friends were interested in pushing every edge they could find. On a campus of kilts, kneesocks, and arrow-collar shirts, they were instantly recognizable in their Salvation Army specials: intentionally tattered and oversized suit jackets, tight jeans worn through at the knees, and bare feet, or fringed hippie skirts and headbands. While I was much too shy to sport the dress code of this crowd, I was drawn to their fiery creative ferment. To my surprise and good fortune, in spite of my age, wardrobe, and inhibitions, they welcomed me. They called me their "jaded freshman," affectionately referring to the sarcasm I held up as a shield to hide my fear and awkwardness.

Failing to find it in myself, I studied spontaneity. I researched sociological theories of play, techniques of improvisation, essays on creativity, and studies of ritual, ceremony, sports, and games. Each of these in its own way liberates participants from the tyranny of what many call the ego[2] or the controlling mind. The baseball fan roaring to his feet and hurling his cap into the air, the devout Catholic weeping with religious fervor in the midst of the mass, the poet pouring forth a stream of words that seem to come from beyond her own thoughts, the actor so taken with his role that utterly uncharacteristic behaviors and speech burst out of him on their own—all of these people have much in common. They are completely spontaneous and in the moment. They are moved by something beyond their ordinary thought. They are free, for a blessed moment, of the steady barrage of habitual thought that usually fills the mind. And they do not care what anyone thinks about them.

I, on the other hand, could remember few such experiences in my own life. I hungered for more, but I felt myself moving in the opposite direction. Underneath the pseudo-sophistication of my sardonic shell, I was becoming more and more self-conscious.

So I wrote research papers on spontaneity, secretly hoping that I would discover how to unlock my own cage and set myself free.

Miraculously, my plan worked. It wasn't until years later, after I had moved to New York City to start a theater company and teach improvisational acting, that I noticed I was actually learning what I was teaching. More and more, a vital moment-by-moment creativity had begun to flow from me, and as it did, I didn't care what people thought. At these times I was able to transcend my own limited mind and be completely present to everything happening within and around me.

Looking back, I see that my study of spontaneity was only the first step. Researching theories of play was an academic obsession appropriate for an industrious college student. Yearning for a direct experience of God, or the luminous void, or whatever existed beyond my mind, was not part of the curriculum. But the heart of the impulse that compelled my research was not a love of games or theater or even poetry. My true longing was to give myself to something greater than my little mind and will.

At the time I had no connection with religion or spirituality. Though my family was Jewish, we rarely went to temple or spoke of anything related to God. This turned out to be a blessing of sorts. For, as my study of spontaneity inadvertently but inexorably awakened me to a vast power and presence beyond my mind, I met it without preparation or programming—exactly as I had hoped was possible: spontaneously.

The Architecture of Freedom

Every circumstance that intentionally evokes spontaneity—whether it is a game of *Monopoly*, a tribal rite of passage into adulthood, or the speaking of a poem—has certain elements in common. Each occurs within a clear structure, the parameters of which serve to create a sense of external control, like an exoskeletal ego. Within that strong boundary, paradoxically, the personal ego can let go.

I remember discovering years ago what remains my favorite natural fact. When a caterpillar enters the cocoon, it turns completely to liquid before the butterfly-to-be begins to constellate. You don't get to retain a few fat little caterpillar legs until you grow an elegant butterfly leg or two. You don't get to hold onto your caterpillar brain while you sprout a wing or an antenna. You turn to mush.

Continuously inspired by this wonderful and terrifying portrait of transformation, years later I wrote this poem:

In Impossible Darkness

Do you know how
the caterpillar
turns?

Do you remember
what happens
inside a cocoon?
You liquefy.

There in the thick black
of your self-spun womb,
void as the moon before waxing,

you melt

(as Christ did
for three days
in the tomb)

conceiving
in impossible darkness
the sheer
inevitability
of wings.

The miracle becomes possible because of the strong walls of the cocoon. Spring a leak and no butterfly. In the case of cultivating spontaneity, the structure—the beginning, middle, and end; the rules of the game or poem or ceremony; and the shared intention of all present—acts as a cocoon. What melts is the self-conscious ego with its need to watch, judge, and control every movement. What is born, again in the words of D. H. Lawrence, is "the wonder that bubbles into my soul"—the pure creative moment.

I spent years courting that wellspring by directing theater ensembles and teaching improvisational acting. Eventually, though, I could no longer pretend that my hunger was about theater. I remember one of the final performances of the theater company I founded and directed in New York City. I led the actors through a 4-hour "warm-up" to perform a 45-minute play. When the audience arrived, I was slightly peeved that they had interrupted our rich explorations. It was then that I had to admit it was consciousness and not performance compelling me.

Inside the architecture of a game, ceremony, or poem, as inside the architecture of a temple, you might taste for a moment the freedom of pure being. But this is only a reminder. Ultimate freedom, of course, cannot be contained in any structure. It has no walls, no rules, no beginning, and no end. The poem and the temple are places to visit this "Self inside self," in the words of the mystical poet Lalla. Through all my research, rehearsals, and theater companies, this was what I was really seeking.

Hungry Ghosts

One of my students, Reba, well understood the power of spontaneous expression. In addition to being a poet, Reba was a dancer and a nurse who specialized in birth. She'd helped innumerable women trust their bodies through their contractions as they labored their babies into the world. And she had a deep trust of her own body, too. Watching her move around the space of the workshop, or even simply sit in a chair, was a lesson in physical spontaneity. Subtle natural movements that most of us have learned to suppress—gentle undulations of the spine in response to a breeze or a fragrance, curling of the toes when the conversation gets uncomfortable—flowed through her constantly.

She loved vibrant color and often sported surprising accessories—bright orange shoes and fruit-shaped earrings—to match the wild tropical hues of her pants and sweaters. A 4-foot-11-inch powerhouse, she was small enough to wear children's sizes and proud of her array of kid's watches that matched every shade of her wardrobe.

So it was all the more startling to hear how unnatural her reading was when she brought her first poem to class. Her toes were spontaneously curling a mile a minute, but her voice had no spontaneity at all. It was thin and tight as a wound wire. Though there was some expression in her delivery, even this seemed exaggerated and disconnected from her body.

From her experience with dance, Reba knew what it felt like to surrender to a creative current, and she knew that was not happening in the way she spoke the poem. She asked me for help. Together, over the next few years, we discovered the keys to the prison around her voice.

"I grew up in a silent home," she told me. "We didn't talk at the dinner table. We didn't talk in the car. It was not okay to express anything out loud, especially not feelings." Then, at six years old, Reba learned to read. "I not only discovered that I loved reading, I discovered I loved reading out loud. I loved the sound of my own voice and the shapes and sensations of the words as I said them." She read to her teachers. She read to her parents. Suddenly people were listening to her. Suddenly she was allowed to talk. She was even getting approval for it.

"In the beginning I was reading out loud just for me, even if other people were listening. But then it changed." Slowly and subtly her delight in the free play of sound and sensation turned into a hunger for approval. What had originated as an innocent explosion of creativity inexorably became a currency that she used to buy a positive reflection in the eyes of others. "When I read out loud, I got approval for being a good reader, but never did I feel my parents loved and valued the real me. So there was still that emptiness."

As is the case for so many, including me in my second Poetry Concert, Reba became caught in a vicious circle. She tried to fill the hole inside her with approval. The more she tried to get approval, the less connected she was to herself and the original pleasure of reading aloud. The less she was nourished by that pleasure and creativity, the bigger the hole inside her became. This caused her to redouble her efforts to fill up with approval, and the cycle continued.

Now the adult woman's true voice was trapped in her hunger for recognition. For how could she allow herself all the bright and involuntary colors of her voice, how could she give over to the pleasure of an uninhibited dance with a poem, if she was so concerned about being judged by those listening?

There's a term in Buddhism, *Hungry Ghost*, that describes a type of supernatural being that is constantly afflicted by an insatiable hunger. No matter how much this being gets, it is not nourished. The creature's agony is not that it cannot get what it wants, but that what it wants does not fill it. In most depictions of its realm, the Buddha holds out a bowl full of Truth, offering the Hungry Ghost the only food that can ever really satisfy this appetite.

The craving to be seen and recognized can be like a Hungry Ghost. No matter how much recognition you get, the hole inside is never filled. The radiance of your original connection with the poem has been hijacked by your craving for recognition. Your

185

expression becomes forced and unspontaneous. You are locked out of the wellspring of the moment.

The Strange Angels

"I had no idea what I was getting into when I first decided I wanted to speak poetry," Reba confided to me later. "I had to show up in my eyes. I had to show up in my body. But even more, I had to show up in my feelings—in relationship with other people."

This, of course, is why she chose to do it. The whole purpose of speaking poetry for her was to release an inner self that did not have a voice. Poetry, the language of the inner life and of feelings, directly threatened her family creed of repressing and denying feelings. "I realized I was going to be more exposed speaking poetry than if I were taking all my clothes off and dancing. It was the most vulnerable thing I'd ever done."

And, no matter how she might wish it to be otherwise, her defenses automatically activated to protect her. Her voice became exaggerated, her body tightened, and, as if there was an actual threat to her safety, her breathing virtually stopped.

This response is common. Even the poet D. H. Lawrence seems to have experienced this sudden, involuntary shutting down. In the last stanzas of his beautiful poem where he speaks of being borrowed by the wind, after arriving at the source of wonder, suddenly he becomes suspicious and afraid:

What is the knocking?
What is the knocking at the door in the night?
It is somebody wants to do us harm.

For many years the end of this poem baffled me. I would even leave out these and the final two lines that follow them when I spoke it, because I was peeved at Lawrence for tainting his message with this sudden descent into distrust and accusation.

Only recently did I recognize that these lines hold the most important message in the poem for me. Often, in my most vulnerable moments, I suddenly become afraid. Just after flinging myself open to "the wonder that bubbles into my soul," just when I've finally taken the risk to give myself fully to whatever I am in love with at the moment—a lover, a vision, a poem, or a "fine, fine wind"—there's that knocking on the door in the dead of night, and I'm sure whoever is there is up to no good. How often have I wanted to lock the door against those uninvited guests, never realizing they are the angels I've been praying to meet?

Sometimes the stranger comes as a human being you don't want to let in. The man who fell asleep in the front row of my second concert, for instance, stymied my craving for approval and knocked me right out of my prideful ego into the heart of why I was there in the first place: to be real and speak the truth. Sometimes the angel comes as a feeling, experience, or thought that you would do almost anything to avoid. Loneliness has frequently knocked on my door in the night. I fight it with busyness, thousands of e-mails and phone calls, even housecleaning. But, though the sound of the knocking may get drowned out for a moment, it doesn't go away. When I finally open the door and instead welcome the loneliness, it always becomes the sweet aloneness that is the source of my most precious moments. I sink into silence, or am inspired to write, or open to places within me calling for healing. For one of my friends, the strange angel was a positive test for HIV. Once he got over his shock and denial, the diagnosis compelled him to quit his boring office job, move to the country, and open the antique store of his dreams—where he is thriving to this day. But his first impulse, like mine, was to bar the door.

Luckily, in Lawrence's case, he catches himself before he locks out the trespassers. Even in the middle of the night, even through his fear, he recognizes at the last minute that these are the "three strange angels" he has been looking for.

For many years, I thought the way to help someone like Reba, who was struggling to let down her defenses, was to create a "safe space" where there were no strange angels knocking at the door in the middle of the night. A space where she could practice taking risks, where she knew that she would be met with receptivity and support, not the judgment she feared. No uninvited guests. No feelings of being unseen or misunderstood or unloved.

Then a wise friend warned me, "Fear tells you, 'I'll make you safe.' Love says, 'You are safe.'"[3] This simple statement woke me up to the truth and revolutionized my approach to all my work. I couldn't possibly create a safe space for anyone! No matter how many agreements the well-intentioned people in the group and I made among ourselves, someone was sure to get their feelings hurt—by a sideways look, an unconscious word, an unavoidable accident—and someone was likely to feel anger or grief or unseen or misunderstood or any of the other unwanted feelings that inevitably arise. In fact, I realized these dreaded experiences might actually be the best things that could happen to my students and to me. Because if you are willing to meet what you fear, not only can you discover that you will survive the experience, but also meeting the fear will give you what you need to thrive.

It turns out that it is not only safety that creates space for risk-taking, but risk-taking that creates a sense of safety. This may seem counterintuitive, but a little investigation can reveal its truth. Think about doing something you fear. It might be swimming out into the sea farther than you've ever gone, or quitting your job, or bungee jumping, or speaking a poem with abandon. Or perhaps it is an emotional "bungee jump," like telling others how much you care about them, or letting yourself cry while a friend holds you, or saying no to someone you love.

At my second concert, after half the audience had walked out and the ruins of my idealized image of myself smoldered around me, I took the risk to welcome the "angels" of embarrassment and defeat, rather than locking the door against them. It wasn't an easy choice to make, but as soon as I did, my world became a safer place. Not only did I survive the experience but I could also breathe deeper and be more fully alive.

When you welcome what you've been running from, your life is no longer shaped by trying to avoid it. You may need to experience feelings that you have feared—consciously or unconsciously—throughout your life. You may need to let them pour through your body: the blush of shame in your cheeks or the sting of tears. A surge of hot rage may move through your belly, or your chest may clench with a chill of despair. When you meet these with presence and patience, even curiosity, they naturally move through you. As they do, your world becomes larger than it was a few moments before. You become freer to be yourself. Not because you finally found a place where you are protected from feeling what you don't want to feel, but because you welcomed those unwanted feelings and lived to tell the tale. Maybe your idealized image of yourself didn't survive, but you did.

With my friend's help, I realized that my job was to remind people that they are already safe—so, paradoxically, they can allow themselves to tolerate fear as they open the door to what they may have spent a lifetime trying to escape.

I think of Martin Luther King, Jr., speaking out in his famous "I Have a Dream" speech. He was not waiting to feel safe. At that time in America, racism had divided the country to such an extent that it was not only outrageous but also dangerous for African American people to express their dreams out loud. I think of Eve Ensler, risking her life all over the world by honoring a word that has been taboo for generations: *vagina*. Her fear of disapproval doesn't stop her. I think of Harvey Milk and Rosa Parks and the girl whose name I cannot remember who stood up for me in second grade when the other kids were teasing me because I didn't know how to jump rope. All of them were willing to risk being attacked and humiliated as they gave voice to what they believed. And I think of the poets, too—Anna Akhmatova, Marina Tsvetaeva, Sylvia Plath, Pablo Neruda, and the young poets of the "Freedom Space" in Baghdad, to name only a few—who have spoken the unspeakable, taboo, and politically dangerous truths that had to be told.

Of course, speaking out politically is not the same as delivering poetry, but there are essential similarities. Both are visionary: they express truths that ask the listener to stretch beyond familiar paradigms into new territory. To be a voice for such change requires the willingness to break out of given protocols, to choose risk over safety, to be a leader.

Two Keys to Authenticity

There are two keys to being freely, simply, authentically your-self as you speak a poem to others. The first is a willingness to welcome feelings of being unseen, unheard, and misunderstood.[4] This may sound ridiculous. You may wonder for a moment if there isn't a typo or two in that sentence. You may say to yourself, *Didn't she mean to say "the willingness to be seen, heard, and understood?" Isn't that, after all, the purpose of self-expression?*

Paradoxically, it is only when you are willing to be unseen that you can be truly visible. Without that willingness, some percent-age of your life energy is always tied up in unconsciously trying to be seen as you'd like to be seen, and along with this, by necessity, you will probably be trying to protect yourself against judgment and rejection.

The second key is seemingly the opposite: a willingness to be seen, yet as you really are, including all sides of yourself, not just the ones you are proud of. It was, after all, an apple from the Tree of the Knowledge of Good and Evil that caused Eve and Adam to grab fig leaves and run for cover. Before they took that educa-tional bite, they knew themselves as only good. Suddenly, they were aware of themselves as good and evil, and shame was born. With it came the impulse to hide: to control what was visible and what wasn't.

This is a very free translation of a story that probably has a thousand other valid meanings. But this reading, offered to me by one of my teachers, Moira Shaw, has helped me hundreds of times when I felt the fear of being exposed. To this day, every time I stand in front of others to express my heart, I carry the message with me in an invisible medicine bag. This lesson helps me to remember that I am both good and evil and to give up the hope that no one will see the "evil" part.

People will see whatever they want to see. I can't control what they think, no matter how much I try to manage how I look, what I say, and how I say it. Once I bring this consciousness to the moment, I realize that I don't even want to control what they perceive. It is a habit, a knee-jerk response of my ego, which always wants to look "good" in order to strengthen its own existence. When I remind myself that I am willing to be visible in all my beauty and imperfection, I may feel a little shyness or shame, but I can welcome these feelings and breathe through them. I know they are "strange angels" that come when I am vulnerable and authentic, which is ultimately much more important to me than looking good.

"The Wonder That Bubbles"

This was the key that freed Reba. One night, when she was reading a particularly long poem she had written herself, I stopped her in the middle. It was a wonderful poem, full of rich imagery and intricately musical language. But there was so much control and urgency in her voice that it was hard to listen to her. Even though the poem was deeply personal, there was nothing personal in her delivery. As usual, she read with her head down and her eyes on the page. She rarely looked at anyone in the room. It didn't feel like she was actually sharing *with* us, but rather that she was trying to do something *to* us and avoid contact with us at the same time, as if she were hiding and trying to get us to see her at once.

She was shocked when I stopped her. "Why did you do that? Now no one will get what I'm saying." I asked her if she thought anyone was "getting it" before I stopped her. She said she didn't think so and that was why she wanted to keep trying. I suggested that instead, she simply look around at the group.

"What do you see in their faces?" I asked her.

"Nothing. I see blank stares. Like I don't matter. I feel as if I've been deflated, like a popped balloon. I used to feel this way when my father ignored me." She paused for a moment. "And I feel very sad."

In childhood, that kind of deflation can be very damaging. A growing child is deeply engaged in creating a sense of self. When her fledgling identity is shattered, the feelings of aloneness and helplessness are often too much for her to bear, so she builds defenses against them. Reba protected herself by cutting off her feelings and trying harder and harder to get approval.

Years of psychological work had helped Reba gain awareness: she knew the wounds of her childhood and the emptiness left by the absence of positive attention from her parents. All her machinations to get approval were attempts to fortify her shaky identity.

The inner strength and self-love she had gained through her years of inner work gave her the courage to stand at a new edge. Now the challenge was no longer about healing or strengthening her identity. It was about letting go of it and "letting the wind blow through." It was time to take a leap beyond all the psychological knowledge she had accrued—beyond her personal story and into her soul.

I asked her if she might be willing to simply let herself feel deflated. To consider the possibility that deflation might even be valuable in this moment. Perhaps whatever identity had been "popped" might not be necessary now. She looked at me for a moment as though I was nuts. But then she nodded and closed her eyes. A few tears slipped out and down her cheeks. We knew she was letting herself fall into that hole inside her.

After a few minutes she spoke without opening her eyes. "It's strange. I feel so quiet and alive now. Being deflated is more spacious than I could have imagined. I would have thought it would be a cramped and broken space. But I feel my heart expanding toward each of you in the most palpable way. I don't feel separated from you at all right now."

I asked her to speak the poem to herself with her eyes still closed. I suggested she simply listen to the sound of her own voice, not worrying about whether anyone else could even hear her, much less understand what she was saying. As she repeated the poem, the hard edges around her voice began to dissolve. She started to play with the sounds of the words, allowing them to burst and whisper, sing and melt into silence. We felt as if we were witnessing a young child discovering the power of speech. Her fingers began to dance in the air and her toes again began to curl, this time in delight. In the poem, she contemplates her own death as she watches how animals die in nature. It had seemed a very serious poem until then. Now, freed of any agenda to fill the Hungry Ghost, the lines revealed innumerable colors—one moment playful, the next tender, the next angry, the next heartbreaking.

Then I asked her to include us in relationship with her and the poem. She looked into our eyes and continued speaking. Her face was shining as she invited each of us into the intimacy of the verses. "I want to die like that crab," she began. Her eyes were sparkling. Suddenly this poem about death was an adventure story, a wonderland, a magical possibility. We could have listened to her all night.

Soon after that class, Reba was invited to speak some of her poetry as part of a gathering of artists and writers. It was the first time she had shared her work with such a large group. "Finally, it wasn't just about the seriousness of getting my needs met. I could play! I was free to get really creative. It was what I had always longed for. I took risks and brought out parts of myself I'd never shown before. I really dropped into the silences and was able to be in connection with the audience as I did. I took up a lot of space. And it happens that I got a lot of praise, but that hardly mattered. I felt so full."

Embodying the Language of Intimacy

"What is our need?" Leonard Cohen asks. "To be close to the natural man, to be close to the natural woman."[5] This simple, human vulnerability is not easy. To be completely natural when speaking a poem, to be "close"—to the poem, to the places within you that are touched and evoked by the poem, and to the people you are sharing it with—this is a call to radical intimacy.

In my early 20s, I had a friendship with a woman from Germany. We had met as members of a summer theater company and, because we both liked to write, had decided to become pen pals. Our communications consisted of weekly letters, handwritten on blue aerogrammes that folded into the shape of envelopes and carried our thoughts across the ocean to one another. We used our missives as an exercise in learning to write as "close to the bone" as we could. Our letters became more and more honest and raw, sharing secrets and dreams and the intimate details of our lives.

When we finally saw each other again, the conversation was strained. We sat in a noisy restaurant in New York City and tried to make small talk. We could barely glance at one another. After about half an hour of this torturous awkwardness, my friend looked me right in the face with tears in her eyes, banged her fist on the table and blurted out, "You're much better on paper than you are in person!"

It was true. I could not live up to the intimacy of my writing. My writer self was far more open and honest than my interpersonal self. My writer self was actually closer to the real me than who I was in a social situation. It took many years and much inner work to free myself to be as real in relationship as I was on the page.

A similar phenomenon can happen with a poem that you love, whether you have written it or someone else has. Poetry is very intimate. A poem is usually written in a moment when the poet is alone with her- or himself. Often, when you first read a poem, you, too, are alone. It speaks to you privately, touching a deeply personal place that you may never have shared with anyone else.

To speak that poem out loud, to one or one thousand people, is to be publicly private. The poem may speak with far more intimacy and presence than you can on your own. Perhaps the voice of the poem is actually closer to your authentic self than the way you speak every day. And if poetry is the language of the soul, speaking a poem to another person is entering into a soul-to-soul intimacy. To give voice to the poem is a wonderful opportunity to incarnate that intimacy. To live it out loud.

The silences just before, during, and just after a poem is spoken can be the most intimate of all. Often people will rush through them, or bury their heads in their books to avoid the eyes of those listening, or fill up the space with talk. When this happens, the most precious moments of the experience are missed. For a poem is made not only of sound but of silence as well. Sometimes the silence speaks louder than the words. To live the silences in companionship with those listening is to enter a quality of meaningful intimacy together that, at least in the Western world, people rarely share outside of romance or deep familiarity.

Years ago I had a theater teacher, the actor Austin Pendleton, who said, "There are two ways to jump off the top of the Empire State Building. You can shut your eyes tight and clench your fists until you hit the ground, or you can look in the windows on the way down." Being present in the silences before, during, and after a poem can feel a little like jumping off the Empire State Building. Your habit may be to squeeze your eyes closed until the moment has passed. But you can also look in the windows: open your eyes, breathe, take in the faces of those listening, silently acknowledging the impact of the poem you are sharing.

When you are about to speak your favorite poem to someone, there is a silence just before you begin. Instead of looking at the words on the page, or talking about the time you first discovered this poem or what it means to you, take a minute to meet the eyes of those gathered. Even the thought that someone is about to read or recite a poem can transform the atmosphere of a room. People automatically ready themselves for "deep listening," as Rumi calls the soul-to-soul communion of poetry. In that moment before you speak the poem, you may feel the very texture of the air becoming saturated with presence. Out of this fertility, the poem can emerge organically.

When it is over, again allow the silence that naturally comes. You have just shared words that have touched and changed your life. Perhaps they have been life-changing for the listeners as well. The poem may have melted their armor and triggered tender feelings. Don't flee this undefended moment. It is the most precious fruit of speaking a poem. Be with your companions in the wave of vulnerability that may wash over you in the wake of the words.

Terrifying Beauty

At the deepest level, what keeps me from allowing myself to be "borrowed by the wind" is not only my fear of someone else's judgment, rejection, or misperception. It is deeper than my concern that someone will see in me what I would rather hide. It is not an interpersonal fear at all. It is not even personal. Behind, before, below, and beyond any personal psychological motive that might keep me locked outside of the spontaneity of the moment is the fact that true surrender means losing the very parameters of who I think I am.

Rilke writes in his "First Elegy,"

> *For beauty is nothing*
> *but the beginning of terror, which we still are just*
>   *able to endure,*
> *and we are so awed because it serenely disdains*
> *to annihilate us. Every angel is terrifying.*[6]

Perhaps you've been in the presence of this overwhelming beauty, as I have, watching the curl of a wave or looking into a baby's eyes. Perhaps you've seen it in the face of a lover or a flower or a mountain. A beauty that is so huge that, if you allowed yourself to receive it totally, you might shatter.

Every poem you love is such a terrifying angel. Add to that the wonder of hearing your own soul's voice and a communion with whoever is listening and it is not surprising that the ego's instinct is to hold on for dear life. The costume of your identity, no matter how resplendent, is too small to contain such beauty. If you are lucky, your identity will burst open at the seams, awakening you to your true nature, beyond form or definition.

When that happens, it is tempting to draw a new outline for yourself, a new identity inspired by the revelation: larger and wiser than before, maybe more empowered, creative, and awake. If you don't follow that temptation, you may find yourself, at least for a moment, in the pure spacious presence that you truly are. You are

Emily Dickinson's "Nobody." You are Rumi's "How aren't you?" Like Whitman, you can say to all sentient beings in the world, "Every atom belonging to me as good belongs to you." You are no one and everyone. You are pure presence and the wind that blows through.

Song of a Man Who
Has Come Through

Not I, not I, but the wind that blows through me!
A fine wind is blowing the new direction of Time.
If only I let it bear me, carry me, if only it carry me!
If only I am sensitive, subtle, oh, delicate, a winged gift!
If only, most lovely of all, I yield myself and am borrowed
By the fine, fine wind that takes its course through the chaos
*   of the world*
Like a fine, an exquisite chisel, a wedge-blade inserted;
If only I am keen and hard like the sheer tip of a wedge
Driven by invisible blows,
The rock will split, we shall come at the wonder, we shall find
*   the Hesperides.*

Oh, for the wonder that bubbles into my soul,
I would be a good fountain, a good well-head,
Would blur no whisper, spoil no expression.

What is the knocking?
What is the knocking at the door in the night?
It is somebody wants to do us harm.

No, no, it is the three strange angels.
Admit them, admit them.

    — D. H. Lawrence

Chapter 10

A SUDDEN GRACE

When the inner and the outer are wedded,
revelation occurs.

— Hildegard von Bingen

When body, mind, heart, and soul align in the voicing of a poem, miracles can happen. This is the power of the word. In recent years, there have been many teachings about using the power of the word to intentionally attract the experiences and things you want in your life. But the power I speak of is not about getting wealth, health, or romance, though these might arrive as side effects. Rather it is about giving. When you speak a poem written in the language of your soul, you join your words with the truth of your deepest being. The potent space created by such alignment can bring gifts not only to you but also to the life around you.

"Tell a wise person or else keep silent . . ." This line is the threshold to Goethe's magnificent "The Holy Longing," the first poem I worked with as I discovered the practice of taking a poem to heart. Though I have known those lines now for more than ten years, each time I return to them, I feel a resonant, holy hush, as if I were entering a great cathedral; the words of the poem are the arches, the ancient stone walls, the stained glass windows enclosing a sacred space. I go there to drop into myself. As I enter, my voice becomes alive with the delicate acoustics of the place, resonant with the voices of all who have spoken these words before me. Just as the light through the rose window changes with the seasons, the poem changes each time I speak it. All the frenetic and disarrayed particles of my attention come into alignment. As Wallace Stevens writes, "We collect ourselves, / Out of all the indifferences, into one thing."[1] My mind quiets and steps aside. I hear the voice of my soul.

When you speak the poems you love—whether to yourself or someone else or many others—a mysterious phenomenon can occur. The sounds and silences become almost palpable with a resonance that seems beyond the sum of the parts. You and whoever is listening are gathered into a kind of grace. The spoken poem smoothes the rough edges of fragmented attention—harmonizing, focusing, and unifying everyone present. As Rumi says of his teacher, Shams, "You make my raggedness silky."[2]

To put this kind of experience into words is difficult. It can so easily sound far-fetched or like a testimonial of a religious experience that may have been authentic at the time but gets lost in translation. Yet this sudden grace is not exotic or unusual. It happens all the time when people give voice to the poems that speak the truth of their souls. The phenomenon saves me, often several times a day, when I am scattered or in pain and I have lost touch with my real self. Though I have never been one to turn to organized religion, I believe I can begin to understand the experience of those who go to church every morning or bow to Mecca five times a day. I turn to poems, the sanctuaries I carry inside me, for the same resonant, absolving holiness.

One of the elements of the feeling of holiness is indeed wholeness, a sense of coherence. Russell Targ, an atomic physicist, has explored the phenomenon of coherence through his work with lasers. When a laser device is too weak to emit a single beam and instead scatters fragmented rays in all directions, even the smallest amount of light from a coherent laser can instantly bring the chaotic one into alignment. "The power of the small but purely coherent laser 'purifies' and 'transforms' the disharmonious, ineffective laser, rendering it highly coherent, and powerful enough to become a potentiating laser itself."[3]

Targ likens this phenomenon to the transmission that occurs in the presence of a saint or guru. Sometimes I have felt a similar transmission while looking out my window at the vast, jagged silhouette of Mount Tamalpais against the night sky, or leaning back into the wizened trunk of a redwood, or hearing the cry of a hawk burst the rattling of my thoughts. The Indian saint Ramana Maharshi felt it in the presence of Arunachula Mountain, where he lived his entire life conveying that pure silence to thousands of seekers.

A poem, spoken from the heart, can also be a direct transmission. A contagion of coherence occurs. It doesn't matter if the poet is an "enlightened" person. He or she may have been as humanly challenged as any of us when doing the dishes or putting the kids to bed. But in writing the poem, the poet experienced a direct connection with a larger field of wisdom. That spark of awakeness is transmitted, like a pure laser beam, through the poem as you speak it aloud, calling all the fragments of yourself into wholeness. And in turn, your wholeness, infused by that of the poet and poem, becomes a "potentiating laser" itself, bringing anyone willing to be touched into resonance.

This contagious wholeness fosters healing and wellness. In the film *Healing Words: Poetry & Medicine,* Dr. Michael Okun, a neurologist at the McKnight Brain Institute of the University of Florida, speaks of the way poetry heals: "Does poetry heal? As a neurologist I can tell you that it does . . . Any poem that I read to you or that you read to me is going to cause a cascade of events in the brain that we don't yet understand. But we do know this can influence brain function—changing chemicals and changing the ways that receptors are receiving information. Changing overall mood can change and improve function . . . Because the brain is smart. It is plastic and it can change."[4]

The experience of this transmission can happen at any point in your relationship with a poem. It might happen the first time you read a new poem aloud. Or one that you've been speaking for years might suddenly take on an amplified vibration, riveting everyone with the awareness that they're experiencing something far more than the sum of the parts. Nor does it matter where you are. You need no literal sanctuary. You might be sitting in traffic amidst a sea of blaring horns and overheating engines, yet as you speak the first words of a poem it is as if a tangible and shining silence descends on everyone in the car. It need not be a mystical poem. Any poem that tells the truth of your soul will do. Sylvia Plath's famous poem "Daddy" begins, "You do not do, you do not do / any more black shoe." When spoken nakedly with the passion of your own experience, even a poem laced with outrage and agony can become an incantation, summoning those listening into resounding, vibrant connectedness.

For that moment, the fragmentation between inner and outer, between body and soul, between heart and mind is healed. All levels—from the most human to the purest spirit—are engaged and aligned in the delivery of the poem. The poem, the listeners, and you seem to be held in a state of revelation. Does it come from the poem? Does it come from the resonance of your own voice? Does it come from those listening or the connection among you? It is impossible to know.

I will never forget the words of Olympia Dukakis about the same phenomenon in the theater. It was the summer of 1976. We were both working at the Williamstown Theatre Festival—I as a student intern and she as part of the acting company. Over lunch in a tiny pizza parlor, I asked her why she thought such a multitude of young actors hoped to make a life on the stage when the statistical possibility of success was so dismal.

"I think that going into acting and staying in acting are two very different things," she began. "When you start out, you are excited by the power that you feel. You want to make audiences laugh. Or you want to make them cry. Or you want to teach them a lesson—possibly for a very good cause, but it's still about the power you have to affect people. If you stay in the theater, you stay for a very different reason." Here, I remember the pause. We were leaning toward one another over the Formica table, straining to hear through the din of hollered pizza orders and clattering plates. Oblivious to the environment, Olympia's eyes filled with tears. "There is something that can happen between you and an audience that I cannot put into words. It is a kind of communion; maybe you could even say a Holy Communion. It is as if something far vaster than the play or the actors or the audience has descended and is holding all of you. You know it, and you know the audience knows it, too. If you keep acting, that is why."

I have found the same to be true of speaking poetry. Perhaps initially you do it because you want to touch people with what you love: to share the beauty or insight or heartbreak, or help a friend in need. But at some point the "communion" that Olympia describes may capture you. Then reading and speaking the poem—or indeed any poem—is no longer a gift from one person to another. It is a grace that happens to both of you at once.

Within that potent space, any and every boundary line we humans draw around ourselves instantly disappears. It is holy without being denominational, political without being sectarian, intimate without being bound by gender, age, or culture.

I discovered how the separating lines of culture and age can dissolve in the presence of a poem the first time I went to Africa. In Kenya, at the Tasaru Ntomonok Rescue Centre for Girls in the Rift Valley, I unexpectedly found myself speaking a poem to a group of Maasai girls, only a few hours after I met them. I had long wanted to visit this miraculous place, ever since it was opened by Eve Ensler and her organization V-Day in collaboration with Agnes Pareyio, a Maasai woman who dedicates her life to stopping the practice of female genital mutilation (FGM). Tasaru, also called the V-Day Safe House, was created as a haven for girls escaping FGM. Fifty or so girls live at the house at any given time. Each has had to leave her family and community. Many have traveled alone for miles, barefoot over the rough roads, spending nights hiding under the bushes for fear of being found by wild animals.

My first few hours there were awkward. My shyness kept me from striking up conversations with the girls, most of whom, though they understood English, did not speak it willingly. They were shy with me too, keeping their distance and watching me in twos or threes, whispering in Maa (the language of the Maasai) and giggling.

Finally I decided to go over to the kitchen, where I heard lively singing as a group cooked ugali (porridge made of cornmeal) and cabbage over an open fire. I listened outside as the last song dissolved into gales of laughter and a cacophony of exclamations in Maa. But the chatter instantly hushed when I walked in. A tall girl who spoke excellent English came up to me and stood directly in front of me: "Do you remember my name?"

I didn't. I had been introduced to about 20 girls in the last couple of hours and could not for the life of me remember which beautiful Maasai face went with which name.

"Salula?" I asked sheepishly, grabbing for the only name I remembered. "No!" The girls shrieked with laughter at what must have been a big mistake on my part. "That is Salula!" They pointed at one of the youngest girls, who had arrived at the Safe House only months before at the age of 9, having been rescued in the midst of a forced marriage to a 42-year-old man.

"I am Jecinta." The tall girl spoke to me with exaggerated patience, as if to a two-year-old. "Do you know any songs?" Clearly she was giving me an opportunity to redeem myself.

"I know some songs," I said. "But what I really love most is poetry."

"I write poems." An older girl with exquisitely chiseled features and piercing eyes was looking at me intently from behind a huge cauldron of steaming cabbage. She was dressed with more sophistication than the others, wearing a tight sleeveless shirt and matching short skirt that made her look more woman than girl. I noticed her gold necklace and earrings as they glinted in the light of the cooking fire.

"Do you know any of them by heart? Can you recite any of them here?" I asked.

"I am too shy to do that." Her beautiful accent made even this simple statement sound like poetry. "I cannot."

"May I recite a poem to you?" I asked her. "Then maybe afterward you will want to recite yours to me."

She nodded. Suddenly I panicked. What poem might these girls relate to? I pored through the archive in my mind. Not one seemed remotely appropriate. Their life experience was so different from mine.

The kitchen had become strangely silent. The clatter of washing and cooking had ceased. The whispering and giggling that had been a constant soundtrack in the background was quiet. All the girls had stopped their work and were waiting for my poem.

Out of nowhere "The Journey" by Mary Oliver, a poem I hadn't thought of in months, burst into my mind. Without even taking the time to run through it silently to see if it was appropriate, I began speaking: "One day you finally knew / what you had to do."

The poem is about leaving home, turning away from the many voices that demand that you stay, risking the anguish of those who seem to need and love you, and walking alone into a wild night in order to save "the only life you can save." The girls listened, transfixed. Each of them had lived through such a turning point. Each of them, at a very young age, had defied tribal tradition and left her parents, friends, and community to save her own life. Who could understand these lines better than they?

It is difficult to describe what happened in that crowded, smoky kitchen as I delivered the poem. There I was, a white, middle-class American woman speaking words written by another white, middle-class American woman, surrounded by Maasai girls who had grown up in tribal villages in the Rift Valley, in families so poor that the two cows their parents would get when they gave their daughter to an old man in marriage were their only hope of a better life.

But as "The Journey" filled the kitchen, there was no separation between us. We were transported into a timeless, placeless, languageless realm where we were the same. By the end of the poem, tears were running down my face and several of the girls were crying as well. Several of them dove toward me, wrapping their arms around my waist. There was a long silence. Then Jecinta asked, "Who is this woman, Mary Oliver? Is she Maasai?"

I shook my head, barely able to speak. "American," I whispered. "*Mzungu*. Like me."

"How did she know?"

In the silence that answered her question, the girl with the gold necklace and piercing eyes came from behind the cauldron of cabbage into the center of the dirt floor.

"I am ready to say my poem," she announced.

In a single wave, the other girls and I moved to one side of the kitchen, spontaneously creating a stage area among boiling pots of food.

"I'm just a girl child." Her voice was surprisingly strong, pulsing with a natural rhythm as contagious as any slam poet's vibe. "It sounds good but oh no— / To my father I'm just a source of income." She continued through the list: her mother who sees her only as a "beast of burden," the boys at school who objectify her beauty, and "the sugar daddy," for whom she was just "a juicy fruit to be eaten raw." The poem ends with the wise and heartbreaking question, "Who cares for me?"[5]

By now there were about two dozen girls packed into the smoky kitchen or leaning in the windows. As the poet spoke her final question, we all cheered and burst into applause. I looked around at the crowd that had gathered. Most girls were melted into each other, their arms draped around their friends. Two girls had maneuvered me into the space between them; one rested her head on my shoulder. For a long moment of silence we gazed at each other through the smoke, our eyes full of light.

In these moments of poetic communion when life comes into a harmony, miracles happen organically: the stroke victim's brain starts making new synaptic connections; a sense of uncanny peace and joy pervades the Freedom Space as bombs explode in the surrounding streets; the armed Sunni soldier embraces the Shiite poet

206

in tears of joy to discover they feel the same grief and longing; a runaway Maasai girl hears her own story told by a white American writer, and she is empowered to find her own voice. When you speak a poem that is written in the language of your soul, you become a voice for the heart in the world, and everyone around you is blessed by a sudden grace.

Many religions say there are holy languages, such as Hebrew or Sanskrit, in which the words themselves are portals between the worlds. The sound of the words *Baruch ata Adonai* or *Gate gate paragate* are said to metaphysically invoke the actual experience they are naming. Supposedly English is not such a language. But if "holy" means the cracking of the mind's shell to let in the direct experience of a reality beyond it, any language, in the form of poetry, can become a holy language.

If you speak the words with love, Mary Oliver writes, "and the felt ferocity of that love, / the fish explode into many." Loaves of bread multiply. Water turns to wine. Poems create holy spaces in the midst of the horror of war. Territorial lines drawn by blood, color, culture, and creed are erased. The veil between the visible and the invisible dissolves in a flood of wonder. "Accept the miracle," Oliver counsels. "Accept, too, each spoken word, / spoken with love."[6]

Annunciation

Even if I don't see it again—nor ever feel it
I know it is—and that if once it hailed me
it ever does—

and so it is myself I want to turn in that direction
not as toward a place, but it was a tilting
within myself,

as one turns a mirror to flash the light to where
it isn't—I was blinded like that—and swam
in what shone at me

only able to endure it by being no one and so
specifically myself I thought I'd die
from being loved like that.

— Marie Howe

EPILOGUE

Here, in the silence that follows this beautiful poem, I want to linger with you. It would be easy to turn away, to go on to the next page, or to step into the thousand tasks that probably await both of us. Pausing instead, swimming in the blinding flash thrown by the mirror of Marie Howe's "Annunciation," turning toward the love that shines through those words, is an unusual and strangely courageous choice.

Rarely does it occur to me that what triggers my headlong rush into the busyness of the next moment might be the fear of love. The other stories are so compelling: e-mails are waiting, the vacuuming hasn't been done, there are calls to return, dishes to wash, errands to run, bills to pay. But the final line of this poem awakens me to a deeper truth: "I thought I'd die / from being loved like that." Like Rilke's terrifying angel, the beam of this love can feel like annihilation.

The truth is, in the wake of every poem that touches me, there is this uncanny sense of being loved. Perhaps that is what it feels like when the soul-door swings ajar. Will I walk through and dwell in the territory of wonder for a while? Or will I turn away and launch into the next task on my perpetually humming to-do list?

In this time of planetary crisis, there is a paradoxical urgency to slowing down, turning toward the mirror's beam, learning to endure—yes, even hunger for—the blinding flashes of brightness. A poem can flash such a beam when it is reflecting your own soul. As you swim in that moment of light there might be a quickening inside you. Some indefinable shining might begin to glow through your cells, your heart, and your mind and spill out of your voice to touch the world.

FURTHER EXPLORATION

THE ALCHEMY
OF POETRY AND MUSIC

The partnership between spoken poetry and music may be older than language itself, according to many archeologists, neuroscientists, and musicologists. As I mentioned in Chapter 1, long before words evolved, there may have been a system of communication that was both music and poetry at once.

In *The Singing Neanderthals,* Steven Mithen conjectures that this "musilanguage," which he called *Hmmmmm,* was used by the early hominids for dozens of millennia, starting around 1.8 million years ago. His theory is that the paths of music and language began to separate about 170,000 years ago with the evolution of the earliest members of our own *Homo sapiens* species.[1] "Music and language diverged in their most characteristic features, pitch organization in music and word and sentence meaning in language," musicologist Fred Lerdahl explains. Poetry, however, "straddles this evolutionary divergence by projecting, through the addition to ordinary speech of metrical and timbral patterning, its common heritage with music."[2]

Throughout the ages, the twin arts have remained inexorably connected. From the *Epic of Gilgamesh* in the 3rd millennium B.C., recited by an unknown bard strumming his lyre, to Michael Franti's rap poetry spoken to hip-hop vibes in the 3rd millennium A.D., music and poetry have always been creative partners. It was not until sometime after Homer's era (750 B.C.) that it even became conceivable that a poem might be recited without music. But even as poets began to speak their work without accompaniment, there were traditions that continued or resurrected the ancient partnership. In the '60s, '70s, and '80s, the Beat Poets, such as Allen

Ginsberg and Anne Waldman, not only took the textures and rhythms of their language from jazz, they often spoke their poems with live accompaniment. Today, as in ancient times, the griots of West Africa recite the history, news, and gossip of their villages in poetry to music. Rap, hip-hop, and spoken-word "dub" artists open the minds of today's listeners to exciting vistas of poetry that, though quite new to the Western mind, are a resurrection of this ancient collaboration.

In my iTunes archive I have a wonderful recording of Anne Waldman speaking her poem "Uh-Oh Plutonium!" to the manic rhythms of an electronic band. The keyboard melody bounces up and down to the point of hysteria, doubling both the playfulness and the horror of the poem. Phrases like "Nails and knuckles glowing! Sore kneecaps glowing! Ankles in despair!" toss in the bucking, frothing waves of synthesized explosions. A little further down the list, the pensive sounds of a jazz band laced with Native American drums and rattles carry Joy Harjo's voice, fierce and broken, as she speaks her elegiac poem "For Anna Mae Pictou Aquash." Further on I find Coleman Barks speaking his translations of Rumi—on one CD to the music of the Middle Eastern tabla and a sitar Rumi himself might have recognized, on another to a single atonal cello, and on a third to flute and piano compositions that sound like Appalachian folk melodies. And of course there are tracks and tracks of my own experiments in the alchemy of poetry and music. I have spoken poetry with every kind of music I can find, merging techno-trance-dance tracks with Rumi and reciting the sonnets of Gerard Manley Hopkins to reggae. I've tried Dr. Seuss to the soundtrack from *Chariots of Fire* and sections of Eliot's *Four Quartets* to everything from contemporary jazz to the Bach Cello Suites. Each different musical setting brings out possibilities within a poem that I might never have conceived of otherwise.

Of course, it is important to note that not all poetry can or should be spoken to music. There are some poems that simply defy musical accompaniment. Perhaps the rhythm, rhyme, or sound-play in the poem is itself so musical that adding another music is cacophonous. I have found this to be true with several of the rhyming poems of William Butler Yeats as well as the verses of Emily Dickinson. Perhaps the silences in the poem are so potent and necessary that to fill them with any sound at all seems criminal. In some of the poems of Marie Howe and Brenda Hillman, for instance, there are so many delicate communications going on in the spaces between the words that to add music can feel heavy-handed and unnecessary. Some poets cringe at the idea of merging their work with music. For them the music is already there, carefully woven into their craft, and any other music, however sensitively it may be chosen, seems to shatter the intentional song and silence of the poem.

However, I have found that many poems, when spoken with music, reveal subtleties of meaning, rhythm, and sound that I had not realized before. In recent years, studies of the brain have offered some scientific explanations of this magic. In general, research has found that the processing of music takes place in the right hemisphere of the brain and that of language in the left. Poetry, as I mentioned earlier, is unique in that it calls on both sides of the brain at once: the rational, linear, and language-oriented left side and the intuitive, kinesthetic, image-oriented right side.

Those who try to understand poetry only through the left side of the brain (usually with minimal reward) will often balk when music is added. The analytical mind cannot get a grip. But this is exactly the purpose of melding poetry with music: the combination so often completely disarms the linear mind. With its strong engagement of the right hemisphere of the brain, music seems to melt the left hemisphere's tight proprietorship of language, thus allowing its more creative, emotional, and nonrational partner to take over so that poetry's way of knowing can be received more fluently. I like to think that speaking poems with music reminds our overly analytical brains of their ancient heritage, when we conveyed poetic, holographic thoughts to one another through song-like "musilanguage." One of my students put it this way: "The music acts as an enzyme that helps the poetry to be metabolized."

When I speak poetry with music, I invite listeners to welcome the inability to understand the words as a medicine that can heal the hyperrational Western mind. I suggest that they give themselves to the river of sound, open all their senses, and make space for another kind of wisdom to awaken from within. Then the poetry, the music, and my own voice can become like the shaman's drum or rattle, which parts the veil between the worlds so that revelation might come to those on the journey.

PRACTICES

Here are some practices, questions, and meditations to help you deepen your direct experience of the possibilities offered in the preceding pages. You need not explore them consecutively; feel free to begin anywhere. Play with those that interest you and leave the rest.

The Medicine of Poetry

1. Is there a line or a poem that has touched your life? Are there a number of poems? Make a list of them.

2. Now see if you can remember how each one came into your life. Did someone pass the gift of this poem to you? If so, who was it? Perhaps you can even remember or imagine how that person came upon this poem.

3. Have you passed these poems on to others? As you contemplate each poem on your list, remember passing it on to individuals whose lives, in turn, were touched by the gift of this poem.

4. Take a few minutes to reflect on how you are a link in a living chain of poem-giving.

Choosing a Poem

I. The Yoga of Poetry

1. If you could experience an aspect of yourself that you have never fully expressed, what would it be? For instance, Hedda

longed to free herself to be a sensual, sexual woman. I wanted to open my heart and my voice to connection with people struggling for freedom around the world. Jordi needed to bring out her vulnerable femininity.

2. Now find a poem that will bring out the aspect you have chosen. If you are unsure of where to look for poems on your chosen themes, www.poetryfoundation.org has a wonderful technology called a "poetry tool" that can help you find just about any kind of poem you can think of.

3. Spend time with this poem reading it, speaking it out loud, and sharing it with others. Notice what it magnetizes to the surface of your consciousness. Welcome the memories, physical sensations, emotions, visions. You may want to write about these. Perhaps you will choose to learn this poem by heart, following the guidance in Chapters 6 and 7.

II. Where I Do Not Wish to Go

1. Look at the list of poems you love from the Medicine of Poetry practice. Even though these are your favorite poems, no doubt many, if not all, of them have lines that you don't relate to or don't particularly like. Choose a poem that has lines that fit this description.

2. Read or speak the poem, paying particular attention to the part of it that isn't easy for you to relate to. Then repeat those lines over and over, noticing what you feel, think, and become aware of as you do. What exactly about these lines is foreign or difficult for you? How might they be "putting a belt around you and taking you where you do not wish to go"? Can you see any benefit in surrendering to the guidance of the lines and inquiring more deeply into this new territory? You may want to write in a journal about this question or contemplate it in meditation.

III. An Autobiography in Poems

1. Make a list of all the poems you've loved, roughly in the order in which they came into your life. As you deepen your relationship with more and more poems, keep a list of them in order. Notice how they fall into themes or "chapters" and tell the story of your inner evolution.

2. Now, choose a poem from among these or elsewhere that you would like to work with through the rest of these practices.

The Anatomy of a Poem

I. Breath

1. Read your chosen poem aloud, paying particular attention to how your breath moves as you speak it. What do you notice about how you have to breathe to speak the lines? Does it lengthen or quicken your breathing?

2. Is there any way you are resisting the pattern of breathing that the poem invites? Are you holding back? Are you breathless?

3. If you fully give yourself over to the breath of the poem, what happens inside your body? Are any subtle sensations or emotions elicited?

4. What can you learn about the poem and yourself when you surrender to letting the poem breathe *you?*

5. What do you notice about the choices the poet has made about the arrangement of lines in the poem? What is the effect of long or short lines on your breathing? Has the poet broken the lines mid-sentence or mid-phrase, or do the lines follow the syntax? How does it affect your breathing when a line breaks in an unexpected place?

II. Drumbeat

1. What do you notice about the drumbeat in your chosen poem? Try speaking the poem aloud, exaggerating the rhythm. Notice where, if anywhere, there is a regular beat and where the poet breaks out of the pattern.

2. What is the effect of this regularity or irregularity on your experience of the poem?

3. Can you feel subtle effects of the rhythm inside your own body as you speak or read the poem? How does this pulse inside the poem's body affect the subtle pulses inside your own?

4. Sometimes it is revealing to read the poem aloud to a piece of music that has a steady pulse. Anything from African drumming to your favorite lullaby will do. Notice how the poem's rhythm dances in and out of the rhythm of the music.

III. Song

1. Read or recite your chosen poem aloud, noticing the sound-play among the words.

- Notice repetitions of the sounds at the beginnings of words.

- Notice repetition of the sounds in the middle or at the ends of words.

- Notice the use of rhyming or chiming among the lines.

2. Now look at a written copy of the poem. For each sound that plays a major part in the poem's symphony, choose a pen or crayon of a different color. Each time a particular sound occurs, underline

or circle its letters with the same color. Thus all *ou* sounds might be green, all strong *s* sounds might be red, and so on. Now draw lines connecting all the sounds that are the same or related.

3. Read your poem again, with a heightened awareness of the infrastructure of the music that gives the poem some of its power.

IV. Image

1. How many metaphorical images do you find in your poem? Remember, some are obvious, such as "the mountains fume like a kettle" or "my mother was the blue wisteria." Some are so embedded in the language of the poem they are harder to discern, as when Kunitz says "you would see yourself, / slipped out of your skin, / nosing upstream." Without warning, you are suddenly a salmon.

2. Become aware of how each metaphor brings two unlike things together in the same thought. Choose one metaphor and, in a meditation, hold both elements of the metaphor in awareness at the same time, allowing your attention to focus simply and only on those two things becoming one in your awareness. Notice the effect on your feelings, thoughts, body, and consciousness as you do this.

Writing Poems on Your Bones

You can do this practice with a partner or alone. You will need to have six to ten lines of your chosen poem written on an index card or piece of paper.

If you are working with a partner, one of you will be the speaker and the other the "listening heart." The job of the "listening heart" is to remain silent and simply listen from the heart. Such compassionate listening can create a powerfully resonant space that allows your partner to uninhibitedly explore both the poem and the many voices it may draw forth.

These instructions are directed to the speaker. If you are work-ing with a partner, go through the practice twice, switching roles the second time.

1.   Reflect on how this poem touches your life right now. If you are with a partner, speak about it to her or him. If you are alone, you may want to do a written meditation about it. In either case, free-associate, without editing yourself, for about five minutes.

2.   For ten minutes, read the poem aloud, over and over.

- Listen to your impulses and follow them, allowing your voice and body to express whatever comes up, whether it makes sense in relation to the poem or not. You may want to get up and move around. You may express strong emotions such as anger or tears. You may explore whispering and shouting. Whatever comes up, however simple or outrageous, is welcome.

- If you are working with a partner, make more and more eye contact as you speak the poem. Notice how this makes you feel and how connection with your partner affects your experience of the poem. If you are working alone, lift your eyes from the page more and more. Close them. Look around. Notice how the poem changes as it is less and less tethered to the page.

- Ten minutes can seem like a long time to keep repeat-ing the same six lines. At times you may feel that you become uncomfortable or "hit a wall." I find that if you stay with the process, a breakthrough can occur at some point, allowing a whole new font of inspira-tion and life experience to infuse the lines.

3.   Now close your eyes. Breathe. With eyes still closed, speak the poem without looking at your card.

4.   Now open your eyes and speak the lines to your partner or yourself without looking at your card.

5.   Notice which words you forget. Use them in the Gift of Forgetting practice below.

The Gift of Forgetting

The steps in this practice can be done in any order. Let yourself be drawn to those that most interest you and leave the rest.

1.   *Learning to pause in the moment of forgetting.* Speak the poem you are learning by heart to yourself. When you come to a point where you can't remember the words, stop. Breathe. Be with the experience of your inability to remember. Perhaps you will even say to yourself, *I can't remember the words.* This inquiry may last only a minute or two, but it can help you develop the capacity to slow down in moments of forgetting and resist the fight-or-flight impulse that autonomically arises at those times.

2.   *Discovering how forgotten words are essential to the poem.* Contemplate how the words you forget are essential to the poem. Why those exact words? Contemplate not only the meaning but also the rhythm, the syntax, the sounds and how they rhyme or chime with the sounds around them, and the way you breathe when you say these words.

3.   *Discovering how forgotten words call you into realms of yourself that are unfamiliar.*

- How is the meaning of the line calling you into new territory in yourself? Here are some questions to contemplate. What are the associations that you have to the forgotten words? What are the feelings and/or memories that come up when you speak them? What are you aware of in your body when you speak them?

Do you have any judgments, fears, or aversions that surface in relation to them? What was the attitude that different members of your family held toward the meaning inherent in these words?

- Do a ten-minute uncensored "writing practice" about these words. Uncensored writing can surprise us, revealing layers of experience that we did not know were in us. It is important to allow anything and everything that arises to spill out of the pen onto the page. It does not matter if it is grammatically correct or even if it makes sense. Let the censor take a break for at least ten minutes and see what pours out.

- Is the rhythm or syntax challenging to you? Say the words out loud and feel how your voice and breath move in your body. Is there something unfamiliar or uncomfortable that rubs against the habits that are woven into your cells?

- Is there something about the voice—that is, the attitude or a quality of presence in the poem—that calls you beyond your usual manner of expression? Is there a power you have not allowed yourself? Or a vulnerability that you have hidden? Is there a texture in the voice of the poet that is threatening some idealized image that you hold of yourself? Contemplate what you need to be willing to experience to risk embodying this unlived voice within you fully.

4. *Getting interested in the silence.* Speak a poem that you are just beginning to learn by heart. When you cannot remember the next word, allow the silence that happens. Be fully present as you bring your awareness to this absence of thought. Notice everything you can about the silence. Does it have light, shadow, color, texture? Can you find the edges of it? What do you notice as it continues;

does it change or remain the same? Let this silence permeate your awareness. Rest into it. Who are you in the space between your thoughts? Explore this until the mind starts up its thinking again, which may happen within seconds or may not happen for quite a while.

5.   *Being willing to openly experience forgetting.* Next time you forget something—the name of an acquaintance or a detail in a conversation or where you put your keys—don't cover up or try to remember. Take a deep breath. Relax. Let your companion know that you don't remember. Feel the flush of embarrassment, shyness, or whatever arises. Now do this when delivering a poem to a friend. Tell your companion what is going on within you as you drop into the moment of forgetting without defending against it.

Undressing Your Voice

Take some time to reflect on your own voice. You can do this alone or with a partner. Sharing this exploration can be a wonderful way of deepening a relationship. The questions that follow may help you become conscious of which sounds are vibrant in your voice and which are costumed and hidden. If you are alone, you may want to write or meditate on the questions that follow. If you are with a friend, take turns asking each other the questions. I recommend that the questioner refrain from responding to the answers or expressing opinions. Give your partner an opportunity to muse out loud uninterrupted, supported by your listening ear and heart.

1.   What part of your body does your voice seem to emanate from? Can you hear or feel what places are resonating in your voice? Can you hear where there are closed doors? What parts of your body are easily penetrated by your breath? Are there areas that feel impenetrable? Does your voice stay "above the waist" or "in your head"? Is it trained to stay away from your belly? Or your pelvis? Or your heart?

2. What feelings do you allow into your voice? What feelings do you prohibit? Do you confine your voice within a boundary of "niceness" or "intelligence" or "toughness" or "softness"?

3. What message does your voice seem to communicate? By this I mean a subtle, unspoken costume your voice wears that usually goes unnoticed. For instance, I have heard voices that, no matter what words they are actually speaking, seem to be saying, "I've got it all under control" or "This is so exciting!" or "There, there, I'll comfort you" or "I know everything" or "Don't bug me!" or "I need you to take care of me" or "Voulez-vous coucher avec moi ce soir?"

4. Contemplate letting go of these vocal limitations and costumes. What thoughts, insights, and feelings come up as you imagine "undressing" your voice? Are there fears or concerns that arise? Do you feel any curiosity or excitement about finding out who you might be if your voice was freed of its habitual garb?

5. In your daily life, play with broadening the spectrum of your expression. What sounds or feelings would be totally out of character for you to express? Try experimenting. If you are someone who speaks softly all the time, try making some noise. See what happens if you speak loudly and emphatically, perhaps first to yourself in the mirror or to a cashier or a waiter. Then try on uncharacteristic expressions with friends and loved ones. (You may want to let them know that you are experimenting with allowing more colors into your voice.) If you always speak with a strong voice full of certainty, try on the opposite. Try speaking softly or with tenderness.

6. As you speak the poem you are working with, venture into some sounds that are "out of character" for you. Speak the poem over and over, to yourself or a partner, trying on a different and uncharacteristic approach each time. Don't worry about whether your experiments make sense with the poem. This is not about finding a "right" way to speak the poem. It is about loosening up limitations of expression.

7. Throughout these experiments, notice what happens emotionally and physically when you consciously disrupt your own vocal patterns. There may be feelings or memories that arise—both of freedom and of fear. After all, when you originally constricted your range of expression (usually in childhood), it was because of fear of what might happen if you didn't. It is important to welcome these feelings if they show up, not numb them or skip over them. The purpose is not to encourage a contrived or exaggerated expression, but to invite you to truly inhabit—emotionally and physically—vocal expressions that are unusual for you. Like stretching a muscle, this can expand your natural "range of motion," that is, the range of sounds available to you as you speak the poem may organically expand. So that when you next speak the poem, you may be surprised by the new tones and textures that play through your voice spontaneously.

8. This is a practice to do with a friend or a few friends. Choose a poem you love, then listen to each person read the same poem as you pass it back and forth among you. Notice how the same poem can be almost completely different when it is voiced by another. Read it many times, being aware of the layers that are revealed when the poem is merged with the life experience in different voices.

Borrowed by the Wind

For this practice you will need a partner.

1. *Releasing agendas.* Having an agenda can often obscure the mysterious beauty of allowing yourself to be spontaneous and authentic when speaking a poem to others. Here, you will exaggerate certain agendas in order to loosen their grip on you. Read or recite your poem to your partner, playfully trying on each of the agendas below. Be sure to really connect with your partner so you know if you are "succeeding" in manipulating them to respond in the way you want.

- Get your point across to your partner. Whatever you love most about this poem, make sure he or she loves it most, too!

- Get your partner to like you as you deliver the poem.

- Get your partner to be moved to tears as you deliver the poem.

- Get your partner to realize how smart you are.

- Think of several more agendas to play with.

Now close your eyes. Feel the effects of these experiments in your body. Breathe. When you are ready, speak the poem quietly to yourself. Don't worry about whether your partner can even hear you. Listen to the poem; notice how its wisdom and music are affecting you. Hear the sound of your own voice and how the poem comes alive when you speak it. Then open your eyes and continue speaking the lines, this time with no agenda but to connect with the poem and your partner. It can be valuable to repeat the poem several times, noticing how it plays through your voice and energy when you surrender to being "borrowed" moment by moment.

2. *Meeting in the silence.* The silence just before you speak a poem, during the poem, and right after it can be the most powerful part of your offering. Yet many of us are uncomfortable with silence and rush through these moments. Practice elongating them instead. Let your partner know you are going to intentionally sink into the wordless spaces. Begin by making eye contact with your partner. Let any discomfort or other feelings come up as you silently be with each other. Now begin the poem. Maintain eye contact as much as possible, and when you are moved to drop into a silence that naturally occurs in the rhythm of the lines, do. When the poem is over, stay with the eye contact without words, letting any

feelings or insights show up. Then talk together about the experience and what arose for each of you in the silences.

Poetry Meditation

This meditation can be done alone or with others. You will need a quiet place, a journal or notebook with pen, and several of your favorite poems readily available. Music is very helpful (a list of my favorite music for reading poems aloud is part of the Resources section that follows). A candle and something of beauty—a flower, a bowl of water, a photo, or a statue—can also help to sanctify the moment.

Begin with few minutes of simply sitting, hearing the music or silence, allowing the outer stillness to provide a space of inner listening. What do you find when you turn your attention inward? Many of us arrive from some degree of rush or pressure, having spent at least part of the day pushing ourselves in one way or another. Now it is as if we stand, perhaps panting a little from the journey, at the door of a sanctuary. This pause is the threshold between daily speech and the sanctuary of poetry, between ordinary habit patterns and the poetic medicine that unlocks them, between impersonal conversations and the deeply intimate language of poems.

After a few moments of silence, pick up one of the poems you have brought. Read it aloud, listening to the words. Perhaps you will read it more than once. If there are others participating in the meditation, they too can read the poems they've brought. It is important that there be no conversation about the poems, just the language of poetry filling the air. Read and repeat the poems aloud for 15 minutes or so. Let the words and sounds of the poems wash over you; do not worry about understanding or retaining anything.

Then fall silent. Breathe. Listen internally for phrases that have stayed with you. They may be from the poems that you have been reading and hearing. Or they may be arising spontaneously from within you. Or they may be from other poems that you hold in your heart. It doesn't matter where they come from. Simply notice which words greet you when you look within.

Begin silently repeating that phrase. Infuse it into your interior, as if it were a mantra given to you by an inner guru. Even if you don't know why this particular message has come to you, trust it as you would a prayer in a holy language. As you repeat it again and again, notice what rises within you, magnetized by these words. There may be feelings or memories or sensations. Imagine that this phrase is the perfect medicine at this moment.

When you're ready, let your voice begin to break the surface. Speak the phrase or word to yourself, only loud enough to send your voice, like an acoustic elixir, directly into your own ears. Notice the texture, the music, the beauty of your voice. Hear the phrase anew each time you utter it.

Let your voice become stronger and continue to repeat the phrase, allowing the words to begin to change, if they do. More words may spontaneously arise from within you—originating in this moment or from poems you've read or learned by heart. Let any words come. Don't worry about whether they make sense or not. Don't worry about where they come from. Let your mind and voice begin to leap from association to association.

If there are others sharing the meditation with you, begin to hear and listen to their voices. Their words and phrases will begin to "cross-pollinate" with yours: you may find yourself echoing lines you hear around you, spontaneously integrating them into your own stream of words.

At some point, let the outflow of words begin to move through your pen and onto the page. It may be helpful to start with the phrase you last spoke aloud and then continue to write, uncensored, anything that follows. Again, don't worry about logic, grammar, or spelling. Just let the words pour onto the paper in whatever way they come. Let the inner critic go out for a coffee break. Write, without editing, for 10 to 15 minutes.

Now read over what you have written. Then read it aloud. Whether you are alone or with others, giving voice to these writings is an essential step. Sometimes feelings, memories, or associations may well up that surprise you. Often you will hear beauty and meaning that you had no idea were there before you lifted the words off the page into your breath, sound, and body.

FIFTY POEMS
TO LIVE BY HEART

There are thousands and thousands of poems that speak the language of the soul. Here are 50 of my favorites. Many of these can be found in the books, CDs, and Websites in the Resources list that follows.

Johann Wolfgang von Goethe, "The Holy Longing," trans. Robert Bly

Mary Oliver, "The Summer Day," "The Journey," "When Death Comes"

Galway Kinnell, "Wait," "Saint Francis and the Sow"

D. H. Lawrence, "Song of a Man Who Has Come Through"

Pablo Neruda, "Poetry," "Keeping Quiet," trans. Alastair Reid

William Butler Yeats, "Crazy Jane Talks with the Bishop," "The Song of Wandering Aengus"

Walt Whitman, "Song of Myself," part 5

Emily Dickinson, "I'm Nobody! Who are you?" "The Soul selects her own Society"

Elizabeth Bishop, "One Art"

William Shakespeare, Sonnet 29, Sonnet 30

Rainer Maria Rilke, "I am too alone in the world, and not alone enough," "You see, I want a lot," "The Man Watching," trans. Robert Bly

Rumi, "Love Dogs," "Undressing," "The Guest House," "A Zero Circle," trans. Coleman Barks

Gerard Manley Hopkins, "As kingfishers catch fire, dragonflies draw flame," "God's Grandeur"

David Whyte, "Self Portrait," "The Well of Grief"

Kabir, "I talk to my inner lover, and I say, why such a rush?" "I don't know what sort of God we have been talking about," trans. Robert Bly

Stanley Kunitz, "King of the River," "The Layers"

Marie Howe, "The Gate," "What the Living Do," "Annunciation"

Jane Hirshfield, "Against Certainty," "It Was Like This"

Derek Walcott, "Love after Love"

Juan Ramón Jiménez, "I am not I," "Oceans"

E. E. Cummings, "i thank you god for most this amazing," "somewhere i have never traveled,gladly beyond"

W. S. Merwin, "Thanks," "Just Now"

William Stafford, "A Ritual to Read to Each Other"

Naomi Shihab Nye, "Kindness"

Theodore Roethke, "In a dark time, the eye begins to see"

Wendell Berry, "I go among trees and sit still"

Marina Tsvetaeva, "I know the truth!"

The Nag Hammadi Library, "The Thunder: Perfect Mind," version by Jane Hirshfield

RESOURCES

Books

Poetry

The list of poetry books I want to share with you is far too long for these pages. The sources of many of my favorite poems can be found among the notes. Here I will list a few excellent anthologies, knowing you will seek out the books of those poets whose work most deeply touches you.

- Aliki Barnstone, editor: *The Shambala Anthology of Women's Spiritual Poetry*

- Jane Hirshfield, editor: *Women in Praise of the Sacred*

- Roger Housden, editor: *Risking Everything: 110 Poems of Love and Revelation, Dancing with Joy: 99 Poems, For Lovers of God Everywhere: Poems of the Christian Mystics*

- Garrison Keillor, editor: *Good Poems*

About Poetry

- Jane Hirshfield: *Nine Gates*
- Roger Housden: The Ten Poems series
- Mary Oliver: *A Poetry Handbook*
- Robert Pinsky: *The Sounds of Poetry*
- Muriel Rukeyser: *The Life of Poetry*

About Self-Inquiry

- Gangaji: *The Diamond in Your Pocket: Discovering Your True Radiance*

- Byron Katie: *Loving What Is: Four Questions That Can Change Your Life, A Thousand Names for Joy: Living in Harmony with the Way Things Are*

- Eva Pierrakos: *The Pathwork of Self-Transformation*

- Pat Rodegast and Emmanuel: *Emmanuel's Books I, II, and III*

Recordings

Spoken Poetry

- Elise Paschen and Rebekah Presson Mosby, eds., *Poetry Speaks: Hear Great Poets Read Their Own Work from Tennyson to Plath*

- Rebekah Presson and David McLees, eds., *In Their Own Voices: A Century of Recorded Poetry*

- Kim Rosen (spoken poetry) and Jami Sieber (music), *Only Breath*

Music for Speaking Poetry

- Peter Kater, *Compassion, Dance of Innocents, Song for Humanity*

- Gary Malkin, *Unspeakable Grace*

- Jami Sieber, *Hidden Sky, Lush Mechanique, Unspoken*

Websites

Poetry Resources

- Poetry Chaikhana, a extensive gathering of mystical poetry: www.Poetry-Chaikhana.com

- The Poetry Foundation, home of the Poetry Tool for finding poems, as well as a wealth of other wonderful resources: www.poetryfoundation.org

Paths and Practices

- The Pathwork: www.pathwork.org
- The Work of Byron Katie: www.thework.com
- Gangaji: www.gangaji.org

Organizations Committed to Art as Activism

- V-Day, a worldwide movement to stop violence against women (my experience at the V-Day Safe House for Girls in Kenya is featured in Chapter 10): www.vday.org

- Organization of Women's Freedom in Iraq, creators of the Freedom Space events: www.equalityiniraq.com

GRATITUDES

Every page in this book is alive with many more voices than my own. Such a richness of soul companions, teachers, and teachings has graced my life that any offering I make is threaded through and through with their wisdom and love.

My deepest gratitude to Eve Ensler, for urging me to reach and risk, for showing me again and again that art can literally change the world, and whose ceaseless friendship infuses everything I do and am.

Karin Aarons believed in this book long before I wrote it, and her deep listening was essential to the creative process. Geneen Roth walked with me through the highs and lows of writing and often offered a crucial hand along the way.

Thanks to Ned Leavitt, my agent, for seeing the heart of this work and guiding it into the world, and to Patty Gift, my editor, for her clarity, caring, and deep, original vision.

I owe much to Susan Griffin for mentoring me through the process of becoming a writer of nonfiction and for helping me bring spontaneity and realness to the page. Laura Koch gave exquisite attention to the myriad details of gathering permissions, and Anne Barthel brought a masterful eye to the final manuscript. I am also grateful for the ideas and guidance of Shoshana Alexander and Elizabeth Rose Raphael, who worked on early stages of this creation.

Special thanks to Marie Howe, for her example of living and writing at the exact intersection of the holy and the human and for the keen insight she brought to this work, and to Jane Hirshfield, whose wisdom and generosity are found throughout these pages.

This book would not exist without the love and inspiration of my friends. Their faith in this work was unswerving and carried me through many moments when I had lost my own. Their companionship keeps me true and touches every chapter in seen and unseen ways. My most tender gratitude to Marjorie Bair, Judi Bachrach, Sagewalker, Paula Allen, Chloe Goodchild, Marri Parkinson, Gary Malkin, Devi and Stan Weisenberg, Debra and George Chamberlin-Taylor, Nonnie Welch, and Carolyn Tilove.

I am thankful beyond words to Jami Sieber for the spring of music and heart that streams from her bow and for her willingness to dive; to David Whyte, whose voice called me back to the path of poetry; and to Pat Rodegast and Emmanuel for taking me under their wings.

The wisdom of the Pathwork Lectures has shaped my life, my voice, and my vision for over 30 years. I spent my 20s and 30s immersed in the community that constellated around those teachings, where I learned practices and possibilities of radical self-honesty and interpersonal authenticity that inform much of this book. There, too, I led my first groups, workshops, and retreats. I am grateful to Eva Pierrakos and The Guide for conveying the lectures, and to the Pathwork teachers and community for showing me how to live them.

In 1997, Gangaji and Byron Katie offered me a portal through my story into the truth of pure presence. For this I am filled with eternal gratitude. I hope that some of the gift they gave me is alive in this book.

Heartfelt gratitude to Maya Angelou, Guy Johnson, C. C. Carter, Sonja Franeta, Yanar Mohammed, Olympia Dukakis, Edward Rockett, and the many others who inspired the stories here.

Thank you to Monnie Reba Efross, Ted Graves, Laurinda Gilmore-Graves, Anna Fischer, Anne O'Reilly, Judith Schwartz, Maria Krekeler, Erin Alexander, Sue Sherman, and all of the Hawaii "pod" for taking the journey with me.

Among the multitudes of people who gave of their time, talents, and love to make this book possible, I thank Andrew Harvey, Christiane Northrup, Thomas Moore, Elizabeth Lesser, Cheryl Richardson, Robert Holden, Joan Borysenko, Genine Lentine, Coleman Barks, Deena Metzger, Grace Yi-Nan Howe, Summer McStravick,

Sally Mason, Michael Smith, Evan Schiller, Mark Matousek, Lou Judson, Coleen Burrows, Kris Gruen, Mary Staton, Michel Saint-Sulpice, Roger Housden, Jan Rostov, Danusha Lameris, and Linda Baldwin.

I will forever be grateful to V-Day for introducing me to Yanar Mohammed in Baghdad and Agnes Pareyio in Narok, Kenya. And I send my thanks to all the girls at the V-Day Safe House there, especially Phyllis Nailois Kamwaro, Jecinta Silantoi, and Salula Naingisa, for showing me how insubstantial the boundaries of culture and creed can be in the face of a poem truly spoken.

I am grateful to my parents, Jerome and Greta Rosen, for giving me a childhood and an education from which I could soar in any direction and for opening their minds to the directions I chose. And I thank my sister, Debora, and my brother, Brad, for their support and companionship.

I am indebted to the many students and friends who have joined me in classes, workshops, retreats, and poetry concerts to explore the frontiers where a poem can lead when taken deeply to heart. You constantly inspire me to new vistas of this path.

Finally, I thank all the poets whose words and silences I have the joy and privilege of delivering, and whose grace saves me every day.

ENDNOTES

Prologue

1. From a question asked of Mary Oliver at a poetry reading at Dominican College, San Rafael, Calif., April 24, 2008.
2. Gaston Bachelard, *The Poetics of Space* (Boston: Beacon Press, 1994), xx.
3. *Encyclopædia Britannica Online,* s.v. "soul," http://www.britannica.com/EBchecked/topic/555149/soul.
4. James Hillman, *Re-Visioning Psychology* (New York: Harper and Row, 1975), x.
5. Thomas Moore, *Care of the Soul* (New York: Harper Paperbacks, 1994), xi.
6. Bachelard, *The Poetics of Space,* xxi.
7. The word *inner,* like the word *soul,* is difficult to use with accuracy, for at the level of pure consciousness there is neither inner nor outer.
8. Emily Dickinson, "The Soul selects her own Society," *The Poems of Emily Dickinson,* ed. R. W. Franklin (Boston: Belknap Press of Harvard University Press, 1998), 409.
9. Jelaluddin Rumi, "Listening," *The Glance,* trans. Coleman Barks (New York: Penguin, 2001), 90.

Invitation

1. Organization of Women's Freedom in Iraq, "OWFI Update," report, March 2008.
2. D. H. Lawrence, "Song of a Man Who Has Come Through," *Look! We Have Come Through,* http://www.gutenberg.org/files/23394/23394-8.txt. The text of this entire poem may be found following Chapter 9.

Chapter 1: Embodying a Poem

1. Steven Brown, "The 'Musilanguage' Model of Music Evolution," *The Origins of Music,* ed. Nils L. Wallin, Bjorn Merker, Steven Brown, (Cambridge, Mass.: Massachusetts Institute of Technology, 2000), 277.

2. Steven Mithen, *The Singing Neanderthals* (Cambridge, Mass.: Harvard University Press, 2006), 235.

3. Jared Diamond, *The Third Chimpanzee: The Evolution and Future of the Human Animal* (New York: Harper Perennial, 2006), 141–167.

4. Jane Hirshfield, *Nine Gates* (New York: Harper Perennial, 1998), 176.

5. Hana Al-Hirsi, "Politics Dominates the Million's Poet," Zawya. com, January 24, 2008, http://www.zawya.com/story.cfm/sidZA-WYA20080124150020.

6. Poetry Foundation president John Barr, as quoted in "The Poetry Foundation Conducts $1,000 National Poetry Recitation Contest," *Foundation: Announcements,* March 2005, http://www.poetryfoundation.org/foundation/release_031405.html.

7. Sam Allis, "Having the final say," *The Boston Globe,* October 31, 2004, http://www.boston.com/news/local/massachusetts/articles/2004/10/31/having_the_final_say.

8. E. E. Cummings, "somewhere i have never travelled,gladly beyond," *100 Selected Poems* (New York: Grove Press, 1959), 44.

9. Robert Bly, "Call and Answer," *The Nation,* December 9, 2002, http://www.thenation.com/doc/20021209/bly.

10. Rainer Maria Rilke, "The First Elegy," *The Selected Poetry of Rainer Maria Rilke,* trans. Stephen Mitchell (New York: Vintage, 1989), 151.

11. Dr. Seuss, *Happy Birthday to You* (New York: Random House Books for Young Readers, 1959).

Chapter 2: How Poetry Saved My Life

1. E. E. Cummings, "somewhere i have never travelled,gladly beyond," *100 Selected Poems,* 44. This poem, in its entirety, can be found at the end of the chapter.

2. Catherine of Siena, "Prayer 20," *Women in Praise of the Sacred,* trans. and ed. Jane Hirshfield (New York: Harper Perennial, 1995), 116.

3. Lucille Clifton, "Album," *The Terrible Stories* (New York: BOA Editions Ltd., 1996), 51.

4. Jelaluddin Rumi, "Say Yes Quickly," *Open Secret,* trans. Coleman Barks (Putney, Vt.: Threshold Books, 1984), 69.

5. William Butler Yeats, "Crazy Jane Talks with the Bishop," *The Collected Poems of W. B. Yeats,* ed. Richard J. Finneran (New York: Collier Books, 1989), 259.

Chapter 3: The Medicine of Poetry

1. Maya Angelou, *I Know Why the Caged Bird Sings* (New York: Random House, 1970), 73.
2. Maya Angelou, interview by Lucinda Moore, "A Conversation with Maya Angelou at 75," *Smithsonian.com,* April 2003, http://www.smithsonianmag.com/arts-culture/angelou.html?c=y&page=4.
3. Angelou, *I Know Why the Caged Bird Sings,* 84.
4. Maya Angelou, interview by Don Swain, "Audio Interview with Maya Angelou," *Wired for Books,* a project of the WOUB Center for Public Media at Ohio University, 1987, http://wiredforbooks.org/mayaangelou.
5. Maya Angelou, "From 'Caged Bird' to 'Delta': A Conversation with Maya Angelou," *The Washington File,* June 6, 2005, http://www.america.gov/st/pubs-english/2005/June/20050606090838pssnikwad0.3981439.html.
6. William Ernest Henley, "Invictus," *Modern British Poetry,* ed. Louis Untermeyer (New York: Harcourt, Brace and Howe, 1920), 10.
7. Maya Angelou, interview by Sedge Thomson, "January 2006 Interview," *West Coast Live,* http://www.prx.org/pieces/8243.
8. C. C. Carter, "The Herstory of my Hips," *Word Warriors,* ed. Alix Olson (Emeryville, Calif.: Seal Press, 2007), 158.
9. C. C. Carter, "What I Remember," *Word Warriors,* 155.
10. Ibid.
11. Walt Whitman, "Song of Myself," *Leaves of Grass: The First (1855) Edition* (New York: Penguin Books, 1984), 28.
12. Ibrahim Al-Shawi, "Poetry Chase," *A Glimpse of Iraq,* January 1, 2005, http://glimpseofiraq.blogspot.com/2005_01_01_archive.html.
13. Ibid.
14. Carl Upchurch, *Convicted in the Womb* (New York: Bantam, 1996), 82.
15. Ibid., 86.

Chapter 4: Choosing a Poem

1. B. K. S. Iyengar, *Light on Yoga* (New York: Schocken, 1966), 19.
2. Sharon Olds, "It," in *The Gold Cell* (New York: Alfred A. Knopf, 1987), 57.

3. Mary Oliver, *The Leaf and the Cloud* (Cambridge, Mass.: Da Capo Press, 2000), 3.

4. Ibid., 4.

5. Ibid., 6.

6. John 21:18 (New Revised Standard Version).

7. Rainer Maria Rilke, "Wenn etwas mir vom Fenster fällt," *Rilke's Book of Hours,* trans. Anita Barrows and Joanna Macy (New York: Riverhead Books, 1996), 116.

8. kin. *Dictionary.com Unabridged* (version 1.1), Random House, Inc., http://dictionary.reference.com/browse/kin.

9. Eve Ensler, *Insecure at Last* (New York: Villard, 2006), 198.

10. Stanley Kunitz, "King of the River," *Passing Through* (New York: W. W. Norton & Company, 1997), 54.

11. Jelaluddin Rumi, "Checkmate," *The Essential Rumi,* trans. Coleman Barks, with John Moyne, et al. (San Francisco: HarperSanFrancisco, 1995), 176–177.

12. Rumi, "Say Yes Quickly," in *Open Secret.*

Chapter 5: The Anatomy of a Poem

1. I have listed some of these books in the Resources section at the back of this book.

2. Emilie Conrad first made me aware of this through her Continuum work: www.continuummovement.com.

3. "What Is EMDR: Frequent Questions," *EMDR.com,* http://www.emdr.com/q&a.htm.

4. Kunitz, "King of the River," *Passing Through.* This poem, in its entirety, can be found at the end of this chapter.

5. Marie Howe, "Prayer," *What the Living Do* (New York: W. W. Norton & Company, 1998), 73.

6. Pablo Neruda, "Poetry," in *Selected Poems,* ed. Nathaniel Tarn, trans. Anthony Kerrigan, W. S. Merwin, Alastair Reid, and Nathaniel Tarn (Boston: Houghton Mifflin, 1990), 457. This poem, in its entirety, can be found at the end of Chapter 1.

7. David Bjerklie, "Does Poetry Make The Heart Grow Stronger?" *Time,* August 2, 2004, http://www.time.com/time/archive/preview/0,10987,994795,00.html.

8. Genesis 1:35 (King James Version).

9. Deuteronomy 1:1 (King James Version).

10. Kunitz, "King of the River," in *Passing Through*.

11. Robert Hass, "Listening and Making," *Twentieth Century Pleasures* (New York: The Ecco Press, 1984), 108.

12. Emily Dickinson, "I'm Nobody! Who are you?," *The Poems of Emily Dickinson*, ed. R. W. Franklin (Boston: Belknap Press of Harvard University Press, 1998), 260.

13. Kunitz, "King of the River," *Passing Through*.

14. Hirshfield, *Nine Gates*, 18.

15. Jason Shulman, *Kabbalistic Healing* (Rochester, Vt.: Inner Traditions, 2004), 118.

16. Richard Miller, "The Principles and Practice of Yoga Nidra," *Center of Timeless Being*, http://www.nondual.com/teachings/articles/yoga-nidra.html.

17. Sharon Olds, "The Last Evening," *The New Yorker*, March 4, 2002, 64.

Chapter 6: Writing Poems on Your Bones

1.   Robert Hendrickson, *QPB Encyclopedia of Word and Phrase Origins* (New York: Facts on File, Inc., 2004).

2.   David Barber, "Does Memory Have a Future?" in *Arts and Letters: Journal of Contemporary Culture*, Issue #15, Spring, 2006 (Georgia College and State University). http://poems.com/special_features/prose/essay_barber.php.

3.   Mary Carruthers, *The Book of Memory*, (New York: Cambridge University Press, 2008), 1.

4.   Frances Yates, *The Art of Memory* (Chicago: University of Chicago Press, 1966), 36.

5.   Ibid., 215.

6.   A *griot* is a West African poet and musician who recites epic poems by heart and has the local history recorded in memory.

7.   Gratitude to Eric Swanson, who collaborated with Yongey Mingyur Rinpoche on his book *The Joy of Living* (New York: Harmony Books, 2007), for relaying these words and ideas to me.

8.   "The Making of Memory: What Makes a Memory?," *BBC*, http://www.bbc.co.uk/radio4/memory/programmes/making_memory1.shtml

9.   Chloe Goodchild, *Your Naked Voice* (Boulder, Colo.: Sounds True, 2006), CD set.

10. "St. Caedmon," *Britannia Biographies*, http://www.britannia.com/bios/saints/caedmon.html.

11. Rainer Maria Rilke, "Just as the winged energy of delight," *Selected Poems of Rainer Maria Rilke,* ed. and trans. Robert Bly (New York: Harper and Row, 1981), 175.
12. See Eva Pierrakos, "The Forces of Love, Eros and Sex," Pathwork Guide Lecture No. 44, International Pathwork Foundation, for an excellent discussion of this phenomenon as it appears in human relationship: http://www.pathwork.org/lectures/P044.PDF.
13. "The Thunder: Perfect Mind," *Women in Praise of the Sacred,* ed. and trans. Jane Hirshfield (New York: Harper Perennial, 1995), 30.
14. Maya Angelou, *Wired for Books,* a project of the WOUB Center for Public Media at Ohio University, http://wiredforbooks.org/mayaangelou/.
15. Rilke, "Just as the winged energy of delight," *Selected Poems of Rainer Maria Rilke.*
16. Dr. Raymond Moody, "Swan Song, The Unexpected Music & Poetry of the Dying," *Oracle 20/20 Magazine,* September 2005, http://www.oracle20-20.com/magazine/2005/0905/swan_song.php.

Chapter 7: The Gift of Forgetting

1. Rainer Maria Rilke, "The First Elegy," in *The Selected Poetry of Rainer Maria Rilke,* 151.
2. Pema Chödrön, *Awakening Compassion* (Boulder, Colo.: Sounds True, 1997), Audio CD.
3. John Keats, from a letter dated December 1817.
4. Eva Broch Pierrakos, "The Idealized Self-Image," Pathwork Guide Lecture No. 83, International Pathwork Foundation, http://www.pathwork.org/lectures/P083.PDF.
5. Ecclesiasticus 33:27.
6. Wendell Berry, "A Homecoming," *The Country of Marriage* (New York: Harcourt Brace, 1973).
7. Gratitude to Emilie Conrad, who first awakened me to this reality through her Continuum work, www.continuummovement.com.
8. Louise Kaplan, *Oneness and Separateness* (New York: Simon & Schuster, 1998), 27.
9. Gratitude to Gangaji, who first asked me this question.
10. W. S. Merwin, "Just Now," *The Pupil* (New York: Knopf, 2001), 62.
11. Jelaluddin Rumi, "Dying," *The Hand of Poetry,* ed. Inoyat Khan, trans. Coleman Barks (New Lebanon, N.Y.: Omega Publications, 1993), 90.

12. Jelaluddin Rumi, "A Zero Circle," in *Say I Am You,* trans. John Moyne and Coleman Barks (Atlanta: Maypop Books, 1994), 35.

13. Much of this section of the chapter is based on the Pathwork Lectures, which are available at http://www.pathwork.org/lecturesObtaining.html. In particular, Lecture No. 83, "The Idealized Self-Image," teaches, "When you muster the courage of becoming your real self, even though it would seem to be much less than the idealized self, you will find out that it is much more. And then you will have the peace of being at home within yourself. Then will you find security. Then will you function as a whole human being. Then will you have eliminated the iron whip of a taskmaster whom it is impossible to obey. Then will you know what peace and security really means. You will cease, once and for all, to seek it by false means."

Chapter 8: Undressing Your Voice

1. Jane Hirshfield, "Remembering Stanley Kunitz," *Poetry Foundation,* http://www.poetryfoundation.org/archive/feature.html?id=178193.
2. Marie Howe, "Remembering Stanley Kunitz," *Poetry Foundation,* http://www.poetryfoundation.org/archive/feature.html?id=178188.
3. Hirshfield, "Remembering Stanley Kunitz," *Poetry Foundation.*
4. Jane Hirshfield, "Against Certainty," *After* (New York: HarperCollins, 2006), 68. This poem, in its entirety, can be found at the end of this chapter.
5. Jane Hirshfield, e-mail message to author, May 15, 2006.
6. Genine Lentine, "Remembering Stanley Kunitz," *Poetry Foundation,* http://www.poetryfoundation.org/archive/feature.html?id=178262.
7. Bachelard, *The Poetics of Space,* xxiii.
8. Jelaluddin Rumi, "The Guest House," *The Essential Rumi,* 109.
9. Edna St. Vincent Millay, "Renascence," *Renascence and Other Poems* (New York: Harper, 1917), 3.
10. Rumi, "Say Yes Quickly," *Open Secret.*
11. T. S. Eliot, "Tradition and the Individual Talent," *Poetry X,* http://articles.poetryx.com/51/.

Chapter 9: Borrowed by the Wind

1. Leonard Cohen, "How to Read a Poem," *Stranger Music* (New York: Vintage, 1994), 287.

2.   The word *ego* has several meanings, depending on the tradition using it. I am using the word here as it is used in Eastern spiritual traditions (not as it is used in many psychological traditions, which have a slightly different definition originating with Freud and Jung). Eckhart Tolle has defined the ego, in the sense I use it here, as an illusory, "mind-made self": a constellation of thoughts composed of memories, plans, successes, failures, and opinions. It is driven by wanting and fearing and is constantly seeking to fortify its own separate existence.

3.   This wisdom was offered to me by Emmanuel, whose publications are listed in the Resources section at the end of this book.

4.   This idea is derived from the teachings in the Pathwork Lectures, particularly Pathwork Lecture No. 84, and the 50/50 Work of Moira Shaw: www.the50-50work.com.

5.   Cohen, "How to Read a Poem," *Stranger Music.*

6.   Rilke, "The First Elegy," *The Selected Poetry of Rainer Maria Rilke.*

Chapter 10: A Sudden Grace

1.   Wallace Stevens, "The Final Soliloquy of the Interior Paramour," *The Collected Poems of Wallace Stevens* (New York: Alfred A. Knopf, 1973), 524.

2.   Jelaluddin Rumi, "Sublime Generosity," *The Essential Rumi,* 135.

3.   Russell Targ and Jane Katra, Ph.D., "Close to Grace: The Physics of Silent Transmission," *Spirituality and Health,* July/August 2003, 42.

4.   Dr. Michael Okun, as featured in the movie *Healing Words: Poetry & Medicine,* produced and directed by Joan Baranow and Dr. David Watts.

5.   Phyllis Nailois Kamwaro, "I'm just a girl-child," unpublished poem, 2007.

6.   Mary Oliver, "Logos," *Why I Wake Early* (Boston: Beacon Press, 2004), 40.

Further Exploration

1.   Mithen, *The Singing Neanderthals,* 249.

2.   Fred Lerdahl, as quoted in *The Soul in the Brain* by Michael R. Trimble (Baltimore: Johns Hopkins University Press, 2007), 130.

PERMISSIONS

Grateful thanks to the following for permission to reprint their work:

Prologue

"Love after Love" from COLLECTED POEMS 1948-1984 by Derek Walcott. Copyright © 1986 by Derek Walcott. Reprinted by permission of Farrar, Straus and Giroux, LLC.

Invitation

Excerpt from "A Voice Through the Door" by Rumi, translated by Coleman Barks, from *The Glance*. Copyright © 1999 by Coleman Barks. Used by permission of Coleman Barks.

"Eternity" copyright © 2009 by the Estate of Jason Shinder. Reprinted from *Stupid Hope* by Jason Shinder with permission of Graywolf Press, Saint Paul, Minnesota.

Chapter 1: Embodying a Poem

"A Word is Dead" by Emily Dickinson. Reprinted by permission of the publishers and the trustees of Amherst college from THE POEMS OF EMILY DICKINSON: VARIORUM EDITION, Ralph W. Franklin, ed., Cambridge, Mass.: The Belknap Press of Harvard University Press, Copyright © 1998 by the President and Fellows of Harvard College. Copyright © 1951, 1955, 1979, 1983 by the President and Fellows of Harvard College.

"Poetry" from SELECTED POEMS by Pablo Neruda, translated by Alastair Reid, edited by Nathaniel Tarn and published by Jonathan Cape. Reprinted by permission of The Random House Group Ltd.

Chapter 2: How Poetry Saved My Life

Excerpt from "Asphodel, That Greeny Flower" By William Carlos Williams, from COLLECTED POEMS 1939-1962, VOLUME II, copyright ©

Chapter 3: The Medicine of Poetry

Chapter 4: Choosing a Poem

Chapter 5: The Anatomy of a Poem

Chapter 6: Writing Poems on Your Bones

Chapter 7: The Gift of Forgetting

Chapter 8: Undressing Your Voice

Chapter 9: Borrowed by the Wind

Chapter 10: A Sudden Grace

ABOUT THE AUTHOR

Kim Rosen, MFA, has touched listeners worldwide with the healing power of poetry. She is an award-winning poet, spoken word artist, healer, and teacher of Self-Inquiry. The co-creator of four CDs of poetry and music, Kim has delivered poems, lectures, ceremony, and workshops in myriad settings from the crypt of Chartres Cathedral to the New Orleans Superdome. She is a graduate of Yale University, with an MFA in poetry from Sarah Lawrence College, and she has been on the faculty of Wisdom University, the Omega Institute, and Kripalu. When not speaking poetry and giving workshops in various corners of the world, Kim lives in California. You can contact her and learn more about her work at **www.kimrosen.net**.

About the Audio Download

1. Kim Rosen speaks "Listening" by Rumi, translated by Coleman Barks. Music by Jami Sieber.

2. Introduction: The Power of Spoken Poetry

3. Robert Holden, director of The Happiness Project and author of ten books including *Success Intelligence* and *Be Happy,* reads and talks about "I Know the Way You Can Get" by Hafiz, version by Daniel Ladinsky.

4. Cheryl Richardson, whose books include *The Art of Extreme Self-Care* and *Stand Up for Your Life*, shares "A Blessing for the New Year" by John O'Donohue.

5. Dr. Christiane Northrup, authority in women's health and wellness and author of *Women's Bodies, Women's Wisdom* and *The Secret Pleasures of Menopause*, discusses Deena Metzger's poem, "Tree."

6. Geneen Roth, author of eight books including *When Food is Love* and *The Craggy Hole in My Heart and The Cat Who Fixed It,* shares "Kindness" by Naomi Shihab Nye.

7. Elizabeth Lesser, cofounder of Omega Institute and author of *The Seeker's Guide* and *Broken Open: How Difficult Times Can Help Us Grow*, reads and talks about "Feast" by Edna St. Vincent Millay.

8. Thomas Moore, whose books include *Care of the Soul* and, most recently, *Writing in the Sand: Jesus and the Soul of the Gospels,* discusses "Name the Gods!" by D.H. Lawrence.

9. Joan Borysenko, whose many books include *Minding the Body, Mending the Mind* and, most recently, *Your Spiritual Compass: What is Spiritual Guidance?* co-authored with Gordon Dveirin, explores Thich Nhat Hanh's poem "Please Call Me By My True Names."

10. Andrew Harvey—scholar, writer, teacher, and the author of over 30 books, including *The Hope: A Guide to Sacred Activism* and *Way of Passion: A Celebration of Rumi*—reads and discusses his own translation of "Look for Passion, Passion, Passion, Passion" by Rumi.

11. Kim Rosen, author of *Saved by a Poem*, shares "Love after Love" by Derek Walcott.

12. Introducing the Poets

13. Stanley Kunitz reads his poem "King of the River."

14. Jane Hirshfield reads her poem "Against Certainty." Music by Gary Malkin.

15. Marie Howe reads her poem "Annunciation."

16. Closing Remarks

17. Kim Rosen speaks "Poetry" by Pablo Neruda, translated by Alastair Reid. Music by Jami Sieber.

18. Grace Yi-Nan Howe reads "If You Are Lucky in This Life" by Cameron C. Penny. Music by Jami Sieber.

254

Audio Download Instructions

Thank you for purchasing *Saved by a Poem* by Kim Rosen. This product includes a free download! To access this bonus content, please visit www.hayhouse.com/download and enter the Product ID and Download Code as they appear below.

Product ID: 4436
Download Code: ebook
For further assistance, please contact Hay House Customer Care by phone: US (800) 654-5126 or INTL CC+(760) 431-7695 or visit www.hayhouse.com/contact.
Thank you again for your Hay House purchase. Enjoy!
Hay House, Inc. • P.O. Box 5100 • Carlsbad, CA 92018
(800) 654-5126

Hay House Titles of Related Interest

YOU CAN HEAL YOUR LIFE, the movie,
starring LouiseHay & Friends
(available as a 1-DVD program and an expanded 2-DVD set)
Watch the trailer at: **www.LouiseHayMovie.com**

THE SHIFT, the movie, starring Dr. Wayne W. Dyer
(available as a 1-DVD program and an expanded 2-DVD set)
Watch the trailer at: **www.DyerMovie.com**

෴

THE ART OF EXTREME SELF-CARE:
Transform Your Life One Month at a Time,
by Cheryl Richardson

CHANGE YOUR THOUGHTS—CHANGE YOUR LIFE:
Living the Wisdom of the Tao, by Dr. Wayne W. Dyer

FOR LOVERS OF GOD EVERYWHERE:
Poems of the Christian Mystics, by Roger Housden

SOLEMATE: Master the Art of Aloneness
and Transform Your Life, by Lauren Mackler

All of the above are available at your local bookstore,
or may be ordered by contacting Hay House (see last page).

We hope you enjoyed this Hay House book.
If you'd like to receive our online catalog featuring
additional information on Hay House books and products,
or if you'd like to find out more about the
Hay Foundation, please contact:

Hay House, Inc.
P.O. Box 5100
Carlsbad, CA 92018-5100

(760) 431-7695 or (800) 654-5126
(760) 431-6948 (fax) or (800) 650-5115 (fax)
www.hayhouse.com® • www.hayfoundation.org

Published and distributed in Australia by: Hay House Australia Pty. Ltd.,
18/36 Ralph St., Alexandria NSW 2015 • Phone: 612-9669-4299
Fax: 612-9669-4144 • www.hayhouse.com.au

Published and distributed in the United Kingdom by:
Hay House UK, Ltd., Astley House, 33 Notting Hill Gate, London W11 3JQ
Phone: 44-20-3675-2450 • Fax: 44-20-3675-2451 • www.hayhouse.co.uk

Published and distributed in the Republic of South Africa by:
Hay House SA (Pty), Ltd., P.O. Box 990, Witkoppen 2068 • Phone/Fax:
27-11-467-8904 • info@hayhouse.co.za • www.hayhouse.co.za

Published in India by: Hay House Publishers India, Muskaan Complex,
Plot No. 3, B-2, Vasant Kunj, New Delhi 110 070 • Phone: 91-11-4176-1620
Fax: 91-11-4176-1630 • www.hayhouse.co.in

Distributed in Canada by: Raincoast Books, 2440 Viking Way,
Richmond, B.C. V6V 1N2 • Phone: 1-800-663-5714
Fax: 1-800-565-3770 • www.raincoast.com

Take Your Soul on a Vacation

Visit **www.HealYourLife.com**® to regroup, recharge,
and reconnect with your own magnificence.
Featuring blogs, mind-body-spirit news, and
life-changing wisdom from Louise Hay and friends.

Visit **www.HealYourLife.com** today!